# THE POLITICAL ECONOMY
# OF EUROPEAN MONETARY UNIFICATION

# The Political Economy of Global Interdependence
*Thomas D. Willett, Series Editor*

---

# THE POLITICAL ECONOMY
## OF EUROPEAN MONETARY UNIFICATION

EDITED BY

Barry Eichengreen and
Jeffry Frieden

Westview Press
BOULDER • SAN FRANCISCO • OXFORD

*The Political Economy of Global Interdependence*

Chapters 3, 5, 6, 7, and 8 previously appeared in *Economics and Politics* 5, no. 2 (July 1993). © Basil Blackwell Ltd. Reprinted by permission.

Published in 1994 in the United States of America by Westview Press, Inc., 5500 Central Avenue, Boulder, Colorado 80301-2877, and in the United Kingdom by Westview Press, 36 Lonsdale Road, Summertown, Oxford OX2 7EW

Library of Congress Cataloging-in-Publication Data
Eichengreen, Barry J.
  The political economy of European monetary unification / Barry Eichengreen and Jeffry Frieden.
      p.   cm. — (The Political economy of global interdependence)
    Includes bibliographical references and index.
    ISBN 0-8133-2081-X
    1. European Monetary System (Organization)   2. Monetary policy—European Economic Community countries.   3. European Economic Community countries—Economic conditions.   I. Frieden, Jeffry A.
  II. Title.   III. Series.
  HG930.5.E428   1994
  332.4'56'06094—dc20                                                                 94-193
                                                                                        CIP

Printed and bound in the United States of America

The paper used in this publication meets the requirements
of the American National Standard for Permanence of Paper
for Printed Library Materials Z39.48-1984.

10    9    8    7    6    5    4    3    2    1

# CONTENTS

# ACKNOWLEDGMENTS

The chapters in this volume are drawn from the work of a study group on the political economy of European integration, convened by the editors on behalf of the Center for German and European Studies of the University of California. The center, funded by a grant from the German government, provided financial support for the research reported here. The editors wish to thank Richard Buxbaum, director of the center, for his support and also thank all participants in the study group for their contributions.

*Barry Eichengreen*
*Jeffry Frieden*

# 1

## THE POLITICAL ECONOMY OF
## EUROPEAN MONETARY UNIFICATION:
## AN ANALYTICAL INTRODUCTION

### BARRY EICHENGREEN AND JEFFRY FRIEDEN

European monetary unification (EMU) – the creation of a single European currency and a European Central Bank – is both an economic and a political phenomenon. Yet few studies have attempted to address simultaneously the political and economic dimensions of the process. In this introduction,[1] we review and extend the relevant literatures. The evidence leads us to conclude that EMU is driven mainly by political rather than economic factors, although our understanding of even these political forces remains incomplete.

EUROPEAN MONETARY unification (EMU) – the creation of a single European currency and a European central bank – is both an economic and a political phenomenon. It is economic in that it will radically transform economic policy and performance in Europe. Transactions costs will be reduced by the creation of a single currency, stimulating cross-border exchange. National monetary autonomy will become a thing of the past, limiting the use by participating countries of the inflation tax and of the exchange rate as an instrument for adjusting to nation-specific shocks.[2]

EMU is also a political phenomenon in that the decision to create a single currency and central bank is not made by a beneficent social planner weighing the costs and benefits to the participating nations. Rather, it is the outcome of a political process of treaty negotiation, parliamentary ratification, and popular referenda. Interest groups support or oppose the initiative depending on how it is likely to affect their welfare, not the welfare of the nation or the Community as a whole. The pressures they bring to bear are amplified and dissipated by the political institutions through which they are communicated.

Despite the flurry of research elicited by the debate over EMU, few studies have attempted to address simultaneously the political and economic dimensions of the process.[3] That is the goal of the symposium published here.[4] Besides showing how both the politics and economics of EMU can be analyzed systematically, the papers are intended to demonstrate how the two dimensions of the

---

[1] The authors wish to thank Benjamin J. Cohen, Geoffrey Garrett, Lisa Martin, Ron Rogowski, and Jürgen von Hagen for their comments and suggestions.

[2] The balance of these costs and benefits is a classic topic in the literature in Economics on optimum currency areas, which we discuss below. For a comprehensive survey, see Ishiyama (1975).

[3] Below we mention a few notable – and important – exceptions to this generalization.

[4] This introduction was revised in August 1993 to take into account late-breaking developments in Europe, and as such differs slightly from earlier versions which some readers may have seen.

process interact. They illustrate how political constraints on the design of the institutions of the monetary union are likely to shape its economic costs and benefits, and at the same time how the changes in economic structure brought about by monetary unification work to alter European politics.

## A SHORT HISTORY OF EUROPEAN MONETARY UNIFICATION

Enthusiasts of European integration have long regarded monetary union as a central goal. Economically, fixed exchange rates or a single currency would reduce the cost of doing business within the European Community (EC); concern with exchange rate volatility is especially strong inasmuch as many European countries are very open to world trade and payments. Politically, movement toward monetary union is seen as a practical and symbolic step toward broader unification of the Community along other dimensions, such as foreign policy and social goals.

Yet movement toward a common EC currency has been hampered by both economic and political factors. Fixed exchange rates and a single currency mean the surrender of national monetary policies to a Community-wide authority. This transfer of responsibility may be desirable in some circumstances for some people. But when major economic dislocations occur, Europe's national governments come under pressure to pursue independent policies tailored to offset national disturbances. Those who shudder at the prospects of common EC foreign, defense, or social policies find monetary union threatening inasmuch as it foreshadows ever greater surrender of sovereign prerogatives in other domains. For these reasons and others, the desirability of European monetary unification has been contested for nearly thirty years, and movement toward the goal has been halting.

Serious discussions within the EC began in the late 1960s, culminating in the 1969 Werner Report.[5] This set forth detailed plans for monetary union but was made obsolete within weeks of its adoption by the beginning of the collapse of the Bretton Woods international monetary regime. Once Bretton Woods crumbled, the most to which the EC's six members could aspire was the maintenance of Bretton Woods-style exchange rate stability. They resolved in 1972 to hold their currencies within a 2.25 percent band against one another. This arrangement, the "snake", was joined by Great Britain, Ireland, and Denmark in the run-up to their 1973 entry to the Community.[6] But divergent economic conditions, associated with the first oil shock of 1973–1974, made the system

[5] It is interesting to note that even at this early date, plans for monetary union were closely linked to broader political problems associated with French ambivalence about the European Community in the aftermath of the franc crisis of 1969. On early monetary plans and developments, see Tsoukalis (1977, pp. 51–111); and van Ypersele (1985, pp. 31–45).

[6] Norway and Sweden also tied their currencies to the mechanism. On the snake, see Tsoukalis (1977, pp. 112–168); Ludlow (1982, pp. 1–36); Coffey, (1987), pp. 6–16. A useful chronology is in Coffey (1987, pp. 123–125).

unworkable. Within three years of its founding only Germany, the Benelux countries, and Denmark remained in the snake. The EC members whose macroeconomic conditions diverged most from those of Germany – the U.K., Ireland, France and Italy – simply left, and the Danes could remain in the union only with continual devaluations.

Renewed discussion of monetary union began in 1977, and in March 1979 a new European Monetary System (EMS) and Exchange Rate Mechanism (ERM) went into effect. All EC members except the United Kingdom linked to the ERM, which allowed a 2.25 percent band among currencies (6 percent for the lira). Realignments were to be allowed within the EMS, although they were expected to be infrequent.[7] Financing facilities were provided for countries attempting to hold their exchange rates stable in the face of temporary balance-of-payments shocks.

Received wisdom at the time was that the EMS was unlikely to succeed. The inflation rates of EMS countries differed too radically for the maintenance of stable exchange rates. Throughout the 1970s the Community's high-inflation countries had been unable to implement the austerity measures necessary to bring their currencies into line with the deutschmark. Optimism about the EMS required some reason to believe that the system itself would strengthen the willingness or ability of high-inflation countries to implement austerity programs.

Initially, the pessimistic view seemed to be borne out. In the first four years of the EMS's operation, exchange rates were realigned seven times. Monetary policies and inflation rates showed few signs of converging. Then, however, things began to change. Rates of price increase in the high-inflation countries began to decline. From April 1983 to January 1987 there were only four realignments, generally smaller than their predecessors. And from January 1987 to September 1992 there were no major realignments within the ERM. Spain, the United Kingdom, and Portugal joined the mechanism. By the late 1980s, the EC appeared to be well on the way toward becoming a zone of monetary stability.[8]

The success of the EMS was both stimulated by and stimulated progress on European integration more generally. In 1985 and 1986, EC member governments developed and signed the Single European Act (SEA), which called for the removal of all controls on the movement of goods, capital, and people within the Community by January 1, 1993.[9] The prospect of a truly common market propelled forward other aspects of European integration, including monetary unification. In this context, and at the urging of the French and German foreign

[7] Ludlow (1982) is especially detailed on the negotiations and early operation of the EMS; see also van Yspersele (1985, pp. 71–95); and Ungerer (1983). Excellent surveys of the EMS experience generally are Fratianni and von Hagen (1992) and Giavazzi and Giovannini (1989).

[8] A good summary of the domestic and regional politics of monetary policy in the EC in the 1980s is Goodman (1992). This discussion side-steps the issue of whether limiting realignments was part of the original EMS plan, or, indeed, was a good thing. For now, we simply pass on the received wisdom of the time, that the fixing of rates within the ERM represented a step toward monetary union.

[9] On the Single European Act, see Garrett (1992) and Moravcsik (1991).

ministries, in 1988 the European Council empaneled a committee headed by European Commission President Jacques Delors to investigate the prospects for further monetary integration.

In early 1989 the Delors Committee recommended that the EC begin moving toward a single currency, and proposed that EMU be approached in three stages. Stage One involved the elimination of all residual capital controls, accession of all EC members to the ERM, and a hardening of the ERM commitment. In Stage Two, with the EMS credible and encompassing, a common set of macroeconomic policies would be adopted by national authorities, and a European System of Central Banks would coordinate the actions of national central bankers. Stage Three would see the development of an EC-wide central bank, a common currency for all EC members, and Community coordination of fiscal policies.

By 1991, with a detailed plan for EMU in place and all EC members except Greece in the ERM, the single currency seemed only a matter of time. This impression was reinforced when in December 1991, at Maastricht in the Netherlands, EC members agreed to a sweeping treaty on political and economic union. [The monetary aspects of the treaty are summarized in Garrett (1994), in this volume.]

Soon, however, unanticipated events and political resistance intervened to interrupt the momentum of monetary unification. German reunification was accompanied by large fiscal deficits, which excited Bundesbank fears of inflation and led the German central bank to implement restrictive monetary policies. British and Italian monetary conditions did not converge to those of the rest of the EMS as rapidly as expected, leading the lira and sterling to appreciate in real terms. And stagnant global economic conditions lowered political tolerance for tight money. The result was pressure on the British and Italian currencies as devaluation expectations grew.

In the midst of the gathering currency crisis, political opposition to Maastricht surfaced. The June 1992 failure of a Danish referendum on the treaty [on which see Martin (1994), in this volume] raised the possibility of an indefinite postponement of EMU and thus increased expectations of instability in the ERM. Opinion polls also indicated that a late-September French referendum on Maastricht would be unexpectedly close.

On September 16, 1992 (four days before the French referendum) Britain and Italy withdrew from the ERM and allowed their currencies to depreciate. This, the most serious setback suffered by EMU since the early 1980s, was followed by realignments that drove the currencies of Spain, Portugal, and Ireland downward.

Turmoil in Europe's foreign exchange markets, including additional forced realignments, persisted into 1993. In the summer of 1993, as unemployment rose throughout the EC, pressure for interest rate reductions increased. However, the Bundesbank, concerned about German inflation, maintained a tight monetary policy that made it impossible for other EMS members to lower interest rates without risking a devaluation. The dilemma was especially serious in France, where a new conservative government had taken office in March amidst a severe recession and high rates of unemployment. Anticipating that the Balladur Government might be unprepared to hold the line, foreign exchange traders attacked the franc and other currencies in the ERM, forcing the French and other governments to raise already high interest rates, thereby exacerbating unemployment, in order to defend ERM parities.

Tensions in European currency markets were exacerbated by characteristics of the Maastricht Treaty itself. Under the Maastricht criteria, a country qualifies for EMU only if it has maintained its currency within ERM bands for two years. (More precisely, it must maintain its currency within the narrow ERM band without "severe tensions" for the two years preceding entry into EMU.) This means that failure to defend a currency may disqualify a country from early participation in the monetary union. Once disqualified, the country no longer retains its previous incentive to pursue the policies of austerity needed to gain entry and has every reason to shift to a more accomodating policy stance. Knowledge that governments possess this incentive gives markets reason to attack, since the shift to a more accomodating policy thereby induced will entail a devaluation and give currency traders capital gains on their investments. Under these circumstances a speculative attack on an otherwise sound currency can succeed.

In August 1993 this confluence of factors gave rise to irresistible pressure on currency markets. In this context, EMS members agreed to widen currency fluctuation bands to fifteen percent (but to keep them at 2.25 percent for the deutschemark and the Dutch guilder). This removed pressure on the EMS but substantially reduced the fixed-rate component of the system.

Despite these setbacks, plans for EMU remain alive. An assessment of its future prospects requires a systematic analysis of both its economics and its politics.

### THE ECONOMICS OF MONETARY UNIFICATION

A standard approach to the economics of monetary unification is to weigh the costs and benefits of replacing multiple currencies with a single currency. In this section, we examine what economic theory and evidence have to say about the balance of benefits and costs. We show that neither economic theory nor economic evidence provides a clear case for or against monetary unification. The direct economic benefits of monetary unification are likely to be relatively small, and may or may not be dominated by the costs. The absence of a clear economic justification for EMU leads us to conclude that events in Europe are being driven mainly by political factors.

A first economic argument for monetary unification is as an antiinflationary commitment mechanism. For much of the 1970s and 1980s, European countries suffered high inflation. Pegging to the deutschmark by joining the EMS was a way to import the credible anti-inflationary monetary policies of the Bundesbank and bring down inflation in a relatively painless way. EMU is portrayed as the final step in this process. As a precondition for entering the monetary union, participating countries will be forced to strengthen the independence of their central banks. [See Garrett (1994), in this volume, for a discussion of the entry conditions.] The Governing Council of the European Central Bank (ECB), on which national central bank governors will sit, will enjoy statutory protection from political pressures. (They will serve long terms in office and be prohibited from campaigning for reappointment, for example.) Hence, by abolishing their national currencies and joining the monetary union, European countries will effectively renounce the option of reverting to inflationary policies. EMU, according to this view, represents an efficient anti-inflationary commitment technology.[10]

A problem with this reasoning is that it is far from clear whether the political independence the ECB possesses in theory will be enjoyed in practice. [Garrett (1994), and Alesina and Grilli (1994), in this issue, touch on this point.] Europe's traditional high- and low-inflation countries will all have equal representation on the ECB's Governing Council. [For further discussion of these arrangements, see Fratianni and von Hagen (1994), in this volume.] To be sure, the costs of defecting from EMU, once in, will serve as an effective exit barrier. But while EMU may serve as a technology for credibly committing to a common monetary policy, the inflationary implications of that common policy remain to be seen.

One might think that the reduction in currency-conversion costs due to replacing 12 national monies with one provides a clear economic justification for EMU. This is not so for two reasons: first, the costs of currency conversion are small; and second, the very measures which deliver the reduction in currency-conversion charges may introduce other, even larger, economic costs such as those associated with the loss of policy autonomy. We consider these objections in turn.

The European Commission has estimated that conversion costs absorb no more than 1 per cent of GDP for the Community's less-industrialized economies, and that they fall to as little as 0.1 per cent of GDP for the large member states for which international transactions are less important.[11] Overall they average only 0.4 percent of EC GDP. This, clearly, is a small return on a monetary unification process riddled with uncertainties and risks.

These calculations may fail to capture the real efficiency gains from a common currency. Such gains may derive from the fact that the creation of a single

---

[10] On this point, see, however, Cohen (1994), in this volume.

[11] See European Commission (1990).

currency, by eliminating exchange-rate uncertainty, will encourage intra-EC trade and investment. In turn this will lead to a more efficient allocation of resources both within and across member states. Existing evidence suggests, however, that exchange-rate variability and uncertainty have only small effects on trade and investment.[12] Traders can use forward markets, hedges and a variety of financial instruments to lessen the risks attendant on exchange-rate changes; it is not surprising, therefore, that most investigators are unable to find much of a relationship between exchange-rate variability and trade. And exchange-rate variability may actually promote foreign investment insofar as it encourages investors to hold diversified portfolios of assets whose income streams are denominated in different currencies.

A more general form of the argument is that monetary unification is necessary for technical reasons if the EC is to succeed in completing the Internal Market and reaping its benefits. A truly integrated European market for capital as well as labor and commodities cannot exist in the presence of exchange controls. It is hardly possible to continue restricting the freedom of Frenchmen to open bank accounts in Germany, for example, while at the same time creating a EC-wide capital market free of restrictions on portfolio capital movements and direct foreign investment. The efficiency gains of the Single Market thus require the removal of capital controls.

The removal of controls, according to this thesis, renders infeasible all monetary arrangements but a single European currency. The EMS, as described above, was a hybrid of pegged and adjustable exchange rates. Extended periods of exchange-rate stability were designed to deliver most of the benefits of fixed rates, while periodic realignments permitted countries to redress serious competitiveness problems. But periods of exchange-rate stability punctuated by occasional realignments were possible only because capital controls protected central bank reserves against speculative attacks motivated by anticipations of realignment. If, for example, France sought to maintain lower interest rates than Germany, huge quantities of financial capital did not flow instantaneously from Paris to Frankfurt, immediately forcing a devaluation. The interest differential had to be large and to be maintained for an extended period before substantial numbers of French arbitragers found it advantageous to incur the cost of circumventing French capital controls and thereby forcing a realignment. The removal of capital controls, by changing this situation, doomed the EMS as it existed in the 1980s.

But it is far from clear, in fact, that monetary unification was the only alternative left by the removal of controls. An obvious alternative is floating exchange rates. But floating retains a bad name in Europe and raises political objections (described below).

Another conceivable alternative stopping short of monetary unification is

[12] See, e.g., Sapir and Sekket (1989); and Cushman (1988).

truly fixed exchange rates among distinct national currencies. A sufficiently credible commitment to intra-EC exchange-rate stability might fix exchange rates even in the absence of capital controls. However attractive in theory, this alternative faces problems in practice. The very existence of distinct national currencies is likely to limit the credibility of policy pronouncements that exchange rates will be irrevocably fixed. [Cohen (1994), in this volume, analyzes this problem further.] In general, it is impossible in a democracy to preclude the possibility that an existing policy instrument like the exchange rate will be utilized. As Cohen shows, only under very special circumstances, rarely present in modern industrial democracies, is it possible to assemble the organizational and institutional prerequisites for credibly fixed exchange rates.

In this sense, then, the Single European Act forced the issue. It required the removal of capital controls, which undermined the viability of the EMS and confronted the Community with the choice of reverting to floating or moving forward to monetary unification. Floating was incompatible with Europe's longstanding aversion to exchange-rate variability. Monetary unification was therefore a prerequisite for reaping the benefits of the product- and factor-market integration foreseen by the Single European Act.

Such are the benefits of EMU. But a proper cost-benefit calculus must also consider the other side of the coin.

The theory of optimum currency areas suggests that the costs come from the loss of monetary policy autonomy that follows from the establishment of a single currency.[13] Whether abandoning policy autonomy is costly depends on the shocks to which participating countries are subjected and the effectiveness of monetary policy in facilitating adjustment. If monetary policy is incapable of affecting output and employment, then abandoning monetary independence is costless. But even if monetary policy is effective, abandoning monetary independence will be costless when the same policy response is appropriate for all members of the union. If all suffer deflationary disturbances simultaneously, for example, then a unionwide reflationary monetary policy will suffice. The larger the change in output relative to inflation due to a monetary initiative and the more asymmetric the shocks, the greater the benefits of monetary autonomy and hence the higher the costs of unification.

The evidence on these questions resists easy interpretation. The rigidity of real wages in Europe gives grounds for doubting that monetary policy is as effective as in the United States. Since many of the same industries operate in many European countries, industry-specific shocks will affect these countries in similar ways. On the other hand, econometric studies have found that both aggregate-supply and aggregate-demand shocks are more asymmetrically dis-

---

[13] Seminal contributions to the theory of optimum currency areas include Mundell (1961), McKinnon (1963), and Kenen (1969).

tributed across European nations than across the regions of existing monetary unions like the United States.[14]

Such asymmetric disturbances do not create a case for policy autonomy if there exist such alternative means of adjustment. Within the U.S., where regional adjustment cannot take place through exchange-rate changes, it occurs mainly through migration. Unemployed auto workers in Michigan load up the U-Haul van and move to the oil fields of Texas when oil prices rise and the auto industry contracts.

By U.S. standards, labor is not very mobile in Europe. Migration between European countries is significantly lower than between U.S. regions. [This generalization neglects the fact, discussed in Eichengreen (1993), that Europe has a secondary labor market in which mobility is very high, comprised of non-EC guest workers. But these guest workers are largely limited to the unskilled, non-unionized segment of the market.] Migration within European countries is lower than in the U.S., as well. Hence region-specific shocks which can no longer be counteracted by exchange-rate changes may give rise to regional concentrations of unemployment more persistent than those characteristic of the United States.

If it is true that shocks to European countries are more asymmetrically distributed than shocks to U.S. regions, while both labor mobility and real wage flexibility are lower in Europe, then the costs of monetary union will be higher than in the U.S. That the U.S. benefits from monetary union is no guarantee that in Europe the advantages of doing so will exceed the costs.

Uncertainty about the empirical magnitude of every one of these benefits and costs suggests the absence of a clear economic case in favor of EMU. Given the risks and uncertainties that pervade the process, there would have to be a clear margin of benefits over costs for economic considerations, narrowly defined, to provide a justification for such a radical departure in policy. The absence of such a margin implies that the momentum for monetary union must therefore derive from other, primarily political, factors.

### THE POLITICS OF MONETARY UNIFICATION

The search for political motivations is hampered by the paucity of theoretical and empirical work on the topic (a gap that this volume hopes to help fill). Nonetheless, as a point of departure we can distinguish three sets of political considerations likely to figure in any such explanation: inter-state bargaining, issue linkage, and domestic distributional factors.

---

[14] On the extent of sectoral specialization, see Bini Smaghi and Vori (1992). One of the first econometric studies of the incidence of aggregate-supply and aggregate-demand shocks is Bayoumi and Eichengreen (1992).

## 1. Inter-state Bargaining

Even if monetary union does not improve social welfare in all participating countries, it still may be in the interest of some EC governments, which then cajole or coerce others into participation. This approach, generally associated with what some political scientists refer to as "intergovernmentalism," interprets international political outcomes as a result of strategic interaction among national governments.[15]

There are several problems with the approach. Concepts like "power" and "coercion" are difficult to define analytically and measure empirically. Inter-state bargains usually appear to be entered into freely (at least in the proximate sense), and thus presumably involve mutually beneficial exchange. This is not to say that there is no coercion in international relations, only that its invocation for analytical purposes requires careful and systematic attention to both the theoretical bases for the argument and the specific details of the case. Neither is common in applications; both are desirable.

Moreover, even where power is defined carefully as one country's possession of bargaining leverage over others, such leverage typically relies on threats and promises, and these threats and promises must possess credibility to be effective. Yet few analyses of intergovernmental bargaining adequately specify what exactly renders credible the threats and promises required for power to be exerted. And as Alesina and Grilli (1994) explain in this volume, there are many circumstances under which pro-EMU countries would be better off keeping more reticent members *out* of a monetary union rather than forcing them to join. Even at the level of theory, then, it is hard to draw explanations of EMU from an inter-governmental bargaining model without further development of the analytical tools used in most such models.

## 2. Linkage Politics

A framework in which governments trade off objectives along different dimensions seems more appropriate than vague invocations of power politics. A systematic analysis of such tradeoffs, however, requires a notion of linkage politics typically lacking in simple analyses of intergovernmentalism.

By linkage is meant the tying together of two otherwise unconnected issue areas, permitting the parties to an agreement to make concessions on one in return for concessions on the other. Thus, one country might "give" monetary union (which it does not inherently favor) in return for "getting" political union

---

[15] For summaries and applications of "intergovernmentalism" in the EC context, see Moravcsik (1991) and Sandholtz (1993).

(which it does) if the perceived benefits of the latter exceed the costs of the former.[16]

Linkage arguments, though compelling, are not unproblematic. Like interstate bargaining generally, effective linkage requires credible threats or promises. Otherwise governments will fear that their foreign partners will renege on the commitment and refuse to enter into it in the first place. But even more when issue areas are linked than when bargaining over each issue occurs in isolation, such threats are unlikely to be fully credible. Not only must commitments on each dimension be credible, but the commitment to link dimensions must be credible as well. What, for example, prevents Germany's partners, once they have obtained monetary union, from reneging on their commitment to move ahead with political union subsequently?

Given the importance of credibility, analyses along these lines must devote a great deal of attention to how the parties bind themselves to the linkages they create. Some recent analyses of such commitment mechanisms have become quite sophisticated.[17]

In addition, the domain of linkage politics is likely to be limited. Linkage can only operate when different nations place different values on different issue areas. If all EC members place similar weight (positive or negative) on EMU, there is little room for trading off concessions along different dimensions, and no room for linked bargaining that might improve the likelihood of agreement on EMU. While linkage politics may operate, its analysis requires caution and detail.

## 3. Domestic Distributional Issues

Just as countries with strong interests in EMU may coerce, cajole or bargain other EC members to participate, specific groups that stand to benefit (or lose) disproportionately may play a similar role domestically. While not benefiting the country as a whole, EMU may still improve the welfare of particular groups within the country, which prevail on the government to pursue their preferred policies. EMU, in this view, is just one example of the distributional politics common in virtually every economic policy arena.

Serious analysis of the distributional implications of EMU is scarce, although there exist some suggestive essays [such as Giovannini (1993)]. A few

---

[16] Early variants of this analysis spoke of the "spillover" from one area of European integration to another. This was one of the arguments associated with the "neofunctionalist" approach to regional integration, although the approach tended to focus even more on how integration would create or reinforce bureaucratic or social interests in further integration. Moravcsik (1991), Webb (1983), and Keohane and Hoffman (1991) discuss this and other perspectives; an early statement of the approach is Haas (1958).

[17] The literature on the credibility of monetary policy is especially well-developed. For two good surveys, see Blackburn and Christensen (1989); and Grilli, Masciandaro, and Tabellini (1991).

observations are probably uncontroversial [for more details, see Frieden (1994), in this volume]. Those for whom currency volatility is most costly stand to gain the most from EMU. They include major banks and corporations with pan-EC investment or trade interests: for them forgoing national macroeconomic policy is a price worth paying for exchange rate predictability. Those for whom cross-border and foreign-currency transactions are inconsequential stand to lose the most. For them predictable exchange rates are of little or no value but national autonomy in the formulation of macroeconomic policies may be extremely important.

It is important to recognize that many distributional concerns raised over EMU have to do with the problems of adjusting to a fixed exchange rate. In a high-inflation country, fixing the exchange rate typically leads to a real appreciation, which puts substantial price pressure on producers of import-competing tradables. They can therefore also be expected to have reservations about both fixed exchange rates and monetary union.

Problems with the distributional approach are not so much theoretical as practical. There is almost no empirical work which successfully measures the distributional incidence of different international monetary regimes. Even if such work did exist, it would tell us little about outcomes because interests are mediated through political institutions. Such institutions can magnify the political influence of some groups and diminish that of others so that, for example, similar interests may be expressed differently when parliaments are chosen by proportional representation than when members come from single districts in a first-past-the-post system.[18] In any case, any rounded account of EMU has to pay close attention to domestic political factors, specifically to the role of interest groups with strong views on EMU and how these interest groups operate within national political institutions.

While additional categories of variables can undoubtedly be brought to bear on the political economy of EMU, these three appear central. We need a clear picture of the domestic interests at stake and the institutional setting within which they are situated. We need to understand how the divergent goals of national governments interact at the EC level. And we need to explore the ways in which EMU is linked to other EC policy areas.

THE POLITICAL ECONOMY OF MONETARY UNIFICATION IN PRACTICE

Though the members of the European Community have pursued the goal of monetary union for more than 25 years, progress has been sporadic. Understanding this trajectory is an obvious prerequisite to predicting whether the EC is likely to achieve this goal.

---

[18] For a summary of such arguments, and an application of one such to the area of trade policy, see Rogowski (1987).

The domestic distributional effects of international monetary policies have been crucial for European monetary developments, as Frieden (1994) and Woolley (1994) explain in this volume. The strongest support for EMU has come from Europe's international banks and corporations, while most of the opposition has come from domestically oriented economic actors, especially those in high-inflation countries where a fixed exchange rate and subsequent real appreciation has led to a large increase in import competition.

In France and Italy in the early 1980s, for example, the greatest opposition to the policies aimed at sustaining commitment to a fixed exchange rate came from workers in such import-competing industries as steel and automobiles. France's commitment to the EMS during the early years of the Mitterrand government was weakened by the unwillingness of Communists and left Socialists – whose principal constituencies were in declining manufacturing sectors hard hit by imports – to agree to austerity measures needed to bring French inflation in line with that of Germany. A similar dynamic was at play in Italy, where the Communist party and its supporters in the labor movement – again concentrated in such import-competing manufacturing as steel production – were reluctant to agree to real wage reductions needed to keep the lira in line with its ERM partners.

While the differential impact of EMU helps explain political conflict over monetary issues within and among EC members, it can explain changes in support for EMU over time only if the relative importance of different groups shifts or changes occur in the intensity with which the groups favor or oppose different international monetary arrangements. Such shifts may have occurred, especially in the 1980s, due to changing levels of intra-EC capital mobility and trade. As the EC became more financially integrated, the choice between monetary policy autonomy and exchange rate stability became starker. At the same time, higher levels of intra-EC trade increased the importance of exchange rate fluctuations for both producers and consumers. And increased cross-border investment among EC members had similar effects, expanding the ranks of those for whom exchange rate fluctuations caused problems. Inasmuch as the increased openness of EC economies involves more economic agents in cross-border economic activities, and these firms and individuals care about reducing exchange-rate volatility, the drive toward the free movement of goods and capital within the Community strengthens support for EMU.

Many accounts of the political economy of EMU emphasize domestic politics [as in Goodman (1992)]. The crisis the EMS experienced in 1992–1993 is a good example. Domestic political factors appeared to impede coordination of EC members' macroeconomic policies. The British government might have raised interest rates to defend sterling, for example, except that the higher rates would have been passed on by mortgage lenders, and many within the ruling Conservative party worried about the objections of property owners. For its part, the Italian government might have enacted drastic fiscal measures to make

its commitment to lower inflation more credible, but in the midst of a deep political crisis this was difficult to achieve over the objections of public employees
and others who feared that their positions would be threatened. The French government could have raised interest rates to defend the franc, but at the cost of
increasing the already-high French unemployment rate. The German authorities
might have loosened monetary policy in order to reduce pressure on their EMS
partners but for the Bundesbank's traditional concern about inflation, which was
reinforced by strong antiinflationary constituencies in the German body politic
such as the country's powerful industrialists.

While there exist many anecdotes about the importance of interest group
politics in debate over EMU, this evidence is hardly systematic. The examples
given above indicate that domestic distributional considerations are undoubtedly important, but have not yet been formulated in ways that allow us to arrive
at clear conclusions as to their effects.

Interstate bargaining has of course been central to the EMU process. The coercive strand of inter-state bargaining theories finds support in the fact that EC
member states appear to have thrown their weight around in the bargaining process. This is in line with assertions that, for example, the Italian government in
the 1980s was not enthusiastic about the EMS but was presented with a fait
accompli by the French and Germans. It also accords with the widespread belief
that the French government in the 1990s has been eager to use EMU to reduce
German influence over European monetary policy while Germany has been
somewhat less ardent in its pursuit of EMU.

But there remain problems with too strong a reliance on inter-state analyses
relying on coercion. Countries can accede to the ERM or not as they wish, and
they can withdraw at will (as they have). Major decisions on the path to EMU
restricting countries' freedom of action in significant ways have typically required unanimous votes. While the Maastricht Treaty certainly narrowed the
permissible room to maneuver of its signatories, for example, no country was
forced to sign. This makes the invocation of power politics questionable.

What most explanations of this type appear to have in mind is not clearcut
coercion, but a bargaining process in which some countries insist to others that
refusing to go along with EMU will impose costs on other dimensions of EC
policy. This means that the bargaining relationship involves explicit or implicit
links between EMU and other issue areas. Linkages are indeed central to what
such analysts as Garrett (1994) and Woolley (1994), in this volume, have in
mind when they argue that the German government went along with EMU –
which it found relatively unattractive on the merits – in return for assurances
that the EC would move forward on political matters, especially a common foreign policy. The analysis of Martin (1994), also in this volume, similarly relies
on institutionalized linkages. The explanation of French and Italian commitments to the EMS in the early 1980s presented by Frieden (1994) in this volume
similarly relies on the domestic political impact of such linkage effects. And

many analysts have pointed to the connection between the EC's search for exchange rate stability and its Common Agricultural Policy (CAP), the operation of which is severely complicated by fluctuations in EC currency values.[19]

Evidence of linkage is not easy to find, however. Formal agreements have rarely tied monetary integration to other EC policies. And any analysis that relies on unstated (implicit) links must carefully explain how we know these links exist. For example, while many analysts and policymakers believe that full participation in the single market might be hampered by non-participation in the EMS, there is no provision in the Single European Act or any other Community document that even remotely hints at this tie. All of this is not to imply that linkage politics are unimportant, only that its analysis requires care and hard evidence.

All of the factors analyzed here have played a role in the process of European monetary unification. None, however, appears to have earned clear pride of place in our explanatory apparatus. The conclusion we draw is not to abandon systematic economic and political analysis of EMU but to encourage it. It is especially important to insist on explicit analytical arguments and on conscious attempts to disentangle the causes of the processes we observe.

## THE FUTURE OF EMU

As we work slowly toward this goal, we should ponder what 25 years' experience with European monetary unification implies for the future of the process. In the wake of the turbulence that afflicted the European Monetary System following the negotiation of the Maastricht Treaty, a number of scenarios are conceivable.

1. *EMU of the 12.* All 12 members of the Community (16 if the EFTA countries, other than Iceland and Switzerland, are admitted to the Community) could rededicate themselves to the task of meeting the Maastricht Treaty's convergence criteria and establish an EC-wide monetary union toward the end of the decade.

2. *Early Two-Speed EMU.* Alternatively, a subset of countries might make substantial progress toward meeting the convergence criteria. If a bare majority of EC countries (including, perhaps, some of the present-day

---

[19] The CAP is far too complex to explore in detail here. Suffice it to point out that in the context of major agricultural subsidies, the EC sets Community-wide food prices. When a currency is devalued, the EC reference price would normally be raised in the devaluing country to counterbalance the devaluation – thus "passing through" the exchange rate change in full to food prices. The inflationary impact of this pass-through would mitigate the devaluation's attempt to restore price competitiveness in non-agricultural sectors. For this reason, the Community devised a series of compensatory arrangements and accounting exchange rates. For our purposes, what is important is only that exchange rate fluctuations complicate Community agricultural policy by changing compensatory farm payments in ways that could disrupt the delicate balance within the EC on farm policy. For more details see McNamara (1993).

EFTA countries) succeeds in doing so, they could establish a monetary union in short order. The version of Maastricht Treaty drafted in December 1991 and signed in January 1992 would permit a single currency to be established by a majority of countries after Stage Two began on January 1, 1994, so long as that majority satisfied the convergence criteria, such as two preceding years of exchange rate stability. Given the exchange rate instability of 1992–1993, in practice it seems unlikely that a majority of countries would satisfy these criteria in the immediate future.

3. *Late Two-Speed EMU.* The attempt to stabilize exchange rates on a Community-wide basis through Stage Two of the transition might fail in the face of market pressures. Only a minority of countries centered on Germany (a "deutschmark bloc" comprised of Germany, Benelux and possibly France and – assuming its admission to the Community – Austria), would succeed in maintaining exchange-rate stability and qualifying for EMU in 1999 (the first date, according to the treaty, when EMU can proceed with only a minority of countries).

4. *No EMU.* Exchange-rate instability could infect even Germany's Northern European neighbors. The Maastricht blueprint would be rendered moot, and would join its predecessors as another failed episode in the effort to achieve monetary unification in Europe.

5. *Forced March to Mini-EMU Outside the Context of the Treaty.* Realizing the scope for renewed exchange rate instability, a minority of strong-currency countries centered on Germany and France (encompassing the rest of the deutschmark bloc, possibly including Austria) would establish monetary union well before 1999. Alternatively, France and Germany could attempt to construct a de facto monetary union between themselves. Either option would require that the Maastricht Treaty be revised, replaced or superseded to permit a small subgroup of countries to establish a monetary union prior to 1999.

Neither economic nor political theory is capable of predicting which scenario will obtain. But the combined body of theory, together with the historical record, suggests that some scenarios are more likely than others.

The first scenario (EMU of the 12 by the end of the decade) is unlikely. The asymmetric shock of 1990–91 (German unification) and Europe's 1992–93 recession revealed that many countries' allegiance to the Maastricht process was a "fair-weather" commitment: opposition resurfaced once it became clear that meeting the treaty's preconditions would have economic costs. Recent experience thus suggests that domestic political resistance to belt-tightening measures will prevent some countries from satisfying the convergence criteria, especially if another recession or another asymmetric shock intervenes. German officials, for their part, have rejected suggestions to relax the preconditions for participation in EMU, and have voiced repeated doubts that all 12 member countries will be ready to participate by the end of the decade.

The second scenario (early two-speed EMU) confronts the same problems as does the first scenario, though for a more limited period of time. Under the provisions of the Maastricht treaty, proceeding with a two-speed EMU before 1999 requires, as explained above, that a majority of member countries qualify. Given the exchange rate instability of 1992–93 and the widening budgetary gaps consequent on Europe's recession, it seems unlikely that a majority of countries would satisfy the convergence criteria at an early date. Given that several of the current applicants for membership (Sweden, Finland) suffered exchange-rate crises in late 1992, the possibility of EC enlargement does not appear to have critical implications for this scenario.

This scenario has other obstacles to surmount, as well. In 1992–93, the instability of some European currencies (those of Sweden, Italy and Britain) spilled over to others, even to those of countries apparently meeting all the conditions for having a strong currency (France, for example). This raises the danger that exchange-rate instability within the bloc of countries proceeding at low speed may contagiously infect those attempting to proceed at high speed [a problem analyzed by Gerlach and Smets (1993)]. The second scenario also raises questions about the viability of other Community programs in a situation where only a subset of member countries form a monetary union. As mentioned above, existing EC programs such as the CAP become difficult to run when intra-European exchange rates are allowed to float. Floating, even over a limited geographical area, is likely to heighten complaints about competitive pressures associated with the Single European Act if some countries are able to depreciate their currencies in order to steal a competitive advantage in international markets. As suggested by Alesina and Grilli (1994), in this volume, this scenario also faces the danger that the early participants will resist the subsequent admission of other countries; knowing this, the others will use their leverage in other issue areas to prevent the strong-currency countries from pursuing the second scenario.

The third scenario (late two-speed EMU encompassing only those EC countries – presumably Germany, Benelux and perhaps also France and Denmark – capable of resisting the contagious effects of exchange rate instability elsewhere) is likely to be viable purely as an exchange rate arrangement. But this scenario, like the second one, may founder on the incompatibility of floating in parts of the Community with the CAP and the SEA, and on the subsequent admissions problem described by Alesina and Grilli.

The fourth scenario (No EMU) is conceivable, but it is a fundamental threat to the SEA. It implies either the indefinite maintenance of capital controls to reconcile pegged exchange rates with national policy autonomy, and hence modification of the SEA, or a return to generalized floating, both of which are subversive to the CAP and the SEA.

On purely economic grounds, then, there is reason to attach a higher probability to the fifth scenario (forced march to mini-EMU outside the context of the treaty) than to the others. There is no obvious economic obstacle to establishing monetary union for Germany, France and some of the small Northern European countries. A quick transition would eliminate scope for exchange-rate instability. Excluding countries with more pervasive inflation and budgetary problems would relieve the members of this mini-EMU of their fear that it would exhibit an inflationary bias.

The question about the fifth scenario is whether it is politically viable since it would require thorough renegotiation of existing EMU agreements and the agreement of Germany. Is the bargain that drew the negotiators of the participating countries to accept the Maastricht draft in 1991 still workable today? One view is that the answer is no: Germany, which otherwise had nothing to gain from monetary unification, agreed to EMU in 1991 only as a quid pro quo for the Community's acceptance of Germany unification. As German unification is now a reality, a new round of negotiations is less likely to meet a successful conclusion. The other view is that Germany will still agree to EMU in return for deeper political union and a renewed foreign policy role. Germany still seeks a renewed foreign policy role within the context of a politically integrated Europe. But the difficulties the Community has experienced in formulating a coherent foreign policy response to the conflict in the former Yugoslavia have dimmed German enthusiasm for this venture. Whether German political leaders and their constituents are really prepared to sacrifice the deutschmark in the short run in order to gain a joint foreign policy role, together with France and the other Community countries, is again an open question.

If not, in which case a forced march to mini-EMU is ruled out, another scenario from the exhaustive list presented above will necessarily obtain. Floating or pegged rates supported permanently by capital controls are the options of last resort: they will obtain if European policymakers cannot agree on a creative solution. If the preferred scenario is a late two-speed EMU, the problem is how to safely navigate the transition without succumbing to additional balance-of-payments crises like those of 1992–93. For countries to rededicate themselves to harmonizing their policies may not be enough. Eichengreen and Wyplosz (1993) argue that perverse incentives built into the Maastricht treaty may give rise to purely self-fulfilling speculative attacks. As explained above, qualifying for participation requires, among other things, two years of exchange rate stability. Hence, a speculative attack which drives a country out of the ERM and disqualifies it from participation may remove the incentive its policy makers previously possessed to pursue policies of austerity. The latter will have good reason to shift toward more accommodating policies following an attack, and knowledge of this fact gives speculators the incentive to undertake it. Currencies are consequently vulnerable to speculative attack even in the absence of any problem with fundamentals, and will grow increasingly so as the 1999 deadline for Stage Three approaches.

If this view is correct, then the EMS requires transitional measures to stabilize its operation over the remainder of the transition to EMU. (This implication follows whether one believes that Stage Three will start early or late.) Eichen-green and Wyplosz propose the temporary imposition of a Tobin tax on foreign exchange transactions or non-interest-bearing deposit requirements on banks taking open positions in foreign exchange as a way of containing self-fulfilling speculative attacks. The first option is a form of taxation like the VAT, while the second is a form of prudential supervision; as such, neither would require modi-fication of the SEA or the Maastricht Treaty. The argument for them is that tem-porary measures are needed to stabilize an intrinsically unstable EMS until the goal of monetary union is reached.

ABOUT THIS VOLUME

The contributors to this volume approach the analysis of EMU from both polit-ical and economic angles. The first chapter, by Jeffry Frieden, looks at the expe-riences of France and Italy in the early years of the EMS. Frieden argues that two factors were central to the domestic politics of currency policy in these countries. First were the distributional effects expected to result from binding the franc and the lira to the EMS. Import-competing manufacturing sectors op-posed fixing exchange rates in ways that would erode their ability to compete with foreign producers; internationally oriented sectors favored currency stabil-ity. The second crucial factor was the linkage made between EMS policy and broader issues in European integration. This forced groups in both France and Italy that were ambivalent about or hostile to the EMS to weigh these concerns against their general attitude toward the EC, and in many cases to go along with monetary policies they might otherwise have tried to block.

The following three chapters, by Geoffrey Garrett, John Woolley, and Lisa Martin, seek to understand how the EMU bargain came about and whether it can be sustained. Garrett analyzes the Maastricht Treaty in terms of linkage politics, portraying it as a bargain between Germany, a country standing to gain little from monetary union per se, and the rest of the Community. EMU must there-fore be understood in terms of issue linkage – a result of trade-offs across issue areas. Germany, he argues, made significant concessions on matters monetary in return for general European support for the process of German unification, as well as for a deepening of valued trade and investment ties with the rest of the EC.

John Woolley's chapter focuses in more detail on the domestic politics of EMU. As Frieden emphasizes the domestic implications of the link between the EMS and European integration in France and Italy in the early 1980s, Woolley insists on the domestic sources of German insistence on tying EMU and Euro-pean political union together in the negotiations that led up to the Maastricht Treaty in the early 1990s. Like Garrett, Woolley regards the German strategy as closely related to the changed environment created by German unification. However, Woolley highlights the foreign policy impact of German domestic politics. He argues, in fact, that German chancellor Helmut Kohl may have had little choice in domestic political terms but to make German support for EMU conditional upon agreements about European political union.

Lisa L. Martin also focuses on bargaining links, but argues that it is important to view the debate over EMU as embedded in an institutionalized pattern of inter-state cooperation on many dimensions. The same set of countries is engaged in institutionalized negotiations over a range of economic and political issues, including defense, social policy, competition policy and, of course, monetary policy. The fact that countries stand to lose all of the joint gains they have made from cooperation on a variety of issues tends to lock in the agreement on monetary matters.

The outcomes thereby produced, Martin argues, are mediated by the institutional arrangements by which differences are resolved – specifically, by the institutions of the European Community. For example, the disproportionate influence of small states in the governance of the monetary union, as reflected in the Maastricht Treaty (all states, ranging from large ones like Germany to small ones like Luxembourg, will have one vote on most matters of policy), must be understood, Martin suggests, as a function of formal decision-making procedures such as unanimity requirements.

Alberto Alesina and Vittorio Grilli also speak to the issue raised by Garrett, Woolley and Martin of "what is in it for Germany." They too suggest that Germany has little to gain in terms of monetary policy outcomes per se. But unlike Garrett, Woolley, and Martin, who contemplate trade-offs across issue areas, Alesina and Grilli concentrate on the implications for monetary policy alone. They argue that the union will prove viable only if Germany is given disproportionate influence over policy formulation. It must be permitted to veto inflationary policies. Since its veto power is likely to be diluted by the admission of additional inflation-prone countries, a two-speed approach to monetary union therefore appears likely.

This leads Alesina and Grilli to examine the viability of two-speed EMU. Their question does not appear to have been addressed in the literature before: will countries which enter EMU initially really wish to admit the laggards? Countries with a strong aversion to inflation, with low debts or experiencing small output shocks may not wish to admit to their monetary union less inflation-averse countries, countries with higher debts, and countries experiencing larger output shocks, since the latter will increase the inflationary bias of the union to the detriment of the early entrants. If the weaker countries succeed in "putting their houses in order" (more generally, in remaking themselves so that their structure and preferences resemble those of the early entrants), this result disappears. Otherwise, the early entrants may have an interest in interpreting entry requirements rigorously when it comes time to consider admission of the laggards.

Jürgen von Hagen and Michele Fratianni analyze the political economy of the European Monetary Institute (EMI), the transitional entity that will coordinate national monetary policies during Stage Two and lay the groundwork for the establishment of the ECB. The authors argue that the institutional design of the EMI will tend to create a bias toward excessively decentralized policy objectives and operating procedures. The poor performance of such an EMU may become an obstacle to future political integration, which in turn could undermine the monetary initiative insofar as EMU needs political integration to be acceptable to the public.

Most of the literature takes as granted that monetary union is irreversible. Benjamin Cohen challenges this assumption. Contrasting the experience of three surviving monetary unions (the Belgium-Luxembourg Union, the CFA Franc Zone, and the East Caribbean Currency Area) with three that failed (the East African Community, the Latin Union and the Scandinavian Union), he asks whether economic, political or organizational factors explain success or failure. He concludes that appropriate economic conditions (high factor mobility, symmetric shocks) and organizational structures (an independent central bank, legal provisions for currency issue) have not always been sufficient to hold a monetary union together. Rather, political factors, broadly defined, are key. The presence or absence of a dominant power (a "hegemon") or sufficient political cohesion ("community") are needed to preserve a monetary union over time.

As the last section emphasized, the convergence criteria which will determine who qualifies for monetary union are among the most controversial provisions of the Maastricht treaty, as well as major constraints on European policymakers. Barry Eichengreen's chapter focuses on the convergence criteria requiring countries to meet debt and deficit targets in order to qualify for EMU, and the so-called excessive deficits procedures that will constrain their fiscal options even after the monetary union begins. He provides a critical review of the fiscal provisions of the treaty, exploring its implications for the EMU debate. He concludes that while the provisions governing fiscal behavior following the inauguration of Stage Three are not without justification, during Stage Two these provisions are difficult to justify on any grounds.

## REFERENCES

Alesina, Alberto and Vittorio Grilli, 1994, On the Feasibility of a One or Multi-Speed European Monetary Union. This volume.

Bayoumi, Tamim and Barry Eichengreen, 1992, Shocking Aspects of European Monetary Unification, in: Francisco Torres and Francesco Giavazzi, eds., *The Transition to Economic and Monetary Union in Europe* (Cambridge University Press, Cambridge).

Bini Smaghi, Lorenzo and Silvia Vori, 1990, Rating the EC as an Optimum Currency Area: Is it Worse than the U.S.? Unpublished manuscript, Banca d'Italia.

Blackburn, Keith and Michael Christensen, 1989, Monetary Policy and Policy Credibility: Theories and Evidence. *Journal of Economic Literature* 27, No. 1, 1–45.

Coffey, Peter, 1987, *The European Monetary System – past, present and future* (Kluwer, Amsterdam).

Cohen, Benjamin J., 1994, Beyond EMU: The Problem of Sustainability. This volume.

Cushman, David, 1988, Exchange Rate Uncertainty and Foreign Direct Investment in the United States. *Weltwirtschaftsliches Archiv* 124, 322–336.

Eichengreen, Barry, 1992, Should the Maastricht Treaty Be Saved? *Princeton Studies in International Finance* (International Finance Section, Princeton).

——, 1993, Thinking about migration: Notes on European Migration Pressures at the Dawn of the Next Millenium, in Horst Siebert, ed., *Migration a Challenge for Europe* (University of Michigan Press, Ann Arbor, Michigan).

Eichengreen, Barry, and Charles Wyplosz, 1993, The Unstable EMS. *Brookings Papers on Economic Activity* 1, pp. 51–143.

European Commission, 1990, One Market, One Money. *The European Economy* 44, special issue.

Fratianni, Michele, and Jürgen von Hagen, 1992, *The European Monetary System and European Monetary Union* (Westview, Boulder, Colo.).

——, 1994, The European Monetary Institute in the Transition to European Monetary Union. This volume.

Frieden, Jeffry, 1994, Making commitments: France and Italy in the European Monetary System 1979–1985. This volume.

Garrett, Geoffrey, 1992, International Cooperation and Institutional Choice: The European Community's Internal Market. *International Organization* 46.

——, 1994, The Politics of Maastricht. This volume.

Gerlach, Stefan and F. Smets, 1993, Contagion Effects of Speculative attacks against fixed exchange rate regimes. Unpublished manuscript.

Giavazzi, Francesco and Alberto Giovannini, 1989, *Limiting exchange rate flexibility: The European Monetary System* (MIT Press, Cambridge).

Giovannini, Alberto, 1993, EMU: What Happened? Exploring the political dimension of optimum currency areas, in: Guillermo de la Dehesa, Alberto Giovannini, Manuel Guitián, and Richard Portes, eds., *The Monetary Future of Europe* (Centre for Economic Policy Research, London).

Goodman, John, 1992, *Monetary sovereignty: The politics of central banking in Western Europe* (Cornell University Press, Ithaca, N.Y.).

Grilli, Vittorio, Donato Masciandaro, and Guido Tabellini, 1991, Political and monetary institutions and public financial policies in the industrial countries. *Economic Policy* 13 (October), 342–392.

Haas, Ernst, 1958, *The uniting of Europe* (Stanford University Press, Stanford, Calif.).

International Monetary Fund, 1988, Policy coordination in the European monetary system. *IMF Occasional Papers* 61 (IMF, Washington).

Ishiyama, Yoshihide, 1975, The theory of optimum currency areas: A survey. *IMF Staff Papers* 22, 344–383.

Kenen, Peter, 1969, The optimum currency area: An eclectic view, in: Robert Mundell and Alexander Swoboda, eds., *Monetary problems of the international economy,* (University of Chicago Press, Chicago) 41–60.

Keohane, Robert, and Stanley Hoffman, 1991, Institutional change in Europe in the 1980s, in: Stanley Hoffman and Robert Keohane, eds., *The New European Community* (Westview Press, Boulder, Colo.).

Ludlow, Peter, 1982, *The making of the European Monetary System* (Butterworth, London).

Martin, Lisa, 1994, International and domestic institutions in the EMU process. This volume.

McKinnon, Ronald, 1963, Optimum currency areas. *American Economic Review* 53, 717–725.

McNamara, Kathleen, 1993, Common markets, uncommon currencies: Systems effects and the European Community, in: Robert Jervis and Jack Snyder, eds., *Coping with complexity in the international system* (Westview Press, Boulder).

Moravcsik, Andrew, 1991, Negotiating the Single European Act: National interests and conventional statecraft in the European Community. *International Organization* 45, 19–56.

Mundell, Robert, 1961, A Theory of optimum currency areas. *American Economic Review* 51, 657–665.

Rogowski, Ronald, 1987, Trade and the variety of democratic institutions. *International Organization* 41, 203–224.

Sandholtz, Wayne, 1993, Choosing union: monetary politics and Maastricht. *International Organization* 47, 1–39.

Sapir, A. and K. Sekket, 1989, Exchange Rate Variability and International Trade: The Effects of the European Monetary System. Ms., Free University of Brussels.

Tsoukalis, Loukas, 1977, *The politics and economics of European monetary integration* (George Allen and Unwin, London).

Ungerer, Horst, 1983, The European Monetary system: The experience, 1979–82. *IMF Occasional Papers* 19 (IMF, Washington).

Van Ypersele, Jacques, 1985, *The European Monetary System: Origins, Operation and Outlook* (Commission of the European Communities, Brussels).

Webb, Carole, 1983, Theoretical Perspectives and Problems, in: Helen Wallace, William Wallace, and Carole Webb, eds., *Policymaking in the European Community* 2nd edition (John Wiley and Sons, Chichester) 1–42.

# 2

## MAKING COMMITMENTS:
## FRANCE AND ITALY IN THE
## EUROPEAN MONETARY SYSTEM, 1979–1985

### Jeffry Frieden

European monetary integration depends on commitments by member states of the European Community to sustain monetary policies consistent with stable exchange rates. These commitments in turn depend on the domestic political support that governments can muster for such policies. Two domestic political dimensions have been central to the development of the European Monetary System (EMS): the role of economic interest groups with preferences toward the policies associated with EMS membership, and the domestic implications of linking EMS commitments with the broader process of European integration. This chapter[1] analyzes the domestic politics of French and Italian policy toward the EMS from 1979 through the mid-1980s, during which the two countries' commitments to monetary integration gradually hardened.

EUROPEAN MONETARY integration (MI) has experienced dramatic twists and turns over the past twenty-five years. The "snake" of the 1970s was a general failure, and in the early 1980s the new European Monetary System (EMS) seemed little better.[2] In the late 1980s the EMS appeared to settle into something approaching a currency union, but appearances of stability were shattered by the currency crisis that began in September 1992. As of late 1993, the monetary future of Europe was still very much in question.

At the center of the problem were national governments' commitments to maintain fixed exchange rates with their European Community (EC) partners. The manifest weakness of such commitments on the part of several important EC members – especially France and Italy – in the 1970s and early 1980s led to great skepticism about the EMS, while the apparent hardening of those commitments in the late 1980s gave rise to equally (and, in the event, perhaps overly) great optimism.

This chapter elucidates the ways in which the French and Italian governments' commitments to a fixed exchange rate became increasingly credible

[1] The author acknowledges support for this research from the Social Science Research Council's Program in Foreign Policy Studies, the German Marshall Fund, the UCLA Institute for Industrial Relations and the UCLA Center for International Business Education and Research and comments from Benjamin J. Cohen, Barry Eichengreen, John Goodman, Jürgen von Hagen, Peter Lange, Lisa Martin, and John Woolley.

[2] It is actually more accurate to speak of the Exchange Rate Mechanism (ERM) of the EMS, which is the agreement to bind currency values. The United Kingdom, for example, was a founding member of the EMS but only tied sterling to the ERM in October 1990. However, inasmuch as the two are closely linked in popular and scholarly discussion, I use the terms more or less interchangeably.

between 1979 and 1985. In this context, I argue for the central role of two factors within the domestic political arena. The first is the confluence of economic interests expected to favor or oppose a system of fixed exchange rates within the European Community. The second is the linkage between monetary integration (MI) and other EC policies, which might lead actors otherwise indifferent about currency developments per se or even hostile to the EMS on its merits to support MI in the interest of broader Community goals.

The first section evaluates a series of common explanations of EC members' decisions to commit to fixed exchange rates over the years, concluding that linkage politics is crucial to the process. The next section discusses both the political implications of the distributional impact of currency arrangements, and the logic of a linkage-based argument. The third section analyzes the domestic politics of French and Italian monetary policies between 1979 and 1985, tracing the operation of the distributional and linkage-related factors that helped the two countries' currency commitments acquire credibility. The final section explores the implications of these experiences for the future of European monetary integration.

## CREDIBLE COMMITMENTS AND EUROPEAN MONETARY INTEGRATION

Monetary integration depends on commitments by EC member governments to particular exchange rates. This implies committing to similar national monetary policies, as currency values depend first and foremost on underlying national monetary conditions. These commitments were, on average, quite lacking in credibility in the 1970s, but gained increasing credibility over the 1980s.

The snake of the 1970s did hold together for Germany, Denmark, and the Benelux countries, but it was widely regarded as a failure. In the late 1980s the EMS and its exchange rate mechanism (ERM) had these countries as members, along with France, Italy, and Ireland, and it was widely regarded as a success. The crucial difference between the failed snake and the relatively successful mature EMS, then, was the adherence of France, Italy, and Ireland. For reasons of size, the French and Italian cases are central.

But this raises a major puzzle. The French and Italian governments had not been able to sustain fixed exchange rates during the 1970s. Nor had either government been able to commit itself to serious inflation reduction over this period. Indeed, bringing them into a German-dominated monetary union was a special challenge: both had run inflation substantially higher than German levels since the late 1960s. There was, therefore, little reason to believe that they would be able to implement the domestic policies necessary to sustain their EMS commitments in the 1980s – and yet they did.

Various solutions to this puzzle have been proposed.[3] The first is that the

---

[3] For a summary of some of these analytical perspectives, see Eichengreen and Frieden (1994, this volume). Other good surveys are Giavazzi and Giovannini (1989) and Fratianni and von Hagen (1992).

formal institutions of the EMS were more effective at sustaining cooperation among member states than those of the less formal snake because an exchange rate agreement requires a number of explicit provisions for consultation about parity changes, and the financing of payments deficits.

It is true that the EMS was a somewhat more developed institutional mechanism than the snake, and that the EMS made more money available to members than did the snake. Much of the difference, at least at the outset, was undoubtedly due to the fact that the snake was planned while the Bretton Woods system was still (barely) alive, which made more formal arrangements redundant. In any event, very short-term financing arrangements were extended from thirty to forty five days, and their capacity expanded from 6 billion to 14 billion European Currency Units (ecus). Medium-term financing ceilings were raised from 5.45 billion to 14.1 billion ecus, and five billion ecus in concessionary loans over a five-year period were made available to Ireland and Italy [van Ypersele (1985, pp. 61–64)]. Certainly the greater resources committed to the EMS made affiliation more attractive.

However, there is little evidence that these organizational factors were particularly important to the process. In fact, many of the new mechanisms were not part of the original EMS but evolved as (or after) it became credible. From the financial side, the money involved was not really substantial, and Italy did not even use its concessionary finance. Certainly there is no evidence that the evolution of French policy was at all related to the formal institutions of the EMS.[4]

A second explanation is that the exchange rate targets chosen in the EMS were more transparent than the monetary targets announced, and not met, by the French and Italian governments in their prior attempts to fight inflation. The idea here is that economic agents are more likely to be convinced by a government's commitment to a specific exchange rate, which the markets can observe, than by a general commitment to reduce inflation or even a specific commitment to a monetary target, which the markets cannot directly observe.

This, however, does not explain why the French and Italian governments were better able to commit to a fixed exchange rate in the late 1980s than in the 1970s. If transparency in and of itself increased a government's credibility, a government serious about reducing inflation would *always* use the exchange rate as such a signal. The fact that the signal sent by the French and Italian governments in the 1970s turned out to be untrustworthy, while it was far more reliable in the late 1980s, simply pushes the question back a step.

A third potential explanation of the greater success of monetary integration

---

[4] This conclusion is analogous to that drawn from a broader historical survey by Cohen (1994, this volume). If one defines institutions more broadly, as does Martin (1994, this volume), then the linkage argument developed below might be regarded as a special case of a broader institutional explanation. However, most of the literature that relies on institutional changes to explain the success of the EMS is referring, as is Cohen (1994, this volume), to the formal organizational mechanisms by which the system itself was governed.

in the 1980s than in the 1970s is that national preferences had converged.[5] Certainly if countries' desired inflation levels had been more similar in 1979 than in 1973, they would have been better able to sustain fixed exchange rates. However, to judge from inflation levels, there is little evidence for such preference convergence. French and Italian inflation rates were higher in the first three years of the EMS than in the first three years of the snake, and differed more from that of Germany. Perhaps politicians and voters *wanted* lower inflation, but they appeared unable to achieve it outside the EMS – which again pushes us back to the need to explain the success of the mechanism as it evolved between 1979 and 1985.

A fourth reason often given for the relative accomplishments of the 1980s is that the international economic environment was easier than in the 1970s, especially in the absence of oil price shocks. This confuses overall *levels* of inflation with *divergences* from German levels. If all EMS members had had lower inflation rates in the 1980s than in the 1970s, this would not necessarily have made fixed exchange rates easier to sustain, so long as national inflation rates differed substantially. For external economic conditions to explain the differential successes of the two decades, these conditions would have to have been asymmetric in such a way that the shocks to Germany were more inflationary than shocks to other EMS countries. Only if this had come to pass – and there is very little evidence that it did – would international conditions have made it easier for other EMS countries to sustain fixed rates against the deutschemark (DM).[6]

[5] Collins and Giavazzi (1993) present the strongest case for this argument, purporting to show a change in national attitudes toward inflation. However, their study does not in fact look at public *policy* preferences, but rather at the weight that household respondents accord inflation (as opposed to unemployment) in formulating their forecasts of general economic outcomes. This is several steps removed from public willingness to support the political measures necessary to reduce inflation, which is the actual shift asserted in the literature.

[6] Fratianni and von Hagen (1992) present one of the more systematic arguments for a combination of the third and fourth arguments (in other words, that national preferences and the international environment changed). They focus more on alleged changes in national preferences, as seen in changes in inflation rates in EMS and non-EMS countries, arguing that there is little evidence that the EMS itself had a significant inflation-reducing impact.

However, questions can be raised about the data they use. Fratianni and von Hagen include successful members of the snake (Benelux) in the EMS sample, but the inflation rates of these countries had already converged with that of Germany by the start of the EMS. Similarly, they include Austria and Switzerland in the non-EMS control group, although the Austrian and Swiss currencies formally or informally tracked the deutschemark for most of the period. Finally, they use average inflation rates weighted by GNP, even though each country is an equally valid observation.

Reworking the data accordingly, in 1977–1978 the average unweighted inflation rate for the eventual new EMS members (France, Italy, Ireland, and Denmark – including this last as it was only a nominal member of the snake) was 11.3 percent, 8.1 percent higher than in Germany. By 1987–1988 the average inflation rate for these four countries was 3.7 percent, just 2.9 percent higher than Germany's. In contrast, the non-EMS group (Australia, Canada, Finland, Greece, Japan, the United Kingdom, and the United States) had an average inflation rate of 9.5 percent in 1977–1978, which came down to 5.8 percent in 1987–1988, 5 percent higher than Germany's. This would appear an appreciable difference in convergence of inflation rates between the two groups.

Perhaps more important is that for my purposes it is not particularly important to show that the EMS was necessarily the only reason for inflation reduction; it is sufficient to show that the EMS required convergence with Germany monetary conditions. This was also the case with the snake, and raises once more the same question: why were these countries willing and able to reduce inflation sufficiently to stay in the EMS when they had been unwilling or unable to do so for the snake?

A fifth explanation for EMS success is that structural economic characteristics of member countries had changed over the course of the 1970s. The principal point here is that the welfare benefits of currency union rise as economies become more financially and commercially integrated, and the members of the EC became more integrated over the course of the 1970s.

There is much truth to this argument, and I have presented the case for it elsewhere [Frieden (1993)]. Levels of economic integration within the EC grew after the late 1960s, and as they grew, so did interest in monetary union. By the same token, those countries most strongly integrated into other EC economies (especially that of Germany) have been most enthusiastic about MI. However, the change in levels of economic integration between 1973–1975, when France and Italy fell out of the snake, and 1983–1985, when they acquired credibility within the EMS, was small. Indeed, a more relevant comparison might be the last years of the snake (1976–1978) and the first years of the EMS (1979–1983), over which time the economies in question changed hardly at all. It is, in any case, hard to believe that marginal changes in structural economic conditions could have such striking effects on national commitments to currency policies.

The final argument made for the success of the EMS in the 1980s rests on linkage politics. Many analysts believe that monetary integration succeeded to the extent that it was tied to other goals at the European level. Countries went along with MI because cooperation on the monetary front was essential to cooperation on other fronts that they valued highly.[7]

In the remainder of this chapter, I develop the argument that linkage between monetary integration and European integration more generally was central to the success of MI in the 1980s, and specifically to French and Italian exchange rate commitments between 1979 and 1985. However, the invocation of linkage politics is not without problems. As Alt and Eichengreen (1989) point out, such linkage effects hold only under certain conditions, having especially to do with different national valuations of the policies in question.[8] Such valuations can best be understood as a function of domestic political factors; I analyze the domestic circumstances in France and Italy that made linkage politics feasible.[9]

### DISTRIBUTIONAL PREFERENCES AND LINKAGE POLITICS IN EUROPEAN MONETARY INTEGRATION

Linkage politics ups the benefits of initial and continuing cooperation because tying two issue areas together enables gains from political trades. A group that

---

[7] Garrett (1994, this volume), makes a variant of this argument. Martin (1994, this volume), presents an explicit linkage-based explanation of EMU in the Maastricht process that is analogous to mine but focuses on the ways in which linkages are made binding by institutional characteristics of the EC itself.

[8] In addition, as pointed out in Eichengreen and Frieden (1994), the invocation of linkage politics simply pushes the credibility problem back one step: if linking two policy arenas raises the costs of defection in each, as it may under certain carefully specified conditions, what makes the link itself credible? I do not address this issue here, but take the tie between the EMS and European integration as given.

[9] A parallel argument is presented in Woolley (1992).

has a strong preference for a policy in one arena and a weak preference against a policy in another arena can compromise with another group that has a weak preference against the first policy and a strong preference for the second policy. In this way, each group gets what it cares about more in return for giving up what it cares about less. Without the linkage process, the two groups would oppose each other in the two arenas; with the arenas linked, exchange is possible.[10]

French and Italian commitments to fixed exchange rates, I argue, were made more credible by the link between MI and broader European integration. This redefined the domestic politics of monetary policy and the choices available to domestic groups in ways that made a previously unattainable outcome possible. To clarify this argument, I discuss the constellation of interests on both dimensions – monetary integration and broader European integration – and show how trade-offs along the two dimensions made domestic political agreement possible.

The first step is to specify preferences in the first issue area, monetary integration.[11] Tying the franc and the lira to the ERM implied a fixed and relatively appreciated exchange rate against the deutschemark. The real appreciation was a function of the fact that France and Italy had inflation substantially above that of Germany, and in any foreseeable circumstances inertial inflation would lead to a transitional real appreciation of their currencies after they were fixed in nominal terms.

Moving from floating to fixed exchange rates provides greater predictability in foreign trade and exchange. However, it makes it impossible for the government to alter exchange rates to affect domestic macroeconomic conditions and relative prices. The level of the exchange rate has straightforward relative price implications: an appreciated ("strong") currency raises the domestic price of nontradable goods and services relative to the domestic price of tradables.

On this basis we can project the positions of economic groups toward fixing the franc and the lira. A fixed exchange rate is favorable to those heavily involved in international trade and payments, especially major international banks and corporations. Exporters of goods or services for which nonprice dimensions (quality, reputation) are very important will also tend to favor exchange rate stability even if the currency's level imposes some cost disadvantage (within limits, of course). Nontradables producers, such as those in the public sector, are pulled both ways: a strong currency is good for them, while forgoing national monetary independence is undesirable inasmuch as they depend upon national economic conditions (and exchange rate stability is irrelevant to them).

---

[10] This is simply a somewhat special case of the common observation that while a median voter result is possible when policy is on one dimension, increasing the number of dimensions makes all outcomes unstable. Linkage politics can, in this sense, be regarded as a process by which a two-dimensional policy space is reduced to one dimension.

[11] I have written at some length about this general analytical problem in Frieden (1991). Here I summarize the implications for the French and Italian cases.

Producers of tradable goods that compete primarily on price, on the other hand, are hostile to both the strong currency and its being fixed. The principal groups in question are producers of standardized manufactures, for whom a real currency appreciation causes substantial difficulties in competing with imports and, where relevant, in maintaining export markets. The fixed exchange rate is of little value, especially inasmuch as these producers are oriented toward maintaining their domestic markets.[12] In the EC, farmers are essentially indifferent, as they are protected against EC exchange rate movements by complex arrangements that are part of the EC's Common Agricultural Policy.

Thus traditional import-competing manufacturing sectors are hostile to a strong fixed currency, internationally oriented firms are favorable, and nontradables producers are ambivalent. Translating this interest group perspective into partisan politics is difficult, as many of the economic sectors in question cut across traditional party lines. It is, however, possible to present a highly simplified picture of French and Italian party positions on the EMS. Generally speaking, in both countries, the Right was oriented toward a mix of international business and nontradables, the center (especially the Socialists) reflected nontradables and manufacturing, and the Left (especially the Communists) represented workers in traditional manufacturing.

In France, the Right was weakly favorable to a strong franc, the Socialists (PS) were weakly opposed, and the Communists (PCF) were strongly opposed.[13] In Italy, the Christian Democrats (DC) were ambivalent about a strong lira, the Socialists (PSI) were moderately opposed, and the Communists (PCI) were a bit more strongly opposed.

These positions on the exchange rate issue made movement toward MI difficult. In France neither Right nor Socialist governments were enthusiastic about a strong franc, while in Italy, neither Right-center nor broad national governments were so inclined. Indeed, only a fraction of the French Right (the Union pour la Démocratie Française) and Left (the Rocard faction of the PS) strongly favored MI, while in Italy only one tiny member of the center-Left coalition

[12] These categories are merely first approximations. Clearly the policy preferences of any firm or individual depend on a wide variety of considerations, and firms' preferences on exchange rates are far more nuanced than is allowed for here. Nonetheless, these divisions are good enough to serve as a starting point for analysis.

It should be also clarified that this abstract discussion ignores the obvious fact that what really matters to such groups is not international trade and payments generally, but trade and payments within the prospective monetary union. This refinement is, of course, crucial to the European case: a British firm say, whose market was primarily in the United States would be far less enthusiastic about European monetary unification than a British firm whose market was primarily in the EC. The discussion also glosses over many important details, such as the relative importance of competition on nonprice dimensions.

[13] In reality one portion of the Right (the UDF) was favorable to a strong franc, while another portion (the neo-Gaullist RDR) was ambivalent; meanwhile, the Socialists were similarly divided between those mildly favorable and those quite opposed. Here I ignore intragroup differences and simply take averages of the two parties.

(the Republican party) was a strong supporter of monetary integration. This made MI on its own merits unattainable in both countries.

The second step is to specify preferences along the second policy dimension, that is, toward European integration more generally. The relative placement of partisan camps on this dimension is amenable to analysis, but for the sake of brevity, here I simply assert such preferences.[14] In France, the PCF was hostile to the EC, while the PS and the Right were moderately favorable.[15] In Italy, all three major parties were strongly favorable to the EC; if anything, the DC was somewhat more ambivalent than the others.

This implies that in both countries there was broad agreement on European integration, despite the disagreement on MI. Both Right and Socialist governments in France were generally pro-EC, as were all conceivable Italian governments. Linking the exchange rate issue to European integration more generally, then, created a new political reality, for a country's inability to join MI implied moving away from the EC.[16]

For political actors, the choice had been on two dimensions: pro- or anti-EC, pro- or anti-strong currency. Linkage collapsed these two dimensions into one: either pro-EC and pro-strong currency, or anti-EC and anti-strong currency. The result was to change the set of likely outcomes. In Italy all major parties were more intensely pro-EC than they were anti-EMS. In France, most of the PS and most of the Right were similarly positioned, while the PCF and a portion of the PS were both anti-EMS and anti-EC (or were more strongly anti-EMS than they were pro-EC).

This stylized discussion is meant simply to illustrate the operation of linkage politics, and its potential application to the French and Italian experiences. I have no illusions that this treatment represents the nuanced nature of the two countries' political debates over the issue between 1979 and 1985. However, I hope that it does help provide a framework in which these debates can be examined.

[14] Such preferences could be derived more systematically with reference to particular groups' or parties' positions relative to national and EC median voters. If, for example, the national median voter is to the right of the EC median voter, the national Left will be favorable to European integration, which will push the country toward its preferred policies. On the other hand, if the national median voter is to the left of the EC median voter, the national Left will be hostile to European integration. I believe that this – rather than political culture or other ideological considerations – explains why in the early 1980s Italian Communists were pro-EC while French Communists and leftist Socialists were anti-EC. However to avoid introducing another controversial set of assertions I restrain myself to observing this partisan placement.

[15] Again, I ignore intraparty divisions (the leftist Socialists and the Gaullists were more hostile to the EC) and take party means.

[16] In this sense, I assume that the linkage was credible, that is, that nonparticipation in MI implied less than full membership in the EC. I do not explore how or why this linkage was made credible, which, of course, is an important question.

## FROM SKEPTICISM TO SUCCESS: FRANCE AND ITALY, 1978–1985

Despite the general failure of the snake in the 1970s, discussion of European monetary union began to gather new momentum in October 1977, when Roy Jenkins, the president of the European Commission, made a prominent public appeal for MI. In April 1978, the French President, Valéry Giscard d'Estaing, and the German chancellor, Helmut Schmidt, proposed a new European Monetary System, which was approved by the European Council in December 1978 and went into effect in March 1979. At that time all EC members except the United Kingdom affiliated with the exchange rate mechanism of the EMS, which allowed a 2.25 percent band among currencies (6 percent for the lira).[17]

The prevailing opinion at the time was that French and Italian inflation rates were too high and intractable to allow the ERM to operate as planned. Indeed, in the first four years of its operation, there were seven realignments of EMS currency values. During this period, deutschemark revaluations and lira and franc devaluations reduced the nominal DM value of the two problem currencies by 27 and 25 percent, respectively – hardly a sign of commitment to fixed rates. But over the following four years, between April 1983 and January 1987, there were only four more realignments, and the lira and franc were brought down only 13 and 9 percent against the deutschemark, respectively. Indeed, after 1983, exchange rate variability within the EMS declined substantially, while monetary policies converged on virtually every dimension.[18] It is generally agreed that the decisive turning point in the evolution of the EMS came between 1981 and 1985, when the French and Italian governments changed course to bring their inflation rates in line with the EC average.[19]

This turning point was in large part made possible by the linkage of the EMS to European integration more generally. The system was launched personally by the French president and German chancellor, and its founding documents explicitly tied monetary stability to broader European integration. There had not been any sense that the snake was essential to the EC, to which in fact two non-EC members (Norway and Sweden) affiliated. Neither national politicians nor Community leaders had staked much political capital on the snake. The EMS was different, and its success was publicly related to other aspects of European integration, in ways that implied that a country not in the ERM would become a second-tier member of the Community.

---

[17] Ludlow (1982) is especially detailed on the negotiations and early operation of the EMS; see also Ypersele (1985, pp. 71–95) and Ungerer (1983). Outstanding surveys of the EMS experience more generally are Fratianni and von Hagen (1992) and Giavazzi and Giovannini (1989).

[18] Relative parity changes are calculated from exchange rate data in International Monetary Fund (1988, pp. 20–34).

[19] See, e.g., International Monetary Fund (1988, p. 48).

Linking MI with EC integration affected the domestic political lineup in many member nations. This was especially the case during the early 1980s, when beset by stagnation and unemployment, many Europeans began to look upon an intensification of economic integration as the last best hope for the region.[20] As the pace of European integration quickened, MI came to be seen as a near-essential component of a broader trend. The process was particularly striking in France and Italy.

*France, 1981–1983*

François Mitterrand and the PS took power in May-June 1981.[21] In the two years since the EMS had begun operation, with French inflation still well above German levels, the franc had appreciated about 12 percent against the deutschemark in real terms, putting serious competitive pressure on French manufacturers.[22] As French prices continued to rise and the trade balance to deteriorate, the government (represented at Brussels by the finance and economy minister, Jacques Delors) negotiated an October 1981 EMS realignment in which the franc and lira were devalued by 3 percent and the deutschemark and Dutch florin were revalued by 5.5 percent. The devaluation proved inadequate in the face of continued French inflation, and in June 1982 another realignment raised the deutschemark and florin by 4.25 percent and lowered the franc by 5.75 percent (the lira was devalued by 2.75 percent). This second realignment gave rise to serious disputes within the French government.

President Mitterrand's government was headed by Prime Minister Pierre Mauroy, and included four ministers from the Communist party. The Communists were unenthusiastic about European integration and hostile to austerity (*rigueur* in French economic policy parlance). The Socialist-Communist differences were especially important because they implicated the trade unions. The largely pro-Communist Confédération Générale du Travail (CGT) was most adamant in its resistance to austerity, even at the expense of French membership in the EC (toward which it had been indifferent or opposed). Inasmuch as the economic policies necessary to control inflation affected real wages, the CGT and the PCF were recalcitrant at best, obstructionist at worst [Kesselman (1980; 1985)].

The PS was divided in several factions, running roughly from right to left as

---

[20] For one among many possible interpretations of this trend, see Katseli (1989, pp. 186–195).

[21] The literature on these years is enormous. Most of the discussion below is drawn from detailed journalistic accounts of the experience, which will be cited as used. More general analyses of the period can be found in Sachs and Wyplosz (1986), McCarthy (1990), Cameron (1992), and Friend (1989). Macroeconomic data are taken, except where otherwise noted, from Sachs and Wyplosz (1986). Among the many edited volumes on the experience, the following contain particularly useful discussions of economic policy: Ambler (1985); Machin and Wright (1985); and Ross, Hoffmann, and Malzacher (1987).

[22] Real bilateral exchange rate calcuated from Wood (1988).

follows. The group led by Michel Rocard was economically liberal and strongly pro-European. Mitterrand's faction was more tied to his personality than to any particular policy stance. The group around Mauroy tended toward standard social democracy – friendly to economic liberalism but committed to traditional socialist goals; Mauroy generally had the support of the Marseilles-based federation led by Gaston Deferre. Finally, the CERES faction led by Jean-Pierre Chevènement was a stronghold of nationalistic and economic policy views similar to those of the Communists [Bell and Criddle (1988); Hanley (1986)]. Mitterrand and his followers dominated the PS, largely by means of a series of tactical alliances with other factions.

In the labor movement, the Socialists' principal allies were the Confédération Française Démocratique du Travail (CFDT) and the Fédération de l'Education Nationale (FEN). The former was a general labor federation that explicitly competed with the CGT; the latter was a teachers' association. There was a Socialist presence in the CGT, but it was a minority of the confederation. A third major labor federation, Force Ouvrière, (FO), was not partisan, although it tended to combine hostility toward the organized Left with general militancy over wage issues [Adam (1983); Mouriaux (1985)].

There were important sociological differences among these parties and labor unions. The Communist party was, as elsewhere in Europe, heavily oriented toward blue-collar workers in traditional industries. The Socialist party was essentially middle class, dominated by managers, professionals, and white-collar workers. The PS membership relative to the population at large in 1973, for example, had a heavy overrepresentation of upper managers (11 percent of the party and 6 percent of the labor force), and of teachers (17 percent of the party and 3 percent of the labor force); workers were underrepresented (19 percent of the PS and 37 percent of the labor force) [Hardouin (1978)]. Of the 169 PS deputies elected in 1981, to take another example, fully 47 percent were teachers; another 22 percent were professionals, and 20 percent were upper managers and senior civil servants.[23]

The trade unions differed quite a bit in their composition. The CGT was especially strong in traditional manufacturing industries. Table 1 shows how much heavier was the industrial bent of the CGT than that of the CFDT and FO: three-fifths of those who voted for CGT in 1979 were in industry, compared to less than half of those who voted for CFDT or FO.

The CGT's industrial orientation is indicated by other measures as well. CGT votes in union elections in 1981 were 32 percent of total votes. In such industries as metalworking, pulp and paper, and chemicals, the CGT vote was between 45 and 51 percent of the total, while in finance and services, the CGT

---

[23] Bell and Criddle (1988, p. 203). Hanley (1986, pp. 177–197), has a useful compilation of his own survey of the PS and that of Cayrol, which address both the party's social composition and the differences among the factions.

TABLE I    FRANCE: SECTORAL COMPOSITION OF VOTES FOR THREE MAJOR LABOR FEDERATIONS AND
FOR ALL FEDERATIONS, 1979 (PERCENT)

|             | CGT  | CFDT | FO   | All Federations |
|-------------|------|------|------|-----------------|
| Industry    | 59.7 | 49.1 | 45.3 | 50.5            |
| Trade       | 23.8 | 24.1 | 26.9 | 23.8            |
| Agriculture | 2.6  | 5.2  | 4.7  | 3.5             |
| Various     | 9.7  | 13.6 | 14.7 | 11.7            |
| Management  | 4.2  | 8.0  | 8.4  | 10.4            |

*Source:* Adam (1983, p. 164).
*Notes:* N = 3.3 million for CGT, 1.8 million for CFDT, 1.36 miliion for FO, and 7.79 million for All Federations. All Federations includes a number of smaller labor unions; percentages do not total 100 because of roundings.

vote was between 10 and 22 percent of the total.[24] Within the public sector, the CGT dominated the steel, chemical, and auto firms, but had little strength in high-technology and financial firms [Mouriaux (1985, pp. 201–202)]. In the 1979 union elections, the CGT received 50 percent of the votes of industrial workers, 30 percent of the votes of agricultural workers, and 33 percent of the votes of other workers.[25]

The CFDT, like the PS, tended to be more oriented toward services and high-technology firms than the CGT. Table 2 shows how some of these differences played out in union elections in several important French firms. While the CGT overwhelmed the CFDT within Renault and led in Michelin, for example, the CFDT dominated such financial firms as the Banque National de Paris and the insurance company Assurances Générales de France. The CFDT and an autonomous union swamped the CGT in IBM-France.

The general pattern within the labor movement, then, was that the CFDT was concentrated in nontradables (service) sectors and competitive high-technology firms, while the CGT was prominent among producers of tradables, especially those most affected by competition from imports. This division was mirrored to some extent by that between the Socialist and Communist parties. In this context, recall the expected policy differences among uncompetitive tradables sectors, competitive internationally oriented firms, and nontradables producers. The first are expected to be especially hostile to a strong currency, the second favorable, and the third ambivalent.

These sectoral divisions were exacerbated by the economic trends of the early 1980s. As the franc appreciated in real terms against other EMS currencies, domestic relative prices moved against tradables and in favor of the nontradables (and cross-border investing) segments of the French economy. In 1981–1982 the prices of industrial products rose 19.5 percent, while prices of private services rose 28.3 percent and those of public services rose 34.8 percent.

[24] Groux and Mouriaux (1992, p. 103).
[25] Adam (1983, p. 164). The elections in question were the *élections prud'homales.*

TABLE 2   FRANCE: CGT AND CFDT STRENGTH IN SELECTED FIRMS, 1979–1981
(PERCENT OF VOTERS)

| Firm and Date of Vote | Votes for CGT | Votes for CFDT |
| --- | --- | --- |
| Renault, 1981 | 61.2 | 16.6 |
| Michelin, 1980 | 46.1 | 43.8 |
| Banque Nationale de Paris, 1980 | 25.1 | 30.0 |
| Assurances Générales de France, 1980 | 22.4 | 50.1 |
| IBM-France, 1979 | 12.4 | 56.2 |

Source: Hervé Hamon and Patrick Rotman, 1982, *La deuxième gauche* (Ramsay, Paris), 423–427.
Notes: The elections in question were for enterprise commissions. In the case of IBM-France, votes for the CFDT include votes for an autonomous union.

This put serious pressure on tradables producers [Fonteneau and Muet (1985, p. 319)]. Indeed, between 1980 and 1983, employment in tradable sectors declined 7 percent. Meanwhile, employment in construction, trade, and services held steady, while that in energy, transport, telecommunications, and finance rose 5 percent.[26] It is not surprising that manufacturers demanded further devaluations.

This cleavage was an important component of French debates over the EMS, which largely became couched in terms of austerity (*rigueur*) and commitment to a fixed exchange rate within the EMS, versus reflation, devaluation, and abandoning the EMS.[27] The Communists and the CGT, along with the CERES faction within the PS, opposed austerity and advocated devaluing the franc and leaving the EMS. The CFDT and the Rocard and Mauroy factions of the PS were pro-European and thus in favor of maintaining EMS commitments, even at the expense of austerity. Mitterrand and his supporters within the PS were in the middle, and they were crucial to the ultimate disposition of the issue.

After the June 1982 realignment, it was clear that the government faced a distinct choice. The franc continued to appreciate in real terms, and after October 1982, it came under constant attack on foreign exchange markets. Battle lines were drawn between EMS partisans and opponents. In March 1983 the issue came to a head in a period that has been called "ten days that shook Mitterrand" [Bauchard (1986, p. 139)]. France had to devalue to avoid running out of reserves in a matter of days, and this devaluation had either to take place within the ambit of the EMS or to represent a definitive break with the monetary union.

At the political level, the Socialists were in trouble. The Left did poorly in the March 6 first round of the municipal elections. Concerned that austerity had

---

[26] These are the figures given, and the aggregations (tradable, nontradable, and "sheltered") used, in Sachs and Wyplosz (1986, p. 275).

[27] For the account that follows, in addition to the general works cited already, I have relied primarily on a series of detailed narratives, by well-informed journalists, of the early Mitterrand years: Favier and Martin-Roland (1990); Bauchard (1986); July (1986); and Nay (1988).

alienated the government's constituents, Mitterrand leaned toward taking France out of the EMS.[28] However, the message of the second round of municipal elections held on March 13 was conflicting. The Left did badly, but the losses were less severe than anticipated and, perhaps more important, the PCF suffered a major setback.

Mitterrand apparently read the election results as an indication that the economic nationalism espoused by the PCF would not succeed in shoring up the Socialists' political base. The municipal elections, in other words, led Mitterrand to conclude that while popular discontent with austerity was widespread, anti-EC sentiment was limited.[29] This apparently pushed him toward keeping France inside the EMS and reconfirming Mauroy in office. At the same time, he increased the hold of the Mitterrand and Mauroy factions on the cabinet, removed several leftist Socialists from office, and appointed Jacques Delors as a super minister in charge of Economics, Finance, and Budget. A series of new economic policy measures were announced, from tax increases and budget cuts to a tightening of exchange controls.

Austerity was the order of the day. Inflation was more than halved, from 12.6 to 6 percent, between 1982 and 1985, and the current account was in surplus by the latter year; but meanwhile unemployment rose from 8.1 to 10.1 percent, and GDP growth stagnated. Nevertheless, the new ERM parities held for more than three years, until the readjustment of April 1986. By then, French commitment to the EMS was credible, and Jacques Delors, as president of the European Commission, was leading the charge to accelerate the process of monetary integration.

Two features of the French experience are worth highlighting. First, there were clear differences, as expected, in the EMS preferences of various sectors of the economy. Import-competing tradables producers, represented especially in the labor movement by the CGT and the PCF, were the strongest opponents of a strong franc. Internationally integrated firms and nontradables sectors, represented especially by the CFDT and segments of the PS, were more enthusiastic about monetary union despite its association with austerity.

Second, the link between the exchange rate and France's relations with its EC and EMS partners was explicit. It was clear by mid-1982 that commitment

---

[28] On this period, see Favier and Martin-Roland (1990, pp. 465–493) and Bauchard (1986, pp. 139–154). Both books, especially the former, are based on extensive interviews with participants both at the time and after the fact.

[29] In the meantime, there is some evidence that many in the business community – including the largely Socialist executives of many newly nationalized French multinational banks and corporations – were pressing strongly for a deepening of French commitment to the EC, which implied staying in the ERM. On this point, see Green (1993). Another argument advanced [by Goodman (1992, p. 136)] is that an internal French government report indicated that the costs of a devaluation would be greater than the costs of conforming to the fixed rate. Without being able to evaluate the evidence fully, I find the report's alleged conclusions, and the likelihood that its arguments were crucial in influencing Mitterrand, quite questionable.

to the EMS required major changes in policy so that French macroeconomic conditions would converge with those of Germany; it was also clear that the EMS commitment was of paramount importance to broadening French participation in the EC. The linkage between MI and European integration was crucial in leading the Socialist government to abandon its economic policies and commit itself to austerity.

## Italy, 1980–1985

The decisions that bound monetary policy to the EMS were less striking in Italy than in France. Italian credibility on this score developed gradually between 1981 and 1986, but several important turning points can be identified. In most instances we observe the sorts of divisions familiar from the French case, and a link between these debates and general attitudes to the EC.

There were two defining characteristics of Italian macroeconomic problems after 1973. The first was a high level of budget deficits, a substantial portion of which was monetized. In fact, in 1975 the central bank committed itself to buy all unsold Treasury securities, thereby ensuring that budget deficits would translate automatically into money creation.

The second feature of Italian macroeconomic conditions was that inflation had taken on something of an inertial character. In 1975 the unions and businesses had negotiated a tight wage indexation scheme, the *scala mobile,* and defense of this arrangement had become a rallying cry for labor. Both the explicit commitment of the central bank to monetize a portion of the budget deficit and extensive wage indexation led to a strong inflationary tendency, which made a fixed exchange rate nearly impossible. Both would have to be altered for Italy to abide by its EMS commitments.

The first major step in reorienting monetary policy was taken in 1981, when the governor of the Banca d'Italia indicated that he would no longer be guided by the 1975 commitment to purchase unsold Treasury securities.[30] This shift in policy, known as the "divorce" of the central bank from the Treasury, was strengthened in 1982 by the implementation of a new, compulsory commercial bank reserve system, and strengthened further in 1983 when administrative controls on credit were eliminated.

Almost immediately after the "divorce" Italian real interest rates shot up from well below German levels to well above them. Real interest rates in Italy went from an average of −1.5 percent between 1977 and 1981 to an average of 3.8 percent between 1982 and 1986. Meanwhile, the share of the public debt held by the central bank declined from 23.7 percent in 1981 to 16.6 percent in 1984 [Tabellini (1988)].

---

[30] The "divorce" is one of the few aspects of Italian economic policy in this period on which there is a substantial literature. See, e.g., Goodman (1992); Tabellini (1987); Salvemini (1983); Addis (1987); and Epstein and Schor (1989).

Restrictive monetary policy was not enough: inflation's inertial component had to be reduced, which required an assault on the *scala mobile*. Attempts to renegotiate the index were frustrated by the opposition of the Communists, and the Communist-oriented labor federation, CGIL. The Socialists and the Christian Democrats, along with the labor federations associated with them, the CISL and UIL, were willing to reduce indexation. Finally, in February 1984, Socialist Bettino Craxi, the new prime minister, simply decreed a reduction in the *scala mobile*. The CGIL and the PCI were outraged, and collected signatures for a national vote on the *scala mobile* [Lange (1986)].

The campaign leading up to the June 9, 1985 referendum was divisive. The costs of austerity were counterposed to the benefits of being in step with Italy's partners in the EMS and the EC. In the event, the no votes prevailed (with 54.3 percent of the total), and the decree loosening the *scala mobile* stood. This was the second crucial set of changes necessary to bring Italian inflation down and make it possible for the country to keep the lira within the ERM.

Domestic political divisions over the EMS and EMS-related issues, such as the *scala mobile,* date back to the original debate over Italian entry into the agreement. Bargaining over these issues took place against the backdrop of important political changes in the country. In 1976, the PCI gave its tacit support to the coalition government led by the Christian Democrats. In early 1978 the CGIL announced a significant moderation of its overall strategy.[31]

Nonetheless, both the PCI and the CGIL were ambivalent about the EMS. In 1978 the Communists voted against the law authorizing Italian accession to the exchange rate agreement, arguing that a delay of at least six months was advisable to avoid too severe a shock to employment and wages. The Socialists abstained, and the bill passed.[32] As discussed above, the PCI and the CGIL similarly fought against the reform of the *scala mobile*.

Some insight into the reason for these divisions is provided by a look at the socioeconomic differences among the major labor federations. The membership breakdown in Table 3 indicates that the Communist-dominated CGIL was more

TABLE 3    ITALY: NONAGRICULTURAL MEMBERSHIP IN THE CGIL, CISL, AND UIL BY SECTORS, 1983 (PERCENT OF MEMBERS)

|          | CGIL | CISL | UIL  |
|----------|------|------|------|
| Industry | 59.4 | 45.6 | 44.8 |
| Services | 40.6 | 54.4 | 55.2 |
| Private  | 18.4 | 16.8 | 21.8 |
| Public   | 22.2 | 37.6 | 33.4 |

*Source:* Calculated from Baglioni, Santi, and Squarzon (1985, p. 196).

[31] On this so-called EUR line see Lange, Ross, and Vannicelli (1982, pp. 165–180).
[32] For two informed discussions of Italian accession see Spaventa (1980) and Andreotti (1981, pp. 284–289).

heavily represented in traditional industries, while the Socialist-oriented CISL and the more independent UIL had larger shares of their memberships in services. Expressed differently, in 1983, CGIL members constituted 55 percent of Italy's unionized industrial workers, with CISL members accounting for 29 percent and UIL members for 16 percent; 48 percent of the country's organized workers in private services, with CISL members accounting for 31 percent and UIL members for 21 percent; and 36 percent of union members in public services, with CISL members accounting for 43 percent and UIL members for 21 percent.[33]

Although quantitative data are not available, impressionistic evidence indicates that the Communist-Socialist social composition mirrored that of their unions, and was therefore similar to that of France. In both instances, the French generalization held for Italy: the Socialists were more representative of those in services and high-technology industries, while the Communists were concentrated in traditional import-competing manufacturing. This, again, helps explain why the PCI was more inclined toward devaluations, with the PSI more favorable to the EMS.

The link between European issues and the EMS was rarely drawn as explicitly in Italy as in France, perhaps because no single decision ever became the focus of popular attention. However, the presence of the link is evident from the beginning of the story. Indeed, when the arrangement was being negotiated in 1978, Prime Minister Giulio Andreotti originally announced that Italy would not participate. Only after substantial pressure was brought to bear on Andreotti by the French and Germans, did the government change its position. On the stick side, both Giscard and Schmidt made it clear that they would regard Italy's non adhesion as a blow to Italy's Europeanist credentials. On the carrot side, they permitted the lira a much wider (12 percent) band of fluctuation and incorporated financial assistance to Italy into the EMS agreement.

Andreotti swung toward EMS entry as the implications for Italian relations with its EC partners became clear. The issue was also tied up with DC-PCI relations at a time when many of Italy's allies were uneasy about the role of the Communists in the government. Extracts from Andreotti's diary for December 1978 are instructive. While still undecided, he noted in frustration: "If we do not adhere immediately it will be said that the Communists are not 'Europeans' and that the government is their slave." Once Andreotti decided to enter the EMS, he named as the most important considerations "the guarantees of Schmidt and Giscard and the need to safeguard our European prestige" [Andreotti (1981, pp. 287–288)].

Indeed, the tie between the EMS and other European policy issues served to mitigate the Communists' opposition. Unlike their French counterparts the PCI and the CGIL were generally Europeanist. The PCI regarded its relations with

---

[33] Baglioni, Santi, and Squarzon (1985, pp. 194–196). Figures exclude retirees.

Chancellor Schmidt, and the German Social Democrats more generally, as crucial to their future as a serious political force, and Schmidt regarded the EMS as a major personal achievement on his part. According to one major PCI leader, "Chancellor Schmidt put a great deal of pressure on both the Italian government and the PCI. In fact, Schmidt called [PCI leader Enrico] Berlinguer to try to get a reassurance that the PCI would not cause a government crisis over the EMS, and Berlinguer gave him that reassurance."[34] In other words, general Communist commitment to the EC, and the specific importance of the EMS for European integration, softened the PCI and CGIL concern about the exchange rate agreement.

There is little doubt among informed observers that the "foreign link" (*vincolo estero*) was crucial to the ability of the government to achieve austerity measures in the early and mid-1980s. A former central bank president put it succinctly: "With a weak government, the external link is a crucial anchor. In this context, a fixed exchange rate is the firmest guarantee of monetary stability when the authorities do not have the ability to impose a responsible monetary policy for *political* reasons."[35] Another Bank of Italy official was even more explicit:

> In the absence of specific *government* commitments to *macroeconomic* policy, we took the EMS as the foundation stone of our policy. The central element responsible for the changes was the desire of the political system and of public opinion for European integration. This is a reflection of the lack of confidence on the part of public opinion in the quality of our own political leaders. This has been exploited by the Bank of Italy. The external constraint was not enough to induce discipline on a full range of policies – fiscal policy is a clear exception – but on monetary issues it did have an effect.[36]

As this last informant indicated, one interesting aspect of the Italian case is the relationship between monetary and fiscal policy. During the 1980s, monetary policy conformed increasingly to the requirements of Italy's EMS commitments. This imposed severe costs on the manufacturing sector, and especially on labor within it. However, although many manufacturing jobs were lost because of the real appreciation of the lira the government picked up a great deal of the slack by running an expansionary fiscal policy. Put somewhat differently, the costs borne by manufacturing were counterbalanced by benefits that accrued to the nontradables sectors, especially those connected to public spending. In fact, over the course of the 1980s, employment in manufacturing declined more than 10 percent, and manufacturing investment was stagnant in real terms. Meanwhile, employment in services rose 27 percent, while investment in nonresidential services grew 5 percent a year in real terms [Confindustria (1992); Rey

---

[34] Interview, Giorgio Napolitano, Rome, July 21, 1992.
[35] Interview, Guido Carli, Rome, July 21, 1992.
[36] Interview, Fabrizio Saccomanni, Rome, July 16, 1992.

(1992, p. 52)]. Eventually, of course, the government's fiscal deficits became large enough to pose economic and political problems for it.

In this light, it is not surprising that adjustment to the EMS was most painful to the PCI's constituencies among industrial workers, while supporters of the DC and the PSI in the public sector were sheltered from the impact of the country's tight monetary policy. It is with this in mind that the man principally responsible for the PCI's economic policies at the time is somewhat bitter about the experience:

> Sectors tied to international competition hoped that the EMS and the single market would serve as a whip against the less competitive, more inefficient sectors, which they saw as a ball and chain around their legs. The most international sectors had to restructure, and had to demand a change in Italian policies.
>
> There is a broad national consensus in favor of European integration, and waving this flag one can ask for sacrifices. In 1984 the reduction of labor costs seemed key. We had indexation that other countries did not have. The inflation issue was crucial, and certainly there was a link to the exchange rate.
>
> The principal costs of this policy were paid by industrial workers. The public sector did well; management did well. But traditional industrial workers were sacrificed.[37]

The Italian experience, then, is one in which the redefinition of austerity and wage restraint as interconnected with the country's European commitments led to the adoption of policies that would probably not otherwise have been accepted. The PCI and the CGIL were forced to support a set of monetary initiatives about which they were very wary, largely because more ardent opposition would have called into question their long standing commitment to European integration. The linkage drawn between the EMS-based austerity measures and Italy's role in Europe allowed the government to change course in a way that had been impossible for over a decade.

## IMPLICATIONS AND CONCLUSIONS

This discussion of the early years of the EMS leads to several conclusions about the reasons for the course of European monetary integration after 1978. Three features of the process deserve to be highlighted. First, the ERM required credible national commitments to austerity measures needed to bring high-inflation countries in line with German macroeconomic conditions. Second, these national commitments depended in large part on the response of various groups to the expected economic effects of the transitional real appreciation that would occur if the EMS commitment were honored. Third, a major component of the domestic political support for the EMS commitment was the linkage of European monetary union with other aspects of European integration: inasmuch as a nation's inability to conform to EMS constraints compromised its ability to be a

---

[37] Interview, Giorgio Napolitano, Rome, July 21, 1992.

full participant in other aspects of the EC, more domestic actors were drawn toward support for the measures required to fix the exchange rate.

It is reasonable to believe that the factors that affected the development of the EMS in the early 1980s will continue to influence the course of European monetary integration. Especially in the aftermath of the currency crisis of 1992–1993, real questions exist about the potential for future monetary integration. Future MI will involve further sacrifices of national policy autonomy, and there is every reason to believe that the forces that operated in the domestic politics of European monetary integration in France and Italy in the early 1980s will continue to operate there and elsewhere in the 1990s.

This implies that the prospects for further MI will depend on factors important to the development of the EMS. Domestic support for MI is essential, and this chapter has emphasized the importance of the link between currency union and other EC agenda items to cement this domestic support. This link was called into question when the ratification of the Maastricht treaty ran into difficulties. Among the results of the ensuing attempt to salvage the Treaty was a separation of economic and monetary unification from more controversial aspects of European integration (such as social programs and foreign policy). Although this might be desirable, the analysis presented tends to indicate that it is precisely the *linkage* among various policies that has been crucial to their adoption. If each component of the EC agenda were taken separately, it might be possible for opponents to prevail on every vote. With European integration taken as a package, the prospects for success are higher.[38]

MI is still closely tied to other aspects of European integration. Whether this linkage is sufficient to bring about a change in national monetary politics large enough to allow the process of monetary integration to go forward in a way that incorporates the entire present (and future) Community, or whether domestic political lineups will force consideration of alternatives to full-fledged MI, will be largely a function of developments in the domestic politics of monetary policy within EC member states.

## REFERENCES

Adam, Gérard, 1983, *Le pouvoir syndical* (Dunod, Paris).
Addis, Elisabetta, 1987, Banca d'Italia e politica monetaria: La riallocazione del potere fra stato, mercato, e banca centrale. *Stato e Mercato* 19 (April), 73–95.
Alt, James, and Barry Eichengreen, 1989, Parallel and overlapping games: Theory and an application to the European gas trade. *Economics and Politics* 1, No. 2, 119–144.
Ambler, John, ed., 1985, *The French socialist experiment* (ISHI, Philadelphia).
Andreotti, Giulio, 1981, *Diari 1976–1979: Gli anni della solidarietà* (Rizzoli, Milan).
Baglioni, Guido, Ettore Santi, and Corrado Squarzon, 1985, *Le relazioni sindicali in Italia: Rapporto 1983–1984* (Edizioni Lavoro, Rome).

[38] This is the conclusion drawn by Martin (1994, this volume).

Bauchard, Philippe, 1986, *La guerre des deux roses: Du rêve à la réalité, 1981–1985* (Bernard Grasset, Paris).

Bell, D. S., and Byron Criddle, 1988, *The French Socialist Party,* 2d ed. (Clarendon Press, Oxford).

Cameron, David, 1992, The franc, the EMS, *rigueur,* and "l'autre politique": The regime-defining choices of the Mitterrand presidency (mimeo, New Haven).

Cohen, Benjamin J., 1994, Beyond EMU: The problem of sustainability. This volume.

Collins, Susan, and Francesco Giavazzi, 1993, Attitudes toward inflation and the viability of fixed exchange rates: Evidence from the EMS, in: Michael Bordo and Barry Eichengreen, eds., *A retrospective on the Bretton Woods system* (University of Chicago Press, Chicago), 547–577.

Confindustria, 1992, *Previsioni dell'economia italiana* 6, no. 1 (Confindustria, Rome).

Eichengreen, Barry, and Jeffry Frieden, 1994, The political economy of European monetary unification: An analytical introduction. This volume.

Epstein, Gerald, and Juliet Schor, 1989, The divorce of the Banca d'Italia and the Italian treasury: A case study of central bank independence, in: Peter Lange and Marino Regini, eds., *State, market, and social regulation* (Cambridge University Press, Cambridge), 147–164.

Favier, Pierre, and Michel Martin-Roland, 1990, *La décennie Mitterrand. vol. 1. Les ruptures (1981–1984)* (Seuil, Paris).

Fonteneau, Alain, and Pierre-Alain Muet, 1985, *La gauche face à la crise* (Presses de la Fondation Nationale des Sciences Politiques, Paris).

Fratianni, Michele, and Jürgen von Hagen, 1992, *The European Monetary System and European monetary union* (Westview, Boulder, Colo.).

Frieden, Jeffry A., 1991, Invested interests: The politics of national economic policies in a world of global finance. *International Organization* 45, 425–451.

———, 1993, Economic liberalization and the politics of European monetary integration (mimeo, Los Angeles).

Friend, Julius, 1989, *Seven years in France: François Mitterrand and the unintended revolution, 1981–1988* (Westview, Boulder, Colo.).

Garrett, Geoffrey, 1994, The politics of Maastricht. This volume.

Giavazzi, Francesco, and Alberto Giovannini, 1989, *Limiting exchange rate flexibility: The European Monetary System* (MIT Press, Cambridge, Mass.).

Goodman, John, 1992, *Monetary sovereignty: The politics of central banking in Western Europe* (Cornell University Press, Ithaca, N.Y.).

Green, Maria, 1993, Setting the agenda for a new Europe: The politics of big business in EC 1992 (mimeo, Cambridge, Mass.).

Groux, Guy, and René Mouriaux, 1992, *La CGT* (Economica, Paris).

Hanley, David, 1986, *Keeping left? Ceres and the French Socialist party* (Manchester University Press, Manchester).

Hardouin, Patrick, 1978, Les caractéristiques sociologiques du Parti Socialiste. *Revue Française de Science Politique* 28, no. 2 (April), 220–256.

International Monetary Fund, 1988, *Policy Coordination in the European Monetary System.* IMF Occasional Paper, no. 61 (IMF, Washington, D.C.).

July, Serge, 1986, *Les années Mitterrand* (Bernard Grasset, Paris).

Katseli, Louka, 1989, The political economy of European integration: From Euro-sclerosis to Euro-pessimism. *International Spectator* 24, no. 3/4, 186–195.

Kesselman, Mark, 1980, The economic analysis and program of the French Communist party, in: Philip Cerny and Martin Schain, eds., *French politics and public policy* (St. Martin's Press, New York), 177–190.

Kesselman, Mark, 1985, The French Communist Party: Historic retard, historic compromise, historic decline – or new departure? in: Philip Cerny, and Martin Schain, eds., *Socialism, the state and public policy in France* (Frances Pinter, London), 42–59.

Lange, Peter, 1986, The end of an era: The wage indexation referendum of 1985, in: R. Leonardi and R. Nanetti, eds., *Italian politics* vol. 1 (Pinter, London), 29–46.

Lange, Peter, George Ross, and Maurizio Vannicelli, 1982, *Unions, change and crisis: French and Italian union strategy and the political economy, 1945–1980* (Allen and Unwin, London).

Ludlow, Peter, 1982, *The making of the European Monetary System* (Butterworth, London).

Machin, Howard, and Vincent Wright, eds., 1985, *Economic policy and policy-making under the Mitterrand presidency, 1981–1984* (St. Martin's Press, New York).

Martin, Lisa, 1994, International and domestic institutions in the EMU process. This volume.

McCarthy, Patrick, 1990, France faces reality: *Rigueur* and the Germans, in: David Calleo and Claudia Morgenstern, eds., *Recasting Europe's economies* (University Press of America, Lanham, Md.), 25–78.

Mouriaux, René, 1985, *Syndicalisme et politique* (Editions Ouvrières, Paris).

Nay, Catherine, 1988, *Les sept Mitterrand ou les métamorphoses d'un septennat* (Bernard Grasset, Paris).

Rey, Guido, 1992, I mutamenti della struttura economica: Fattori produttivi, distribuzione del reddito, domanda, in: Confindustria Centro Studi, ed. *L'Italia verso il 2000: Le istituzioni, la società, l'economia* (SIPI, Rome), 2: 3–55.

Ross, George, Stanley Hoffman, and Sylvia Malzacher, eds., 1987, *The Mitterrand experiment* (Polity Press, Cambridge, Mass.).

Sachs, Jeffrey, and Charles Wyplosz, 1986, The economic consequences of President Mitterrand, *Economic Policy* 2 (April), 262–322.

Salvemini, Maria Teresa, 1983, The Treasury and the money market: The new responsibilities after the divorce. *Review of Economic Conditions in Italy* 1 (February), 33–54.

Spaventa, Luigi, 1980, Italy joins the EMS: A political history, Occasional Paper, no. 32, Johns Hopkins University Bologna Center (June).

Tabellini, Guido, 1987, Central bank reputation and the monetization of deficits: The 1981 Italian monetary reform. *Economic Inquiry* 25 (April), 185–200.

———, 1988, Monetary and fiscal policy coordination with a high public debt, in: Francesco Giavazzi and Luigi Spaventa, eds., *High public debt: The Italian experience* (Cambridge University Press, Cambridge) 90–134.

Tsoukalis, Loukas, 1977, *The politics and economics of European monetary integration* (Allen and Unwin, London).

Ungerer, Horst, 1983, *The European Monetary System: The experience, 1979–82*. IMF Occasional Paper, no. 19 (IMF, Washington, D.C.).

van Ypersele, Jacques, 1985, *The European Monetary System: origins, operation and outlook* (Commission of the European Communities, Brussels).

Wood, Adrian, 1988, *Global trends in real exchange rates, 1960 to 1984*. World Bank Discussion Paper, no.35 (World Bank, Washington, D.C.).

Woolley, John, 1992, Policy credibility and European monetary institutions, in: Alberta Sbragia, ed., *Europolitics: Institutions and policymaking in the "new" European Community* (Brookings Institution, Washington, D.C.).

# 3

## THE POLITICS OF MAASTRICHT

### Geoffrey Garrett

The Economic and Monetary Union (EMU) treaty signed at Maastricht does not guarantee the recreation of German-style economic policies and outcomes at the European Community (EC) level. Membership was not limited to countries that mimic the German commitment to price stability. National representatives may outvote inflation-averse EC central bankers in monetary policy decisions. The Council of Ministers has the power to set exchange rate policy vis-à-vis third currencies. The treaty does not provide binding constraints against fiscal profligacy in member states. The German government agreed to this suboptimal outcome because in the wake of the demise of the Soviet Union and German unification it had broader political interests in maintaining the pace of European integration at Maastricht. The Bundesbank's policy of high interest rates in 1992, however, has effectively guaranteed a two-speed monetary union, in which the first group of members will be limited to a narrow deutschemark zone. Given the waning enthusiasm for integration across the EC, the German government has no incentive to alter this outcome.

THE CREATION of an Economic and Monetary Union (EMU) by 1999 was the principal component of the 1991 Maastricht Treaty on European Union, entered into by the twelve European Community (EC) member states.[1] The common wisdom about the Maastricht agreement on EMU is that it will recreate at the EC level the current German monetary regime: a central bank that is immune from tampering by politicians and that can impose the goal of price stability on the EC, even at the cost of higher unemployment (at least in the short term).[2] Two central pieces of evidence are used to support this argument. First, the provisions of the EMU treaty are deemed at least as stringent as those of the German Bundesbank. Second, demanding economic criteria, the so-called convergence criteria, are attached to EMU membership, which purportedly will limit admission to countries that already mimic German economic policies and outcomes. From this perspective, the Maastricht treaty appears to entrench in the EC Germany's preferred set of institutions and macroeconomic policies.

I would like to thank Peter Hall, Torben Iverson, Peter Lange, David Soskice, Wolfgang Streeck, George Tsebelis, and John Woolley for helpful comments and suggestions on various aspects of the paper. Special thanks to Barry Eichengreen and Jeffry Frieden for their tireless criticism and enthusiastic support.

[1]The other important elements of the treaty include institutional reforms to increase the power of the European Parliament, the extension of qualified majority voting to certain areas of social policy, and agreements for coordinating defense and foreign policies.

[2]For a recent influential elaboration of this position, see Kenen (1992).

This paper offers a different interpretation of the treaty. In terms of the institutional arrangements of the European System of Central Banks (ESCB), there is no doubt that the EMU agreement will create a sort of super-Bundesbank. But the success of the German model is contingent upon much more than the institutional structure of the central bank [Hall (1993); Scharpf (1991)]. The memory of Nazism renders price stability a more important objective for all actors in Germany – political parties, trade unions, and voters, as well as central bank officials – than is the case in other countries. Moreover, coordination between organized business and labor mitigates wage-price spirals more effectively than in other member states [Soskice (1990)].

Thus, the correspondence between the institutions of the ESCB and the Bundesbank is not sufficient to generate price stability in Europe. Rather, low inflation in EMU would be generated only if

- membership in the union were limited to countries that have demonstrated a strong commitment to price stability;
- all decisions affecting macroeconomic policy were made by actors with Bundesbank-like aversion to inflation; or
- the Bundesbank itself were allowed to set European macroeconomic policy – as is the case, de facto, under the exchange rate mechanism (ERM) of the European Monetary System (EMS).

Clearly, the Maastricht treaty did not entrench the Bundesbank's hegemony over monetary policy. Neither did it ensure price-stable members or inflation-averse decision-makers.

The convergence criteria are merely guidelines for determining membership in the monetary union, which ultimately will be settled by a qualified majority vote by member governments.[3] Deals could thus be struck in which governments displaying less than rigid macroeconomic discipline would vote one another into the monetary union. If membership in the EMU is not restricted to a narrow deutschmark zone, the only other guarantor of price stability would be a macroeconomic policymaking procedure that eliminates the influence of less inflation-averse actors. The Maastricht treaty did not do this. Decisions in the ESCB will be by simple majority, permitting national representatives on the ESCB to outvote the EC's central bankers to accommodate other objectives with looser macroeconomic policies. Furthermore, the governments of member states will retain significant influence over EC macroeconomic policy through their power to establish guidelines for external exchange rates – irrespective of ESCB decisions

---

[3]Qualified majority voting pertains to many decisions made by the Council of Ministers (meetings of different cabinet ministers from member governments) and the European Council (meetings of heads of state). Votes are apportioned as follows: ten votes each for Britain, France, Germany, and Italy; eight for Spain; five each for Belgium, Greece, the Netherlands, and Portugal; three each for Denmark and Ireland; and two for Luxembourg. Fifty-four of the total (76) votes constitute a qualified majority.

over monetary policy. Finally, EMU will generate strong incentives for members to free-ride on the union by running large budget deficits, and the treaty does not provide automatic and binding sanctions against this.

This interpretation of EMU suggests that the fundamental puzzle of Maastricht is not why the other members acquiesced in the institutionalization of German macroeconomic hegemony, but rather why the German government agreed to an EMU that weakened its position. My answer is that the German government accepted an economically suboptimal EMU (from its perspective) because after the implosion of the former Soviet bloc and German unification, it had a very strong interest in maintaining the momentum for ever-greater European integration. It simply could not allow the Maastricht summit to fail.

In turn, this implies a reading of post-Maastricht politics that does not concentrate on the anti-Brussels reaction of mass publics across Europe. Rather, I argue that the major obstacles to the creation of EMU should have emanated from within Germany, particularly from the Bundesbank, whose leaders have long voiced grave concerns that German price stability not be sacrificed in the name of the EMU. The Bundesbank's proximate objective in 1992 was to quell the domestic inflationary pressures associated with German unification. Nonetheless, the bank's steadfast refusal significantly to cut German interest rates – to revive other European economies and to stabilize the EMS – has ensured the evolution of a two-speed union, if not cast serious doubt on the whole project. It is implausible to argue that this was not anticipated by the Bundesbank.

Finally, the German government acquiesced in this behavior not merely because its control over the Bundesbank is limited, but also because it now prefers a two-speed EMU. While it was essential that the German government support EMU at Maastricht – when Euro-enthusiasm was pervasive – the situation has changed since mid-1992. Euro-skepticism is now the dominant political trend in Europe, and hence it is today much easier for the government to mold European integration in the manner it sees fit – especially since the government can always hide behind the independence of the Bundesbank.

In the following sections, I elaborate on this analysis of the pre- and post-Maastricht politics of monetary union. I put the EMU treaty under the microscope, so to speak, to determine precisely what the governments agreed to; to explain the outcome of the treaty negotiations; to explore the aftermath of Maastricht; and finally, to lay out my conclusions.

## INTERPRETING THE MAASTRICHT TREATY

The part of the Treaty of European Union pertaining to EMU can be divided into two components: provisions regarding the transition to monetary union, and those that will govern macroeconomic policy in the completed union. The former include the convergence criteria; the latter set forth decision-making structures.

The protocols attached to the treaty outline the following economic preconditions for EMU membership:

- for one year prior to membership, an inflation rate that is less than 1.5 percentage points higher than that of the three lowest national inflation rates in the EC;
- for one year prior to membership, long-term interest rates that are less than 2 percentage points higher than those of the three EC countries with the lowest inflation rates;
- for two years prior to membership, no devaluations within the narrow band (±2.25 percent) of the exchange rate mechanism of the EMS;
- a national budget deficit of less than 3 percent of GDP; and
- a public debt of less than 60 percent of GDP.

These convergence criteria, however, are not hard-and-fast rules for admission. All decisions about membership in the union will ultimately be made under the qualified majority voting rule described in the Single European Act of 1987 (Article 109i). Moreover, the Maastricht treaty explicitly directs governments to base their decisions only on whether members have made good faith efforts to meet the criteria. Article 109j, paragraph 1, states that eligibility for EMU is contingent upon "the achievement of a high degree of sustainable convergence" and that "(t)his will be apparent from a rate of inflation which is *close to* that of at most the three best performing Member States". The treaty also asserts that the relevant deficit criterion is whether it has "*declined substantially and continuously* and has . . . reached a level that comes *close to the reference value*" (Article 104c, para. 2a). The appropriate consideration with respect to the public debt is "whether the ratio is not *sufficiently diminishing* and not *approaching the reference value at a satisfactory pace*" (Article 104c, para. 2b; all emphases added).

When the EC governments agreed to the reference values for the convergence criteria in December 1991, only France and Luxembourg satisfied them all (see Table 1). Assuming, however, that the costs of German unification begin to fall in the next few years, Germany will likely meet the convergence criteria when the initial EMU membership decisions are made at the end of 1996. If Britain chooses to reenter the ERM and to move from the broad (6 percent) to the narrow (2.25 percent) band, it will probably have little difficulty attaining the Maastricht desiderata. Denmark and the Netherlands also will likely be able to satisfy the criteria. So, too, might Portugal and Spain, given their strong growth rates and the manifest commitments of their governments to EMU. It is thus possible that up to eight current EC members may satisfy the Maastricht criteria by 1996.[4]

The picture is much less optimistic for the remaining four members. Belgium's public debt is very high, and growing. The amount of austerity that would be

---

[4]The applications of Austria, Finland, Norway, and Sweden for EC membership will likely be settled by the date of the first EMU decisions, and it is likely that at least Austria will also be eligible for membership in the monetary union.

TABLE 1   NATIONAL ECONOMIC PERFORMANCE AND THE EMU CONVERGENCE CRITERIA, 1991

| | Inflation Rate (%) | Long-Term Interest Rates (%) | Budget Deficit (% GDP) | Public Debt (% GDP) |
|---|---|---|---|---|
| Convergence criterion | 4.0 | 10.6 | 3.0 | 60 |
| Belgium | 2.8 | 8.9 | − 6.4 | 129 |
| Britain | 3.7 | 9.7 | − 1.9 | 44 |
| Denmark | 1.8 | 8.8 | − 1.7 | 67 |
| France | 2.5 | 8.8 | − 1.5 | 47 |
| Germany | 4.1 | 8.1 | − 3.6 | 46 |
| Greece | 17.6 | 20.8 | − 17.9 | 96 |
| Ireland | 3.5 | 9.3 | − 4.1 | 103 |
| Italy | 6.2 | 12.6 | − 9.9 | 101 |
| Luxembourg | 2.4 | 8.1 | 2.0 | 7 |
| Netherlands | 4.8 | 8.6 | − 4.1 | 78 |
| Portugal | 9.8 | 14.1 | − 5.4 | 65 |
| Spain | 5.5 | 11.7 | − 3.9 | 46 |

*Source: The Economist*, Dec. 14, 1991, 52.
*Notes*: The convergence criteria are based on the economic performance of the EC countries in 1991. Values for a fifth criterion, the permissible devaluation band, are not shown. Bold face figures indicate performance that exceeds the convergence criteria.

required in Greece, Ireland and Italy to satisfy the Maastricht objectives is enormous [Eichengreen (1992, p. 52)] Given the deleterious consequences of trying to meet the Maastricht criteria for growth and unemployment in the short run, it is unlikely that governments in any of these countries will seriously attempt this.

But does this mean that these countries will be excluded from the monetary union? Not necessarily. The issue is simply whether a qualified majority of EC governments will vote to include poorer-performing members in order to maintain what is widely viewed to be a desirable congruence between the membership of the EC as a whole and each of its constituent institutions. The tension between economic prudence and political expediency will be most clearly manifest with respect to Italy. Will a majority of members be prepared to exclude a founding and central member of the EC from what is probably the most important development in Europe since the creation of the EC? This is an open question, but it is clear that the provisions of the treaty do not eliminate the possibility than there will be union without convergence.

Once created, the monetary union will be run by the Executive Board of the European Central Bank (ECB) and the national central bank governors of participating countries. Together these constitute the Governing Council of the ESCB, which is deemed to be fully independent, that is, immune from political intervention (Protocol on ESCB/ECB, Article 7). The primary objective of the ESCB is price stability. Other goals, such as promoting employment and output, may be pursued only where they do not prejudice price stability (Article 105, para. 1). The ESCB cannot monetize national deficits through the provision of credit to member governments (Article 104). The treaty also reinforces the independence of the ESCB with appointment rules designed to reduce the influence of governments, not only collectively over the members of the Executive Board, but also individually over national central bank governors sitting on the Governing Council.[5]

It is these provisions that lead to the characterization of the ESCB as a "super-Bundesbank". But will this institutional structure ensure stable and low rates of inflation? There are at least three reasons to be skeptical about such a conclusion.

First, the Maastricht treaty is ambiguous as to who determines exchange rate policy. Article 105 delegates authority to the ESCB not only to control monetary policy, but also to manage external exchange rates. However, this provision is qualified – if not contradicted – by Article 109, paragraph 1, which declares that the Council of Ministers – which comprises relevant government ministers from the member states, may (acting unanimously) "conclude formal arrangements for an exchange rate system for the ECU [the new single currency] with respect to non-Community currencies". Paragraph 2 goes further, declaring that the Council of Ministers (voting by qualified majority) may "formulate general guidelines for exchange rate policy vis-à-vis these currencies". Paragraph 2 then states that these guidelines should be "without prejudice to the primary objective of the ESCB to maintain price stability", but it is unclear how in practice the tension between monetary policy – controlled by the ESCB – and exchange rate policy – determined by the Council of Ministers – will be resolved.

Second, even assuming that effective control of monetary and exchange rate policies rests with the ESCB, its decisions will be by simple majority, with each member of the Governing Council having one vote (Protocol on ESCB/ECB, Article 10.2). The Governing Council will have up to eighteen members: six members of the Executive Board of the ECB and the governors of the national central banks of countries in the union (Article 109a). Simple majority voting would allow national governors interested in looser monetary policies to outvote members of the Executive Board (even if the latter always pursue "sound money"). The treaty acknowledges this problem by mandating reforms for national central banks intended to ensure their independence, but there is no guarantee that this will be sufficient to turn all central bankers into would-be members of the Bundesbank. In turn, the larger the membership of EMU, the more likely that more members of the Governing Council will wish to stray from the path of price stability. This is because the poorer the economic performance

[5]Article 14 of the Protocol stipulates that all members of EMU must alter their domestic regimes so that the terms of governors of national central banks are at least five years (i.e., no shorter than electoral cycles in any of the member countries). The term of the president of the ECB shall be eight years; the vice president will serve for five years; and the four other members of the Executive Board (who will also serve on the Governing Council of the ESCB) will have terms from five to eight years. Furthermore, the terms of members of the Executive Board are not renewable (Protocol, Article 50).

of members, the stronger will be their incentives to push for looser macroeconomic policies [Alesina and Grilli (1992)].

Third, other things being equal, the creation of the single currency will lessen the constraints on national fiscal policies by decoupling them from national money supply growth and exchange rate movements, thereby creating strong temptations for individual governments to free-ride on the monetary union as a whole by running large national deficits. If governments and economic actors within a member country believed that others would view their national economy as "too big to fail" (and hence would cover their debts, rather than allow them to default on loans), this would generate even stronger temptations to pursue expansionary fiscal policies. Thus, national governments that wished to engage in deficit spending would be constrained only by their ability to raise capital in international markets. Governments undoubtedly would have to pay higher interest rates when borrowing, but it is unlikely that the disparities in real interest rates across member states would be more than a couple of percentage points.[6]

The Maastricht treaty responds to these incentives for fiscal profligacy by providing that governments with "excessively" loose fiscal policies may be fined or required to maintain non-interest-bearing deposits in the ECB (Article 104c). But the structure for enforcing these sanctions is weak and indeterminate.[7] Most significantly, the decision to take any action against a high-deficit or high-debt government rests with a qualified majority in the Council of Ministers, not with the ESCB (Article 104c). Thus a blocking coalition in the Council of Ministers could make it impossible to sanction EMU members who were using the protection of the single currency to pursue expansionary fiscal policies.

In sum, even given the independence granted to the ESCB in the Maastricht treaty, there is no guarantee that EMU will generate low inflation across Europe. While it would be patently false to assert that the treaty mandates macroeconomic laxity in the EC, it is equally clear that neither will the monetary union necessarily be a paragon of price stability. For this to transpire, actors in all participating countries – not only central bank governors, but also government leaders – will have to behave in ways that mimic the stance of the Bundesbank.

## INTERGOVERNMENTAL BARGAINING OVER THE TREATY

Why did the member governments of the EC agree to this form of EMU at Maastricht? Conventional economic accounts are not particularly helpful. There is an extensive literature on optimal currency areas [McKinnon (1963)] and on the desirable consequences of central bank independence [Barro and

---

[6]During the late 1980s, for example, real interest rates in Italy were only two points higher than those in Germany, even though the Italian national debt was very high, and even though a considerable part of the interest rate differential was caused by the risk premium attached to the possibility of a devaluation of the lira.

[7]It is instructive that the EC did not choose to follow the practice that has evolved in the U.S. to meet this problem: balanced budget amendments to almost all of the state constitutions.

Gordon (1983); Rogoff (1985)]. It is doubtful, however, that the EC represents an optimal currency area, and this significantly weakens the putative benefits of central bank independence [Eichengreen (1992)]. The monetary union would eliminate currency transaction costs, increase the credibility of commitments to price stability, and reduce the uncertainty associated with the possibility of exchange rate movements. But it is not clear that these benefits outweigh the large costs associated with asymmetries in economic shocks, the limited prospects for efficient adjustment to them by less mobile factors (such as fixed capital and labor), and the likely respones of governments to these conditions.

The absence of a compelling economic justification for EMU has led economists to conclude that the prime motivating force behind the Maastricht treaty was "politics" [Fratianni *et al.* (1992)]. But what does this mean? A political explanation should start with the preferences of the governments who signed the treaty, and then move on to an analysis of the bargaining between them.

### Government Preferences

Let us begin with the preferences of the critical player in EMU negotiations: the German government of Helmut Kohl. The most important point to note here is that the government was quite satisfied with the EMS status quo. Germany possesses considerable macroeconomic autonomy in the ERM as the $n$th currency in a de facto "$n-1$" fixed exchange rate regime. So long as the currency markets view the deutschemark as "good as gold" – and this seems not to have been shaken by the massive economic costs of German unification – the German government may set its own fiscal policy, and the Bundesbank can maintain its preferred monetary policy,[8] while policymakers in other ERM member states are constrained to follow the German lead.

There were, nonetheless, two economic incentives for the German government to contemplate EMU. The government believed that the stability of the EMS would be prejudiced within Europe by the removal of capital controls in the EC, as mandated by the Single European Act, and stability in the external environment is very important to the exporters and multinationals that form the base of the German economy [Frieden (1992)]. With respect to the rest of the world, the government believed that the creation of a single European currency (dominated by Germany) would create a counterweight to the U.S. dollar and the yen, which in turn would lessen the effects of U.S. and Japanese policy choices on Germany [Scharpf (1991)].

These reasons for German support of EMU should not conceal the fact that the government had very clear preferences as to the precise form the monetary union should take (and these preferences were very faithfully followed by the

---

[8]The government and the Bundesbank, of course, may pursue conflicting policies, as has been the case in German unification. However, this does not detract from the central point that German policymakers possess considerably more macroeconomic autonomy than do their counterparts in other European countries.

governments of the Benelux countries and Denmark, whose economies and policies were already inextricably connected with Germany). First, it wanted membership limited to countries whose economic policies and outcomes mirrored those in Germany ("convergence before union"). In the negotiations over Maastricht, German representatives opposed the qualified majority voting rule for membership in EMU, favoring instead a unanimity rule, under which Germany could veto the admission of any country [Woolley (1991, p. 16)]. Second, the German government believed that the operating rules for EMU should generate policies wholly consonant with the preeminence of price stability. Indeed, the government proposed that the ESCB should be given complete control over both monetary and exchange rate policies, with no role at all for the Council of Ministers [Cameron (1992b, pp. 38–39); Woolley (1991, p. 18)]. The Germans also advocated the automatic imposition of large fines (by the ESCB) on union members whose budget deficits and public debts exceeded specific, previously determined levels [Cameron (1992b, p. 39)].

The preferences of the other EC member governments were quite different from those of Germany and the other existing members of the de facto deutschemark zone. There is little doubt that all the other governments sought to appropriate some of the German reputation for monetary stability. This was the basic impetus after the demise of the Bretton Woods regime for the creation of the "snake" exchange rate system and subsequently the EMS. However, by the end of the 1980s, it had become apparent to a number of EC members that large costs were associated with participation in the ERM. By far the most important was being forced to acquiesce in the Bundesbank's hard line on macroeconomic policy even if this generated very high levels of unemployment during national recessions. Thus, for the EC members outside the deutschemark zone – France, Italy, and the four less industrialized countries, Greece, Ireland, Portugal, and Spain – the primary objective in moving to EMU was to "soften" the EMS. They sought to maintain a credible commitment to low inflation through participation in an international institution with a strong reputation for price stability, but without having to suffer the full consequences of the Bundesbank's uncompromising policy stance.

France's president, François Mitterrand, was in the vanguard of moves to limit Bundesbank power. Mitterrand and his advisers believed that the government's "socialism in one country" experiment of the early 1980s had been undermined by German unwillingness to accommodate the French expansion within the ERM [Cameron (1992a)]. This position was strongly supported by the Italian government, as a result of the large economic costs associated with ERM membership, even though Italy did not join the narrow band until 1990 [Giavazzi and Spaventa (1989)]. Ireland, too, suffered within the ERM in the 1980s [Dornbusch (1989)]. The other European less industralized countries realized that they, too, would in all likelihood soon have to join the narrow band of the ERM, and bear the consequences. For the governments in all these countries, the deleterious consequences of participating in the ERM were underlined in the period after German unification in 1990. High German interest rates greatly reduced the scope for other governments in the ERM to ease monetary policy, even though most were in the middle of deep domestic recessions. It is thus not surprising that Mitterrand was able to find strong allies for his basic position in other EC members.

These governments also disagreed with the German insistence that economic convergence precede union. All the governments – with the probable exception of Mitterrand's French administration – needed to transform their reputations for macroeconomic laxity by attaching themselves quickly to an international institution with strong counterinflation credentials. Obviously, this could be achieved by stable participation in the narrow band of the ERM, but the costs of attaining some of the Bundesbank's reputation were very high. EMU offered a more attractive prospect so long as its rules allowed some room for using countercyclical policies during deep recessions or, alternatively, provided some compensation for adhering to the dictates of macroeconomic rectitude. France and Italy pushed most strongly on the former front, whereas the European less industrialized countries, led by Spain, argued persistently that agreement on EMU should be coupled to the creation of a large new program for financial assistance to the poorer countries, in the name of cohesion.

The only government that did not neatly fall into either the deutschemark zone or what might be called the counter core[9] group was the conservative British government under John Major. Major's government is not as inveterately anti-European as was Thatcher's. Nonetheless, protecting British sovereignty is still a fundamental element in the government's calculus. In the run up to Maastricht, the Major government sided with the German camp on the importance of price stability and on a long transition to EMU. However, Major was constrained from aligning too closely with the German government because of the popular perception that the decision in 1990 to participate in the German-dominated ERM had eroded British sovereignty. The ambivalence of the British government was reflected in Major's bargaining stance at Maastricht: basic support for the German position, but with the proviso that Britain obtain an opt-out clause that would delay the final British decision on EMU until the membership and form of the union were complete.

In sum, the primary cleavage in the intergovernmental bargaining at Maastricht was between Germany, its Benelux allies, and Britain – who favored convergence before union, a slower transition to EMU, and strict operating rules – and France, Italy, and the southern countries – who preferred union before convergence, a fast transition, and looser operating rules. Given the differences between these two basic camps, what outcome might have been expected?

[9]I wish to thank Jeffry Frieden for suggesting this term to me.

*Bargaining over EMU: A First Cut*

During the intergovernmental conferences that culminated at Maastricht, there was no indication that any of the member governments – not even the British one – would consider moving to a more flexible exchange rate regime. Thus, the governments were faced with two choices. The first was whether to maintain the basic structure of the EMS or to move toward full monetary union. The second was whether the EMU would primarily reflect the preferences of the German government or those of the countercore.

On the basis of the economic dimension of monetary politics in Europe, one would have expected the German government to have been in a very strong position to impose its preferences on the countercore. The German government was quite satisfied with the EMS. It had an economic rationale to support a move to EMU, but these incentives were far smaller than those for the governments of the countercore, which were suffering badly at the hands of the Bundesbank within the ERM. Given this simple bargaining structure, the German government should have been able to hold out for an agreement at Maastricht that would have reflected its primary concerns for convergence before union and for the most stringent possible central bank independence reforms.

As discussed above, however, the final EMU treaty diverged considerably from these German preferences. In addition, the British government secured its opt-out clause. The less industrialized countries also gained agreement to development of a cohesion fund, the details of which were finally settled at the Edinburgh summit in the Delors II package. Thus, the outcome of the intergovernmental bargaining at Maastricht cannot be explained purely in terms of monetary politics. Rather, the bargaining must be understood in a much broader political economic context.

*EC Bargaining in Post–Cold War Europe*

Why was the German government unable to impose its EMU preferences on the other EC members at Maastricht, given its hegemonic position in European monetary politics? It is commonly suggested that the German government has a strong federalist impulse – as a result of German history – and that this explains its acquiescence in a suboptimal EMU. However, more tangible reasons can be adduced to explain the government's behavior at Maastricht. There is little doubt that in the period up until the all-Germany election in December 1990, Kohl was prepared to trade acquiescence in a rapid movement towards EMU (and political union) for the acceptance by the other EC members of rapid German unification (such as allowing the new Germany into the EC without any revisions of the EC treaties). Indeed, it was in the calendar year 1990 that the firm pro-EMU (and pro–political union) alliance was formed between Kohl and Mitterrand [Cameron (1992b, pp. 40–43)].

But the Maastricht treaty was not signed until December 1991 – one year after the process of German unification was formally complete and internationally recognized. Why didn't the Kohl government then push harder for its preferred EMU? An abrupt about-face would have been difficult to manage diplomatically. More important, however, German interests changed significantly in the wake of the implosion of the Soviet bloc in 1989, moving beyond the short-term goal of gaining international acquiescence in German unification [Anderson and Goodman (1993)]. The clearest manifestation of these new German interests was the importance the government attached to convincing not only its European neighbors but also the U.S. that unification would not be the harbinger of a bellicose remilitarization; creating powerful institutional ties to the EC was viewed as the best way to achieve this end.

The economic consequences of the momentous events of 1989–1990 have been at least as significant as these security concerns. In virtue of its geographic location, the historical ties of the former East Germany to the former Soviet bloc, and unified Germany's position as the economic hegemon in Europe, the German government has been forced to play a central role in dealing with the problems that have arisen from the revolutions to the east. The government committed itself to a very large aid program to Russia in return for the latter's acquiescence in unification. It has made the largest contributions of aid and other forms of economic assistance to the emergent capitalist democracies in Eastern Europe. Germany has also borne the brunt of immigration pressures from the east, as hundreds of thousands of people have sought to take advantage of the asylum provisions of the Basic Law and of a common cultural and ethnic heritage to migrate to Germany.

Moreover, the internal German economic outlook has deteriorated significantly since unification. Projections of the time it will take fully to integrate the former German Democratic Republic into the Federal Republic continue to grow, as do the costs associated with the transition, in terms of unemployment benefits, other welfare provisions, and direct aid for adjustment and development. The official central government deficit increased from 0.5 percent in 1989 to 5 percent in 1991, largely as the result of spending U.S. $83 billion on investment, unemployment benefits, and employment subsidies [Anderson and Goodman (1993, p. 10)] And recent estimates suggest that the costs of unification are still growing.[10] The dire economic consequences of unification have been layered on top of longer-term demographic developments that will place ever-greater stress on the economy and the government in the coming decades – most significantly the graying of the population and the increasing propensity of Germans to take early retirement.

From this perspective, the German government's commitment to "Europe" can be readily understood. The partial socialization of the costs among all EC members of integrating the old eastern bloc (including the former East Germany)

[10]See, e.g., "Germany: A survey", *Financial Times*, Oct. 26, 1992.

into Europe is very appealing, although it seems that the burden the other members are willing to assume is considerably smaller than the German government would prefer.[11] More important, the most viable route for the German economy to dig its way out of its current plight is through exports, and further penetration of EC markets would be the best method of achieving this objective. This prospect would be enhanced by further progress toward ever-greater European integration at Maastricht, whereas stalemate may have proved very damaging to broader German interests.

In sum, the German government had powerful reasons to hope that the Maastricht summit would result in a clear and significant advance in European integration. Other things being equal, the government would have preferred that this include an EMU based on an ironclad commitment to price stability. However, given its preferences for "more Europe", the government was prepared to compromise. The other member governments understood this, and thus they were able to gain significant concessions from Kohl in the wording of the Maastricht treaty, notwithstanding Germany's monetary hegemony and the bargaining power over EMU one might have expected this to have generated.

## POST-MAASTRICHT POLITICS

In contrast with the relatively straightforward ratification of the SEA and the success of subsequent moves toward the completion of the internal market, the post-Maastricht period has been a very trying one for the future of European integration. As discussed above, the greatest opposition to the treaty should have come from economically conservative forces in Germany, particularly the Bundesbank (and finance minister Theo Waigel of the Bavarian Christian Socialist Union). A cursory analysis of events in 1992, however, suggests that this was not the case; instead, the greatest obstacles to the ratification and implementation of the Maastricht treaty arose from populist opposition in other member states (Britain, France, and above all, Denmark) and from the instability in the foreign exchange markets this opposition generated. These factors undoubtedly played a significant role in the post-Maastricht turmoil. But it is equally clear that the Bundesbank's intransigence with respect to lowering interest rates was a major catalyzing factor in lessening the prospects for the early completion of monetary union across all the EC member states.

Each of the governments seeking to ratify the Maastricht treaty confronted a difficult political problem: how to persuade a majority of its citizens (in the cases of popular referenda) or parliamentarians (in the cases of legislative decisions) that giving up the national currency and formal authority over

---

[11]The EC extended approximately U.S. \$4 billion in structural funds to the eastern portion of Germany in 1991, but the Bonn government continues to shoulder the bulk of financial assistance, not only to the former East Germany, but also to Eastern Europe.

monetary policy was in their best interests.[12] As discussed above, the
countercore governments had good reasons to be content with the economic
implications of the EMU treaty. However, the arguments supporting this position
are complex, and they require a sophisticated understanding of both open
economy macroeconomics and the arcane details of the EMU treaty itself.
Governments sought to convince mass publics that under the EMS they had very
little effective macroeconomic autonomy, and that autonomy would actually be
increased under EMU as a result of diminished Bundesbank power, majoritarian
decisions over monetary policy, and the like. This task was made all the more
difficult by the depth of the recession in Europe in 1992, and the attendant feeling
that "Europe" was at least partially to blame for this. In this environment, naive
nationalism rather than sophisticated realpolitik was likely to be the dominant
force in domestic politics.

The task confronting the French government after Mitterrand decided to tie
the treaty's ratification to a popular referendum is illustrative. The Socialists
were convinced that France's economic interests would be best served by ratifying
the treaty since it would increase the government's influence over French (and
European) macroeconomic policy by mitigating the power of the Bundesbank.
For many French voters, however, it was an absurd proposition that the best
means of gaining economic independence was giving up the franc.

The ratification problems that plagued the Maastricht treaty were clearly highly
significant on their own. But the popular backlash against Maastricht also had
very harmful effects on the EMS (and hence indirectly on the transition to EMU).
After the removal of virtually all controls on capital flows within the EC by 1991,
many economists argued that the future stability of the exchange rate mechanism
would depend crucially on expectations in the currency markets that the EMS
was only a stepping-stone to EMU. So long as speculators believed this, they
had little reason to fear prospective devaluations by members – even those whose
economies were performing very badly.

Once the treaty's ratification became problematic, however, the markets'
confidence in the weaker currencies in the EMS – and the disciplines imposed
by the exchange rate mechanism – declined precipitously. The credibility of the
ERM was contingent upon the commitment of all participants to defend their
currency parities, come what may, and agreement to EMU was the most
important tangible evidence of this commitment. As the credibility of the ERM
eroded, the probability of speculative runs against the weaker currencies increased
significantly. With hindsight, it is clear that some currencies were overvalued
in the EMS, most notably, sterling and the lira. But their parities might have
been sustainable if the ERM had continued to be perceived as a stepping-stone
to EMU. When this connection was called into question, the foreign exchange

---

[12]Referanda were constitutionally mandated only in Denmark and Ireland. In France, Mitterrand
decided to seek a referendum in order to capitalize on what he thought to be very strong popular
support for the treaty. German Länder have argued that portions of the treaty require revisions of
the Basic Law, but this argument was not accepted by the federal government.

markets began making speculative runs on currencies whose economic "fundamentals" were not sound. Indeed, even the "sound" franc was subject to extensive speculative attacks, particularly at the time of the French referendum.

In essence, this is the story of September 1992 and its aftermath. For present purposes, however, two elements of the politics of the currency crisis should be highlighted. First, the governments with currencies that were under attack struggled valiantly to maintain their ERM parities, with public pronouncements of commitment to the system, the raising of interest rates, and the spending of reserves in the currency markets. In this context, it should be remembered that both Prime Minister Major and Chancellor of the Exchequer Lamont both continued to insist that sterling would remain in the ERM right up until the moment it was announced that, in fact, Britain was suspending its membership. This behavior was consistent with preferences for more, rather than less, monetary integration in Europe. There was little evidence before September 1992 that any of the EC members wished to turn to more flexibile exchange rates.

Second, and more important, the Bundesbank was under political pressure – from the German government and from the rest of Europe – to ease interest rates throughout the crisis period. For the German government, the Bundesbank's tight monetary policy was counterproductive with respect to reviving the German economy. The bank argued precisely the opposite: that tight money was the only antidote to the government's fiscal laxity during the euphoric months after the fall of the Berlin Wall. It was also clear to government leaders throughout the EC that the Bundesbank's policy was critical to the economic fortunes of other EC members, to the stability of the EMS, and ultimately to the prospects for the EMU.

In this regard, it should be noted that the Bundesbank studiously adhered to its EMS obligations to intervene in the foreign exchange markets to support currencies that reached their floors against the deutschmark.[13] For example, the German central bank bought DM 24 billion worth of lira in the second week of September to defend the Italian currency. At the same time, however, the bank was not prepared to take the more important step of significantly lowering its interest rates, which would have lessened the speculative pressures that were pushing the weak currencies to their ERM floors. When the lira was devalued by 7 percent on September 12, the Bundesbank cut Germany's Lombard rate by one-fourth of a percentage point and its discount rate by one-half point, but these cuts were considered far too small and too late. Moreover, in the ensuing months of speculative runs against other currencies, the Bundesbank refused to take any significant action on interest rates, confining its activity to the EMS-mandated interventions in the foreign exchange markets (while speaking out against this practice as encouraging speculation) [Norman (1992)].

---

[13]It is less clear whether the Bundesbank followed the 1987 Basle-Nyborg guidelines for intramarginal interventions.

One might argue that the Bundesbank merely acted myopically, focusing exclusively on the German economy, in 1992, rather than trying willfully to break up the EMS and to lessen the prospects for an EC-wide EMU. However, in the months after September, the three highest officials of the bank – Helmut Schlesinger, the president; his vice president, Hans Tietmeyer; and the Bundesbank's chief economist, Otmar Issing – gave numerous speeches detailing their opposition to the EMU negotiated at Maastricht [Norman (1992)]. Predictably, their speeches emphasized three points. First, while EMU is a worthwhile objective in theory, it cannot under any circumstances prejudice German price stability. Second, membership in the union should be determined by a monetary survival of the fittest, in which only those economies that match German performance should be admitted. Finally, the operating rules of the EMU are not stringent enough to mandate price stability, and the political control that remains in the treaty should be eradicated.

What explains the behavior of the Bundesbank? Here, it must be recognized that even before Maastricht, there was a cleavage in Germany between Kohl and his foreign minister, Hans-Dietrich Genscher, both of whom were prepared to compromise on EMU agreement in the context of broader political and economic objectives, and the Bundesbank, for which domestic price stability was the preeminent concern. Kohl possessed the formal authority to sign the Maastricht treaty to commit Germany to EMU, but this did not guarantee that the Bundesbank would then fall into line. Rather, as had been the case after the government's decision quickly to create a monetary union in Germany (with its hallmark one-to-one deutschmark-ostmark exchange rate for individuals' savings), the bank used its autonomy with respect to monetary policy to counteract the government's decision. With respect to German monetary union and the government's subsequent fiscal expansion, the Bundesbank's response was ever-higher interest rates. This policy carried over to the EC level, where the bank insisted that given the German economy's domestic problems, it was imperative that inflation be held in check, irrespective of the consequences of this policy for the other European economies and for the Maastricht treaty. The signing of the treaty by the twelve EC members only strengthened the Bundesbank's resolve to hold the line on stable money.

The most likely consequence of the Bundesbank's tight money policy will be the creation of a two-speed EMU, with initial membership limited to the current deutschmark zone, plus France and perhaps Britain and Ireland (and Austria, if it accedes to the EC by 1997), and with high barriers to the admission of other states. The partial disintegration of the EMS has made real convergence in the EC economies by the end of the decade far less probable. In turn, this will make it more difficult for governments to vote politically on membership in EMU by discounting the importance of strictly meeting the letter of the convergence criteria. While it may have been possible to argue for good faith (but failed) efforts to converge to justify membership in a stable and encompassing ERM, such arguments will be much less credible if participation in the narrow band is reduced to half a dozen or fewer currencies.

The final point that should be noted about post-Maastricht monetary politics in Europe is that a two-speed EMU might accord with the interests of the Kohl government. Recall that the government shared the Bundesbank's preferences regarding the EMU, but given the political conditions that surrounded Maastricht, especially the wave of Euro-optimism, it was impossible for the government to hold out for its preferred EMU. The situation after mid-1992 was very different. The enthusiasm for ever more European integration cooled considerably. The partial breakdown of the ERM jeopardized a swift transition to EMU for all EC members. In this environment, it would have been far easier for the Kohl government, too, to voice some reservations about the EMU. But the German government did not behave this way. All one can observe is that the Bundesbank pursued its tight money policy. Government officials criticized this behavior, with respect to its consequences both for the German economy and for the EMU. But given the Bundesbank's celebrated independence, the government could credibly argue that it had no capacity to change the central bank's stance. Thus, the Bundesbank's structure provided the government with a very helpful blind behind which to hide, if, indeed, the government had second thoughts about the deal it signed at Maastricht.

## CONCLUSION

The future of the monetary union in the EC has waxed and waned considerably in the past few years. Little of this checkered history can be explained in terms of traditional economic analyses. Rather, it seems that a broader political economic understanding is required. This paper has focused on two interrelated facets of European monetary integration.

First, with respect to the intergovernmental bargaining which culminated in the signing of the Treaty on European Union, the EMU agreed to at Maastricht in December 1991 does not recreate the German model at the EC level. It does not rule out the admission of less disciplined and lower-performing members. Moreover, its operating rules are not designed to minimize political control over monetary policy. How can this be explained? The simple answer is that after the tumultuous events of 1989 and 1990, the German government was prepared significantly to compromise on the details of the EMU treaty in order to make tangible progress on European integration at Maastricht, for both political and economic reasons. Notwithstanding the hegemonic German position in the EMS, the Kohl government acceded to the demands of seemingly less powerful member governments for less stringent admission rules and a less than airtight commitment to price stability. Among other things, these potential outcomes reflected a tacit acceptance by the German government that it should bear a considerable economic burden within the union, either by accepting higher rates of inflation or by granting substantial assistance to the weaker member economies.

Second, Bundesbank leaders were not happy with this outcome. For them, monetary stability should not be compromised at any price. Unlike most other domestic actors who were unhappy with Maastricht, however, the Bundesbank was able to voice its disapproval in a manner that had an enormous impact on the European political economy – by maintaining high interest rates at a time of deep recession in most member states. Other factors – most notably, popular opposition to the Maastricht treaty and uncertainty in the currency markets – had considerable effect on events after September 1992, but it is clear that the behavior of the Bundesbank was a powerful catalyst in the destabilization of monetary integration, the behavior of European economies, and the future of European integration. It is unclear whether the Kohl government was unable or unwilling to influence Bundesbank policy. Either way, the prospect of a two-speed Europe is much more likely than was the case in December 1991.

REFERENCES

Alesina, Alberto, and Vittori Grilli, 1992, The European Central Bank: Reshaping monetary politics in Europe, in: Matthew Canzoneri et al., eds., *Establishing a central bank: Issues in Europe and lessons from the U.S.* (Cambridge University Press, Cambridge).
Anderson, Jeffrey, and John Goodman, 1993, Mars or Minerva? A united Germany in a post-cold war Europe, in: Stanley Hoffmann, Robert Keohane, and Joseph Nye, eds., *The post-cold war settlement in Europe* (forthcoming).
Barro, Robert, and David Gordon, 1983, Rules, discretion and reputation in a model of monetary policy. *Journal of Monetary Economics* 12, 101–122.
Cameron, David, 1992a, Exchange rate policy in France, 1981–1983. Paper presented at the Conference on Labor and the Left in France: A Decade of Mitterrand, Wesleyan University.
——, 1992b, *The Maastricht agreement on Economic and Monetary Union: Initiation, negotiation, implications.* Ms., Yale University.
Dornbusch, Rudiger, 1989, Credibility, debt and unemployment: Ireland's failed stabilization. *Economic Policy* 4, 173–209.
Eichengreen, Barry, 1992, *Should the Maastricht treaty be saved?* PEEI Working Paper 1.10, University of California, Berkeley.
Fratianni, Michele, Jürgen von Hagen, and Christopher Waller, 1992, *The Maastricht Way to EMU.* Princeton Essays in International Finance 182, Princeton University.
Frieden, Jeffry, 1992, *European Monetary Union: A political economy perspective.* Ms., University of California, Los Angeles.
Giavazzi, Francesco, and Luigi Spaventa, 1989, Italy: The real effects of inflation and disinflation. *Economic Policy* 4, 133–172.
Hall, Peter, 1993, *Independence and inflation: The missing variables.* Ms., Harvard University.
Kenen, Peter, 1992, *EMU after Maastricht* (Group of Thirty, Washington, D.C.).

Magee, Stephen, et al., 1989, *Black hole tariffs and endogenous policy theory* (Cambridge University Press, New York).

McKinnon, Ronald, 1963, Optimum currency areas. *American Economic Review* 53, 717–725.

Norman, Peter, 1992, The day Germany planted a currency time bomb. *Financial Times*, Dec 12–13, 2.

Rogoff, Kenneth, 1985, The optimal degree of commitment to an intermediate monetary target. *Quarterly Journal of Economics* 100, 1169–1190.

Scharpf, Fritz, 1991, *Crisis and choice in European social democracy* (Cornell University Press, Ithaca, N.Y.).

Soskice, David, 1990, Wage determination: The changing role of institutions in advanced industrialized countries. *Oxford Review of Economic Policy* 6, 36–61.

Woolley, John, 1991. *Creating a European Central Bank: Negotiating EMU and the ESCB.* Ms., University of California, Santa Barbara.

# 4

## LINKING POLITICAL AND MONETARY UNION:
## THE MAASTRICHT AGENDA AND
## GERMAN DOMESTIC POLITICS

JOHN T. WOOLLEY

An important and fateful decision early in the Maastricht process was to conduct two parallel intergovernmental conferences: one on economic and monetary unification, the other on political unification.[1] This linkage was effected primarily because Germany insisted on it, with Helmut Kohl playing a key role in formulating and negotiating from the German position. The German strategy of linking monetary and political union is analyzed in terms of the "two-level game" metaphor developed especially by Putnam. The strategy cannot be understood without taking account of both levels of the game: the dramatic changes in the international environment (especially the collapse of the East German regime) and the constraints imposed by German domestic politics. German domestic political commitments and institutions deserve special emphasis.

A MOST IMPORTANT – indeed, fateful – development early in the Maastricht process was a decision to broaden the agenda of reform by launching two parallel intergovernmental conferences: one on economic and monetary unification, the other on political unification. Like so much of the history of the development of European institutions, the joining of these sets of issues seems to have occurred at the initiative of the leaders of Germany and France. Many accounts identify as critical a joint Franco-German declaration of April 19, 1990, favoring the launching of a second intergovernmental conference to deal with political unification.[2] This intent was echoed immediately thereafter in a decision of a special European Council meeting in Dublin. In that decision, the Council instructed foreign ministers to develop proposals for a second intergovernmental conference for consideration at the June 1990 summit.[3]

[1] This paper was originally prepared for the research group on the political economy of European integration, Center for German and European Studies, University of California, Berkeley. An earlier version was presented at the 1993 Conference of the European Community Studies Association in Washington, D.C., in May 1993. I am grateful for the very useful comments on earlier drafts received from David Andrews, Benjamin Cohen, Barry Eichengreen, Jeffry Frieden, Geoffrey Garrett, Jürgen von Hagen, Randall Henning, Peter Henning Loedel, Kathleen McNamara, and Lisa Martin and for the research assistance of Dirk Nowack. Financial support from the Center for German and European Studies of the University of California, Berkeley, and the Georgetown University School of Business is gratefully acknowledged.

[2] Bartsch (1990). The declaration stated that the goals of the conference would be: "to reinforce the union's democratic legitimacy, to make its institutions more efficient, to ensure economic, monetary, and political cohesion and to define and set in motion a common foreign and security policy." On the dynamics of previous reform initiatives, see Moravcsik (1991) and Cameron (1992).

[3] See Nelson and Revzin, 1990; *Europe Daily Bulletin,* May 1, 1990, p. 5.

It is important to examine the conditions within which this linkage was created because, with hindsight, it is clear that most of the misgivings expressed in the course of the ratification process – not least in Denmark, but also dramatically in France – have had to do with the political union elements of the Maastricht treaty.[4] Moreover, many observers maintain that the linkage appears to have been unnecessary and therefore problematical.[5]

The historical evidence reviewed in this chapter indicates that the support of the German chancellor, Helmut Kohl, was especially critical in linking political to economic and monetary unification. While many others, especially Jacques Delors, the president of the European Commission, promoted the issue and gave it visibility and specificity, it was Kohl, more than any other participant, who made sure that the whole array of issues appeared on the formal agenda for negotiations.

Several explanations for the linkage appear to be especially promising. One explanation is framed exclusively in terms of the international negotiating strategy of the Germans. In this view, the linkage was either a means of deliberately burdening the negotiations with many complex issues in order to increase the probability of failure, or a means of enlarging the scope for possible compromises. A second explanation is framed in terms of the dramatic change in the external political environment with the collapse of the Communist government in East Germany. In this view, the increased uncertainty caused by the East German collapse made Western states more willing to consider dramatic changes in order to ensure stability of the regional international system. A third explanation refers to domestic politics. According to this view, negotiators sought the linkage in order to satisfy domestic political interests – for example, by acknowledging principled commitments of critical coalition partners.

This chapter argues that each of these views depends on the others. It would be mistaken to try to choose among them as if they were mutually exclusive. Of course, the German support for linking economic and monetary unification to political unification was part of a negotiating strategy. The task is to see how that strategy responded to both international and domestic circumstances.[6] In

---

[4] The Danish rejection of the treaty in June 1992 was later interpreted by Danish politicians as a rejection of common defense policy, European citizenship, and transfers of sovereignty in justice and police matters. Danish officials restated their opposition to participating in Stage Three of Economic and Monetary Union (EMU), which was already anticipated in the terms of the treaty. Concerns were also expressed about ensuring greater openness in the Council of Ministers, a stronger role for the European parliament, assurances that the social dimension set minimum rather than maximum requirements, and greater clarity about the principle of subsidiarity. The Danish position is stated in a document entitled "Denmark in Europe," published in *Europe Daily Bulletin* Document no. 1806, November 5, 1992.

At the time of the 1990 Dublin summit, when formal agreement was reached to launch the two intergovernmental conferences, the Danish foreign minister, Uffe Ellemann-Jensen, was quoted as saying that there should be "no misunderstanding that we support a strengthening of the Community structures."

[5] For example, in 1990 two close observers noted Kohl's interest in strengthening the European Parliament and characterized it as "somewhat of a mystery." Colchester and Buchan (1990, p. 48).

[6] I am particularly indebted to David Andrews for his suggestions along this line.

order to understand the linkage of the parallel political union and monetary union negotiations, we must examine commitments in German domestic politics and the evolving international context. Without the domestic commitments, German leaders could not have credibly pushed the political union issues onto the agenda. Without the international changes, the pressures to move swiftly toward economic and monetary unification would have been significantly reduced.

This analysis draws on the work of others on the logic of so-called two-level games [e.g., Putnam (1988), Alt and Eichengreen (1989); Tsebelis (1990); and Putnam and Bayne (1987)]. In a two-level game, players have to play simultaneously in two games. For example, international negotiators have to deal with the representatives of other states and with their domestic constituencies. The characteristics of each level of the game affect the definition of strategy, and a negotiator must select a specific strategy that has consequences simultaneously in both levels of the game. Analysts have been especially interested in how the domestic political game affects strategic choice.[7]

Domestic politics can shape the behavior of international negotiators in at least three ways which may interact to reinforce one another. First, domestic institutions specify whose preferences count by specifying whose agreement is required in formal ratification and subsequent implementation of the international agreement. Second, the fundamental policy commitments to critical coalition partners or decisive ratifying institutions must be honored in order to ensure their continued support. Fundamental commitments may be created in various ways, but a common one is through reiterating a principled position and taking action consistent with that position over time.[8] Third, electoral challenges to the governing majority on issues of importance in the negotiations can lead negotiating partners to be more accommodating than they otherwise would have been, so long as they prefer the current government to its potential challenger. Fundamentally this approach asks us to look at negotiators as simultaneously solving two strategic problems with a single act (or set of acts). One strategic problem is in the domestic game; one is in the international game.

## PUTTING POLITICAL UNION ON THE AGENDA

"Political union" is a very large umbrella. It covers a wide array of issues, including the set of relationships among European Community institutions, the

---

[7] Putnam (1988), for instance, discusses the way the size of the domestic "win set," or set of ratifiable agreements, will constrain and guide the behavior of negotiators.

[8] A detailed discussion of the issue of credible commitments is beyond the scope of this chapter. The importance of general principled positions is stressed in Schelling (1980). Promises to a national parliament or to a national audience in advance of negotiations may have a commitment effect analogous to that of a contract between a principal and agent [see Dixit and Nalebuff (1991)]. Commitments of the latter kind were made only by the UK government of John Major prior to Maastricht. A useful general review of the issue of credibility and commitment is in Blackburn and Christensen (1989).

conduct of common foreign and defense policy, regional policy, industrial and regulatory policy, and the social charter. At the core, and especially so for Helmut Kohl, formation of a European Political Union (EPU) was about how to create and balance new institutions that could be the repository of significant transfers of national sovereignty to the European Community. The issue came onto the negotiating agenda in a context dominated by the collapse of the East German government and by a concern that the momentum for formation of an Economic and Monetary Union, the EMU set forth eventually in the Maastricht treaty, not be lost. Kohl played an especially important role in propelling the issue of political union onto the agenda and in defining its content as being about new powers for European institutions, especially the European Parliament.

Political union had long been a goal of European federalists, although it had never been so seriously and prominently on the agenda as in the spring of 1990.[9] There was an easy juxtaposition of the goal of political union with concern about a European "democratic deficit."[10] Concern about the democratic deficit demonstrably increased in the course of 1989 as excitement grew about the 1992 project and observers contemplated the political implications of the Delors Report, on EMU, released in April.[11] Thus a body of ideas was available to be exploited by any large-country leader who wished to press for action on political union.

In mid-1989, no focal program for advancing political union or addressing the democratic deficit had been embraced by any of the major European leaders. There was no sense of urgency about beginning work on political union until Kohl – and Delors – began to press the issue in late 1989. President Mitterrand of France, who was president of the European Council in the second half of 1989, was focusing attention on striking an interstate bargain on adherence to a social charter. Mitterrand was also agitating for convening an intergovernmental conference (IGC) on EMU as soon as possible after July 1, 1990, the date for starting Stage One of EMU as described in the Delors report. Mitterrand showed an interest in strengthening the links between national parliaments and the European Parliament, but little or no enthusiasm for reforms that would strengthen European institutions relative to the European Council.[12]

[9] Indeed, monetary union has sometimes been characterized as essentially a means to the end of political union.

[10] This refers to a belief that the power of European institutions is not matched by sufficient accountability to elected officials [see Williams (1991)].

[11] See European Communities, Committee for the Study of Economic and Monetary Union [Delors Committee], 1989 Report on Economic and Monetary Union in the European Community [Delors report] (Commission of European Communities, Brussels). A NEXIS search of press use of the term "democratic deficit" prior to 1990 turned up only eleven articles, eight of them in 1989, two in 1988, and one in 1985. The search included all sources in the NEXIS archive; sources identified in the search included the *Financial Times*, the *Telegraph* (daily and Sunday issues), the *Reuter Library Report*, and *The Economist*. The search excluded official EC documents, such as the *Journal of the European Parliament*.

[12] Mitterrand, as president of the Council, and Kohl, in an unusual break with custom, both addressed the European Parliament on November 22. Mitterrand stressed the need to move forward swiftly on EMU, the social charter, and environmental policy. Kohl stated the German government's full support of "implementation of European union" and strengthening the process of European integration [see Johnson (1989)].

In a speech at Bruges in October 1989, Jacques Delors urged acceleration toward EMU in order to counteract any tendency to become distracted from the Single Market program by political changes in Eastern Europe. Delors suggested the need for a "qualitative leap in our conception of the Community," suggesting that reforms in the Community's institutions would be needed to respond to the contemporary challenges.[13] This speech was seen as part of a "campaign" by Delors to step up the pace of movement toward EMU – a campaign endorsed at least in part by Helmut Kohl [see Jukes (1989)].

Delors expanded on this notion in late November, suggesting that an EMU treaty should include measures to "improve the decision-making process and to fill what has come to be called the democratic deficit in the Community."[14] Delors seemed most clearly to have in mind measures to strengthen the power of the Commission, but he also mentioned the possibility of reforms in the Council, enhanced powers for the European Parliament, and creation of a set of independent agencies to manage some regulatory matters [Kellaway (1989b)].

Just prior to the meeting of the European Council in Strasbourg in December 1989, Kohl upset Mitterrand by proposing to delay the start of the IGC on EMU from mid-1990 to after December 1990 and use the added time to expand the conference to include consideration of the structure of Community institutions and the European Parliament.[15] Kohl's position was that the next European Parliament (elected in 1994) must have increased power [see Buchan (1989b); Buchan and Davidson (1989)]. In my view, this act by Kohl is extremely important. It was one of the first unambiguous indications by Kohl of his interest in linking EMU and EPU.

The response to Kohl's initiative was primarily hostile and suspicious. Delors repeated his own support for institutional change, but cautioned that strengthening the European Parliament should not be made a precondition for EMU negotiations. Delors further warned that the need for changes in EC institutions was being used as a pretext for delay on EMU.[16]

The Strasbourg summit concluded with an agreement to move forward on an intergovernmental conference on EMU in late 1991, after the German elections, as Kohl desired. The issue of political reform was still inchoate and by no means

---

[13] Delors did not make specific proposals beyond calling for adopting and ratifying an EMU treaty [see Buchan (1989d)]. This led the *Financial Times* to editorialize that a decision on radical institutional reform, implying a new treaty, "would surely be the most difficult and time-consuming [course of all]" (October 18, 1989, p. 18). *The Economist* perceived in Delors's remarks the "hint that the coming intergovernmental conference on EMU should also take on board another reform of the Community's decision-making" (October 21, 1989, p. 50).

[14] Buchan (1989a). See also The building of Europe, *Financial Times*, December 7, 1989, 16.

[15] Kohl breaks with Paris on Delors plan, *Times*, (London), December 7, 1989, 1.

[16] Bonn bid to cover EMU talks rift. *Financial Times*, December 8, 1989, 1. Simultaneously, the president of the European Parliament demanded that any EMU treaty dramatically increase the powers of the Parliament.

clearly on the negotiating table.[17] It was obvious to many observers that the issue of political reform was likely to resurface and cause controversy. Shortly after the Strasbourg summit, Delors suggested that a second IGC on political and institutional issues take place one or two years after the EMU conference.[18]

In speeches by Delors, Kohl, and Bundesbank president Karl-Otto Pöhl, January 1990, issues were raised relevant to the question of political reform. Pöhl (1990), speaking in Paris on January 16, described in considerable detail his image of a politically independent monetary authority, which he argued should be created at the intergovernmental conference on EMU. Of particular interest, Pöhl stated that he saw no problem with the creation of an independent central bank prior to the perfection of a political union: "To give the system democratic legitimacy, it would suffice that it be set up by a treaty among democratic governments and ratified by democratically elected parliaments, and provided with a clearly defined mandate." However, Pöhl left no doubt about his deep concern that other EC institutions be clearly committed to the same objectives as those sought by the central bank.

In a counterpoint to Pöhl's speech, the next day Kohl and Delors made coordinated presentations in which they both stressed the need for reforms in Community institutions and progress toward political union. In a speech before the European Parliament, Delors explicitly called for addressing the Community's democratic deficit and endorsed Kohl's earlier suggestions that the upcoming intergovernmental conference should deal not only with EMU but with institutional reform. In these remarks, Delors emphasized "political cooperation" (i.e., a common foreign policy) and the creation of a responsible executive power.[19] It was clear at the time that the French were not particularly enthusiastic about Delors's proposals [Trean (1990b)]. In an address to the French Institute for International Relations in Paris, Kohl repeated his call for political union and institutional reforms [Johnson (1990)].

For a period in February 1990, discussion shifted back to the issue of the timing of the meeting of the EMU intergovernmental conference, with the Italians and French again proposing to accelerate it to July. The issue was scheduled for discussion at a special European Council summit in Dublin in April.

The discussions on political union gained form and specificity in March 1990. In mid-March the Martin report, a detailed program of political reforms, was adopted by the European Parliament.[20] Shortly thereafter, the Belgian for-

---

[17] The summit's final communique included this Delphic statement: "The European Council emphasized, in this context, the need to ensure the proper observance of democratic control in each of the member states. With a view to the new term of the European Parliament, which will begin in 1994, it calls for Economic and Monetary Union, to comply fully with this democratic requirement."

[18] Delors adopted a much more positive tone toward parallel negotiations a month later [Kellaway (1989a); Dickson (1990)].

[19] M. Jacques Delors propose de mettre en chantier dès 1990 les institutions de la "Fédération" Européenne, *Le Monde*, January 18, 1990, 4. See also Usborne (1990).

[20] Among other things, the Martin report called for majority voting in the Council of Minsters, public debates in the Council of Ministers, codecision for the Parliament, a parliamentary right to initiate legislation, and the right of the Parliament to elect the Commission president. Buchan and Dickson, (1990).

eign minister, Mark Eyskens, circulated a working paper outlining proposals for institutional reforms.[21] In late March, Kohl again raised the issue of political union, calling for a decision at the April summit to launch an intergovernmental conference on EPU to begin at the end of the year and run parallel to the EMU conference.[22]

In short, while the issue of political union had been on some agendas for a long time, it emerged as a serious issue only in the context of decisions to proceed with EMU negotiations. These decisions were being made while the players were trying to respond to the changes taking place in Eastern Europe. Jacques Delors was an important voice for reform, and for a broad conception of the issues to be considered. Others, including the European Parliament and Belgian officials, helped contribute relatively highly detailed programs for reform. However, the history of European reform suggests that unless a leader of one of the major countries embraces a proposal, it has little chance of becoming a viable option [see Moravcsik (1991)], and the critical, initial proponent of political union was Helmut Kohl. The sequence of events supports the interpretation that Kohl conditioned meaningful progress on EMU on broadening the agenda to include EPU.

### A GERMAN NEGOTIATING STRATEGY FOCUSED ON EMU

How should we understand the German strategy of linking EPU and EMU? One interpretation of this strategy is loosely and very generally couched in terms of a trade-off between perceived German national economic interests and international influence. Many observers argued that the purely economic benefits for Germany from EMU were ambiguous, at best. EMU, of course, held out the prospect of imposing a German-style central bank on all of Europe, with no coherent counterbalancing political institution. German influence in such an institution would surely have been substantial, providing Germany with a legitimate and important forum for exercising political influence.

However, since Germany already controlled the de facto European central bank, the increment in international influence would be small, and some serious risk existed of eventual loss of control over monetary policy. Given that the expected economic gains from EMU were small, the strategy of adding EPU to the negotiating agenda could be seen essentially as a hostile strategy intended to derail EMU. Placing an additional set of difficult issues on the negotiating agenda would increase the odds of deadlock and stalemate in the negotiations. Thus, a status quo acceptable to Germany would be preserved without the

[21] Eysken's proposals, which paralleled the ones in the Martin report, included proposals that virtually all decisions be taken by a majority vote of ministers; that the European Commission should become powerful executive, with its president elected by the European Parliament; and that other new powers be accorded to the Parliament, including the right to propose legislation. See Belgium calls for accelerated EC integration, *Reuter Library Report,* March 21, 1990.

[22] Trean (1990b). At the time it was clear especially that the Spanish government supported Kohl, and the French indicated that they and Kohl "were both going in the same direction."

potential embarrassment of having to defend it explicitly.[23] At the least, introducing an additional set of issues might allow Germany to extract further compromises on EMU – thereby doubly assuring that a German conception of EMU would be reflected in the outcome.

There is reason to believe that some German interests would have welcomed the adoption of a strategy intended to increase the likelihood that negotiations would ultimately fail. However, there are serious weaknesses in this stylized account, which are precisely the ones the "two-level game" metaphor is intended to address. First, why did Germany not adopt a more straightforward approach to resisting EMU if that were its true objective? The government of the United Kingdom tried to do so by advancing the so-called "hard ecu" plan. I will argue that international pressures on Germany in late 1989 and early 1990 made straightforward opposition a difficult option for Germany to adopt,[24] and that in domestic terms, such a straightforward strategy would have been very hazardous for Helmut Kohl.

Second, if the EPU-EMU linkage was at bottom a negotiating strategy hostile to EMU, why was that strategy not embraced by other negotiating partners also hostile to EMU, such as the UK leaders? I argue that in the absence of a genuine domestic commitment to political union, which did exist in Germany, such a proposal would not have seemed serious. John Major, for example, could not possibly have embraced EPU as a hostile negotiating strategy. The domestic reaction from his own party would have been one of repudiation; internationally, no negotiating partner would have considered the negotiating position to be a serious one.

The goal, then, must be to supplant a stylized, oversimplified account of a negotiating strategy with an account that is more sensitive to the domestic and international political circumstances of the time. Doing so will help to illustrate how the range of credible options open to international negotiators arises from the circumstances of domestic politics.

### THE FOREIGN POLICY CONTEXT

To understand the strategic problems Kohl faced, we need to be reminded of the international challenges he faced. This especially includes the cataclysmic changes under way in Eastern Europe and the radical implications of those changes for the international balance of power.

It is difficult to overstate the dizzying speed of change in this period. The

---

[23] As noted in Treverton (1991), "Economically, though, achieving the 1992 program and not much more would suit unified Germany just fine."

[24] As already noted, while Kohl's advocacy of political union talks was essential, Kohl was not alone. The importance of Delors at critical moments in promoting and underscoring the idea of political union talks cannot be ignored. No story constructed purely in terms of German negotiating strategy can adequately account for the role of Delors as an agent.

rapid weakening of the Communist government in East Germany in the Autumn of 1989 – the Berlin Wall fell on November 9 – dramatically altered the West German and European political agendas. In late November 1989, without prior consultation with European allies, Kohl outlined a ten point plan for eventual German reunification. The lack of consultation on an issue so fundamental to postwar European security arrangements was regarded as disturbing, especially in London and Paris. Mitterrand met with Gorbachev to advise against allowing the German reunification to occur too swiftly. By January 1990, East Germans were fleeing to West Germany at the rate of more than two thousand a day. In late January, East German parliamentary elections planned for May 6 were abruptly advanced to March 18, as the Communists' capacity to govern slipped away.

Within days of the January crisis in East Germany, monetary union between the two Germanies was high on the agenda. French and British leaders were notably cool toward the prospect of German reunification and found renewed interest in discovering their own common ground in areas of defense and foreign policy. The French and Italian governments renewed proposals for accelerating the start of the EMU conference to midyear – a proposal Kohl had rejected in December on domestic political grounds (he wanted to avoid negotiations on this issue prior to national elections in December).[25] He again rejected the proposal – for the same reasons [Marsh and Cooke (1990)].

At the time, commentators saw strong opportunities for negotiating partners to exercise leverage against Germany in EC negotiations. Fears of "the German problem," it was asserted, could be invoked to press Kohl to move faster than he would prefer on EMU. Further claims were made that the process of German monetary union showed how Kohl could override Bundesbank objections in a decisive way – and thus, how little domestic constraint he really faced.

It was in this foreign policy context, after a lengthy period of negotiation between Bonn and Paris, that the joint Kohl-Mitterrand statement on political union was issued in mid-April. The joint statement was widely interpreted as part of a move to reassure Germany's allies that a reunified Germany would be firmly anchored in Western institutions.[26] The statement was also understood as representing a recognition of the need to reconsider issues of European security arrangements in light of the changed strategic context.

The collapse of East Germany is without doubt an important element in comprehending the pressures on the German government to reassure its partners and adjust its policies. It helps us to see why Germany's negotiating partners felt a sense of urgency about making sure that Germany would be more closely tied

---

[25] Raising this issue again in light of the clear prior indications that it caused domestic political problems for Kohl suggests, among other things, a certain willingness on the part of the French and the Italians to push Kohl in a direction that would subject him to possibly significant domestic political challenges.

[26] So editorialized the *Financial Times* (April 20, 1990, 22).

into Western Europe.[27] It is especially important in showing why Kohl had to frame a response that did not reject EMU. Yet why these actions should have taken the form of a major initiative for European political union is not obvious from the international circumstances. The most prominent requests for reassurance from Kohl's partners, moreover, were not for the set of reforms that Kohl advanced. Kohl had other ways to reassure his European partners without proposing large and difficult institutional reforms. He could have simply expressed renewed interest in EMU and undertaken additional intensive consultations about reunification, the Oder-Neisse line, and NATO defense arrangements.[28]

Kohl's December 1989 proposal to examine and strengthen Community institutions clearly antedated the period in which German monetary unification was an immediate reality. Moreover, the proposal was by no means presented in a context of trying to reassure and mollify aroused negotiating partners, and it did quite the opposite. Prior to Kohl's initiative, his negotiating partners were urging a renewed commitment to European union, but that commitment was framed primarily in terms of a redoubled effort to achieve EMU. Ironically, the emergence of a renewed European (especially French) commitment to achieving EMU along the lines already approved by the Bundesbank president, Pöhl, in the Delors report, heightened the pressure on Kohl. The new foreign policy context is clearly a necessary element in our understanding of the German strategy to link these two large initiatives. However, without further knowledge of Kohl's domestic political constraints, it is not a sufficient explanation.

### GERMAN DOMESTIC POLITICAL COMMITMENTS
### TO POLITICAL UNIFICATION

A more nearly sufficient account, I believe, must take account of the domestic commitments and calculations of Kohl and other leading German politicians.[29] With the collapse of East Germany, foreign and domestic politics were suddenly and dramatically fused in Germany. Consequently, these external stresses provoked a reassertion of German domestic policy commitments that shaped the

[27] The German reunification did clearly raise one kind of institutional question that involved the weight of German representation in EC institutions, especially the European Parliament. The pressures created by international events may have made it much more difficult than it otherwise would have been for Germany to engage in relatively straightforward delaying tactics about EMU.

[28] Moreover, if Kohl needed to reassure his partners, those partners also needed to reassure him. They had been cool, if not hostile, to one of the defining objectives of West German politics, the reunification of Germany. The depths of the mistrust they revealed about fundamental German intentions must have been disturbing to the Germans. Did these leaders have any rational basis for confidence that the German response would be positive? Would any have had a basis for objection if Germany had responded by trying to constrain the EMU negotiations as narrowly as possible to the issue of making a European Bundesbank?

[29] To reiterate, this by no means rules out the relevance of international circumstances. As Hanrieder has written, in the postwar period, "the meshing of domestic and foreign policies became the essence of West Germany's political culture" (1989, p. 332).

two-level play in the Maastricht negotiations. They also revealed a certain am-bivalence about European unification in German domestic politics. These cir-cumstances provided the conditions for Kohl to embrace an ultimately ambig-uous strategy – one that echoed deeply held German commitments while exploiting their potential for producing stalemate. Domestic political commit-ments, coalitions, and institutions all reinforced the logic for Kohl of putting EMU and EPU on the same agenda.

### West German Consensus

One important element was the existence of a strong consensus (at least at the rhetorical level) in favor of European unification on the part of virtually all the major players in German politics. In this context, Kohl had to advance the polit-ical union issue together with EMU, or, to frame the argument more modestly, it was very unlikely that any major domestic participants could challenge him successfully when he did so.[30]

As early as 1982, Kohl had committed his government to "opening new routes to European Unification" [Bulmer and Paterson (1987, p. 81)]. But even in 1982 this was hardly a new commitment. Support for European federalism had been a fundamental assumption of West German politics from the earliest days of the Federal Republic [see Bulmer and Paterson (1987, pp. 6–7); Kirch-ner (1991, p. 154)]. In the 1950s, this goal had been particularly closely asso-ciated with parties of the CDU/CSU center-Right coalition, Kohl's core constit-uency [Sturm (1989)]. Over time, however, European union ceased to be an important source of partisan division in German politics. Indeed, one of the dominant features of recent German politics has been the gradual creation of a strong area of compromised agreement on foreign policy objectives, such as supporting European integration [Hanrieder (1989, p. 334)]. The view that Ger-man influence and German reunification could come about only in the context of a politically unified Europe was widely shared among German political lead-ers and "Parliamentary opinion, with the exception of the Greens, [was] solidly in favor" of union [Bulmer and Paterson (1987, p. 247)].

Thus, there was a long-standing principled commitment in German domestic politics to the idea of West European unification. If some observers detected a waning enthusiasm for European political union in the years prior to 1989–1990 [see, e.g., Kirchner (1991, p. 157)], it was also true that there had been no rejec-tion of that long-standing commitment. Indeed, consistent with this general sup-port for European unification, there had been significant criticism of the limited enhancement of the powers of the European Parliament as part of the Single

---

[30] Indeed, given the relative weakness of the economic benefits for Germany in EMU as estimated by some economists, it may be appropriate to see Kohl's linkage of political union and EMU as a rhetorical device to explicitly evoke the deepest commitments of German politics in order to preclude issues from being framed in strictly cost/benefit terms.

European Act [Bulmer and Paterson (1987, p. 249)]. As the moment for German reunification suddenly presented itself, there was no possibility of retreating from the associated commitment to European unification.

## Institutions and Coalitions

By linking EMU to political union, Kohl also had a means of simultaneously addressing some of the most important commitments of his coalition partner, the Free Democratic Party (FDP), and of an institution important for implementing EMU, the Bundesbank. Although a small party in terms of votes, the FDP provided the decisive Bundestag majority for Kohl. The FDP drew its support overwhelmingly from the urban middle and upper-middle class, and had been supported financially by industry [Sturm (1989, pp. 465–466)]. These constituencies were particularly attracted by the contributions European unification could make to liberalism and free markets. The Bundesbank, the highly independent German central bank, had always been perceived as implacably opposed to any form of EMU that would result in a diminished commitment to the goal of price stability.

The FDP, and especially Hans Dietrich Genscher, the German foreign minister since 1974 (and party chairman from 1974 to 1984), was clearly and strongly committed to EMU, European federalism, and common European defense and foreign policies.[31] Genscher had been associated with a major contribution to reinvigorating the movement toward European unification: the Genscher-Columbo proposal, which promoted various forms of cooperation, especially in foreign and security policy, and became the basis for the Stuttgart European Council's Solemn Declaration on European Union in 1983.[32] Genscher played a key role in promoting the Delors Committee as an important step toward European unification. The radical aspirations implicit in Genscher's vision would suggest that EMU alone was not a sufficiently large ambition.[33] Kohl could hardly ignore the FDP leader's deep commitments in this area without risking the stability of his coalition, nor is there any evidence that he desired to do so.

The Bundesbank, by contrast, had a well-known and long-standing commitment to price stability, which was potentially threatened by EMU. Price stability, in the Bundesbank's own view, was not simply a result of the legal position of the central bank, but was even more fundamentally a result of the commitment of social institutions, broadly conceived, in supporting the goal of price stability.

---

[31] This treatment may overstate the unity of the FDP; some elements in the party were quite close to the Bundesbank position. However, the political strategy for Kohl would not have been different in light of that.

[32] See Colchester and Buchan (1990, p. 18); Bulmer and Paterson (1987, pp. 134–135). This proposal itself had domestic political goals of differentiating the FDP from the SPD more clearly.

[33] As noted by Marsh (1989), "Mr. Genscher puts forward a vision of a federal Europe of East and West, and says that 'no one thinks any more in the category of nation-states.'" See also Buchan (1989c).

The view that convergence had to precede economic union had been evident in the German (and especially Bundesbank) view expressed in earlier European debates about monetary union. Only convergence, it was argued, could guarantee that there would not be problems of economic coordination in a monetary union [Tsoukalis (1977); Ludlow (1982)]. Indeed, it is precisely the Bundesbank's long-standing suspicion of monetary union that underpins the belief of some observers that the Bundesbank supported EPU because of a desire to see the EMU negotiations fail.

It is possible to see the Bundesbank position in a somewhat different, and possibly more favorable, light. Pöhl's January 1990 statement explicitly challenged the notion that democratizing political reforms at the European level must precede the creation of a European Central Bank.[34] His statement read, nonetheless, as a brief for EPU, although the basis differed from Kohl's. Unlike Kohl, the Bundesbank was not concerned with political legitimacy, or the democratic deficit. Rather, it was with the current and possible future existence of centers of power external to the central bank that might be opposed to the bank's goals. Thus the Bundesbank's view was that EMU should not proceed without simultaneously ensuring a supportive environment for the central bank's anti-inflation goals. Pöhl went on to say in his speech that public authorities, labor and management must all adopt a responsible attitude, involving acceptance of realistic limits, in order for the central bank to fulfill its mission "without problems" [Pöhl (1990)].[35]

The Bundesbank reiterated its concern for the terms of political union in a statement on EMU that was released in September 1990, prior to the start of the intergovernmental conferences. At that time, the Bundesbank said: "In the final analysis, a Monetary Union is ... an irrevocable sworn confraternity – 'all for one and one for all' – which, if it is to prove durable, requires, judging from past experience, even closer links in the form of a comprehensive political union" [Deutsche Bundesbank (1990)].[36] Beyond this particular phrase, the Bundesbank had little to say publicly on political union. In its most concrete expres-

---

[34] Pöhl (1990) did note explicitly that "of course European integration cannot be limited to monetary policy. Improvements in other domains are also necessary, as the German Chancellor has urged for the European Parliament".

[35] In a post-Maastricht statement, the Bundesbank characterized its earlier position as one maintaining that monetary policy "will be crucially influenced by the economic and fiscal policies of, and by the behavior of management and labour in, all the participating countries." *Europe, Daily Bulletin,* Documents no. 1764, March 2, 1992. A more cynical interpretation of the Bundesbank's position would involve noting that it began to embrace political union as it became clear that the French were going to agree to an independent central bank along the lines of the Bundesbank.

[36] *Europe Daily Bulletin,* Febuary 14, 1992; Koelle (1992). The Bundesbank statement is reproduced in full in *Europe, Daily Bulletin,* Documents no. 1655, October 5, 1990. See also *Financial Times* September 20, 1990. A review of major European press sources (*Financial Times, Le Monde, Frankfurter Algemeine Zeitung, Handelsblatt, Der Spiegel*) covering the Bundesbank's statement, found none that singled out this particular phrase as especially significant or reflecting a novel policy departure. Of the sources surveyed, only the *Financial Times* treated the story as worthy of the front page.

sions, the Bundesbank stressed the need to create institutions ("binding rules and sanctions") to ensure "effective budgetary discipline."

However, in the period after the negotiations, spokespersons for the Bundesbank again emphasized the importance of the political and social environment in which monetary policy functions [Schlesinger (1992)]. In a statement published in early February of 1992, the Bundesbank criticized the Maastricht agreement as inadequate: "Future developments in the fields of the political union will be of key importance for the permanent success of the monetary union."[37]

Kohl's decision to move political union to the fore makes sense in terms of an effort to address both the preferences of his coalition partner and the view of the Bundesbank. Both positions were held with great conviction; ignoring either while pursuing EMU alone could have been very politically costly to Kohl.[38] The Genscher/FDP position favored expanding the agenda in order to achieve the long-standing goal of creating a European union capable of defining a common defense and foreign policy. The support of the FDP was essential to the Kohl government's continued majority in the Bundestag. The Bundesbank position favored attention to "political union" in order to ensure the success of monetary union. The Bundesbank would have substantial ability after the fact to affect the progress toward effective implementation of EMU – it could be ignored only at great political peril.

### Elections and Kohl's Calculus

One reasonable expectation from the logic of two-level games is that domestic and international politics may be linked especially in the periods around elections. At such times, domestic challengers may try to turn issues in international negotiation into salient domestic issues. Alternatively, international negotiating partners may shape negotiations in order to try to influence the other party's domestic election.[39] Kohl's electoral circumstances were of some importance in this period, as elections were pending, and it is worth exploring how this might have affected the decision to link EMU and EPU.

In June 1989 elections for the European Parliament, the CDU-CSU coalition

---

[37] *Europe Daily Bulletin,* Document no. 1764, March 2, 1992.

[38] As early as August 1989, German EMU preparations were guided by a working party that included representatives from the Chancellery, Foreign Ministry, Economics Ministry, Finance Ministry, and Bundesbank. Granted, it might have seemed unlikely that a difference of views on Europe great enough to provoke FDP defection would emerge, but the willingness to do so in principle could not be doubted since the FDP provoked Schmidt's fall in 1982.

[39] It is quite likely, for example, that such calculations led Chancellor Kohl to decide to agree to the ploy of putting the social protocol outside the body of the Maastricht treaty, as an agreement between all parties except the United Kingdom. This provided electoral protection for Major, who had committed himself on the issue before Parliament; preserved an already complex agreement; and increased the prospects that the United Kingdom would continue to be led by Conservatives rather than Labour. See, e.g., *The Economist,* December 14, 1991, 61; and Boris Johnson, After Maastricht: How "King" Kohl saved the day for Britain, *Daily Telegraph,* December 12, 1991, 6.

lost seats. Nationalist right-wing parties did particularly well, winning more than 14 percent of the vote in Bavaria, the CSU stronghold. The right wing was especially hostile to suggestions that the deutschemark be surrendered under any circumstances in the future. In 1989, an important right-wing party, the Republican party, was predicting further substantial gains in state elections in 1990. As early as December 1989, right-wing posters were proclaiming, "Hands off the deutschemark!"[40]

It is not surprising that the German government insisted, successfully, against opposition from the French and Italians, that the EMU intergovernmental conference not start prior to the German national elections in December 1990. According to many press reports at the time, the Kohl government made clear its concern that the EMU negotiations not become an occasion for right-wing politicians to raise alarms about loss of control of the deutschemark, weakening of the Bundesbank, or allowing European unification to disrupt progress toward German reunification. This threat suggests a domestic rationale for delay and foot-dragging. However, if Kohl moved forward on EMU and thereby lost right-wing support, could he compensate by occupying more centrist ground?

Länder (state) elections in Germany during the period of preparation for the IGCs provided further confirmation (at least to some observers) that Kohl was under domestic pressure – this time from the left. For example, in January 1990, Oskar Lafontaine catapulted to the national leadership of the Social Democratic party (SPD) as a consequence of his decisive victory in the Saarland elections. In contrast to the right-wing threat, Lafontaine may have presented an attractive alternative to Kohl for some negotiators – particularly Mitterrand's Socialist government.[41]

In fact, however, Kohl could use the issue of political union to divide the SPD opposition while laying claim to the middle of the political spectrum. The SPD, like Kohl, opposed the right-wing nationalism that threatened to take votes from Kohl. However, unlike Kohl, the left wing of the SPD was suspicious of the probusiness themes in the larger Single Market program and in European unification generally. To the SPD's left wing, these seemed to promote the interests of large firms, environmental destruction, and loss of European democracy. By promoting political union, encouraging the power of the European Parliament, and endorsing the social charter, Kohl presented the SPD with a dilemma. How could the SPD oppose just some aspects of the current proposal for European unification and avoid seeming to be in alliance with the extreme right [see de Weck (1991)]?

---

[40] See Europe: The prospect of a reunited Germany promises to reshape Europe's own 1992 reunification plans, *Institutional Investor,* December 31, 1989, 43.

[41] See A tale of three cities, *The Economist,* June 2, 1990, 54; Trean (1990a). Ironically, Lafontaine's own opposition to the Maastricht treaty not only worked against his leadership of the SPD, but reduced his usefulness to German bargaining partners who might have wished to encourage the fortunes of an opponent to Kohl. See Busche (1992).

*German Federalism*

The Länder was another source of German domestic concern for clarifying the details of political union. An EMU that created a new European Central Bank replacing the Bundesbank would infringe on the rights of the Länder to have representation on the Bundesbank council.[42] Indeed, Länder rights had been adversely affected by prior European reforms, such as the Single European Act. It was almost certain that any treaty on EMU would have to be approved by the Bundesrat. Since the Länder had aspirations to achieve independent regional representation within the EC, for Kohl to advance an EMU treaty that promised to reduce Länder powers without any compensating benefits might have seemed unwise and put ratification in jeopardy.

Since 1985, the Länder had had observers participating in meetings of the European Council of Ministers. The Single European Act had infringed on the rights of the Länder by extending EC policy into such areas as regional policy and training and the environment [Bulmer and Paterson (1987, pp. 250–251)]. The Länder established their own representation in Brussels, and created a new committee in 1988 to search for a common Länder position on pending EC legislation.[43] The Länder concerns were rarely partisan in any straightforward sense; rather, they reflected the deep commitments of Länder politicians to preserving the prerogatives of the Länder.

The CSU (based in Bavaria) also emphasized the need to protect Germany's federal structure (and the rights of the Länder) during the process of European integration [Sturm (1989)]. Since the CSU was a quasi-independent grouping within the dominant coalition, Kohl could hardly ignore these views.

Federalism had long been a major issue in German politics. Because of the complex implications of any further steps toward European unification for the German federal system, and given the importance of federalism in the German system, it would have been surprising if a German chancellor had failed to try to ensure that spheres of authority be as precisely demarcated as possible in any moves toward creating stronger European institutions. Moreover, given the disagreements within Germany over the independent representation of the Länder in the EC (i.e., opposition from Genscher and the Foreign Ministry), inclusion of such an issue on the agenda for negotiations would allow Kohl an opportunity to externalize an internal political dispute, thereby taking advantage of the inherent logic of the two-level game.

---

[42] After German reunification, the Bundesbank itself proposed to reduce the number of seats occupied by Länder representatives in order to avoid having the Bundesbank Council become too unwieldy. This was greeted with hostility by the states, and none other than Oskar Lafontaine began trying to recruit other states to assist in challenging the move in the Federal Constitutional Court. Terence Roth, German reunification creates problems for Pöhl in bid to realign Bundesbank, *Wall Street Journal,* October 12, 1990, B5A.

[43] For some additional interesting views on the Länder representation in Brussels see Hauser (1991).

*Confirmation of Commitments*

Additional evidence of the existence of important and relevant domestic commitments in support of political union came while the Maastricht negotiations were under way. In November 1991, the CDU's draft Dresden Manifesto called for the development of the EC into a political union [Vorkoetter (1991)]. At about the same time, the SPD warned that failure to enhance the power of the European Parliament would lead to the treaty's eventual rejection in the Bundestag. One observer noted that "the feeling in favor of granting co-decision-making powers to the European parliament is running strongly in all parties in the Bundestag" [Peel (1991, p. 2)]. The point of the SPD warning was to criticize the Kohl government for not having done enough to strengthen the European Parliament.[44]

In the immediate aftermath of the Maastricht summit, Kohl was roundly criticized at home for not having made enough progress on political union, given the commitment made to enter EMU in 1999 [Parkes (1991)]. As Marsh (1991a) put it, "An influential part of German opinion, from both the right and left, declare[d] that Chancellor Helmut Kohl ha[d] given away control over the D-Mark for too low a price" (p. 7). This influential opinion included both FDP leader Otto von Lambsdorf (a "sad event") and SPD leader Bjorn Engholm ("the chancellor simply buckled at the knees") [Landrey (1991, p. 2.A); Berlin (1991)]. Reimut Jochimsen, president of the regional central bank of North Rhine-Westphalia, criticized Kohl's compliance as "maybe suicidal" [Marsh (1991b)].

The hostile reaction to the prospect of losing "our lovely money" was, of course, not a surprise [de Weck (1991)]. It was precisely in anticipation of such a reaction that Kohl had insisted that the intergovernmental conference on EMU not begin prior to national elections in 1990. However, it confirmed the wisdom, in domestic political terms, of his earlier move to broaden the agenda of the EMU negotiations beyond the creation of a new currency.

## CONCLUSION

Building on ideas suggested by prior work on two-level games, this chapter has examined how German negotiating strategy came to embrace the linking of EMU and EPU. This was one of the most important decisions of the Maastricht negotiations, and one that arguably had the ultimate consequence of significantly slowing the progress toward EMU. Without the dramatically changed conditions in Eastern Europe, the pressures on Germany to move rapidly toward

---

[44] *Europe Daily Bulletin,* November 15, 1991, 4–5. On the same day, Kohl was quoted as reiterating, "The Treaty on Political Union is the indispensable counterpart of the Treaty on Economic and Monetary Union." If a reunified Germany received significantly more seats in the European Parliament, enhanced power for the Parliament would indirectly augment German power in Europe.

EMU would surely have been much less. Without the commitments in German domestic politics, Kohl's support for EPU would have lacked credibility, and he would surely have had to take a different kind of approach if he wished to slow or derail EMU.

Kohl's strategy clearly involved large risks: He opened a second agenda whose content he could not precisely control. The conflicting domestic pressures that made political union an important issue to raise also made it almost certain that some interests would be dissatisfied with any possible outcome. For example, if EMU had to be accompanied by a specific version of political union to be acceptable to the Bundesbank (and other domestic constituents), then Kohl was running a great risk that he would not be able to deliver the required agreement. In the aftermath of Maastricht, we can see that many of these risks were substantial. However, we can also see that Kohl's strategy was in many ways an excellent response to Germany's international and domestic political environment at the time. The risks to Kohl of almost any other approach to the start of the negotiations would have been greater than those of the path he chose.

## REFERENCES

Alt, James E., and Barry Eichengreen, 1989, Parallel and overlapping games: Theory and an application to the European gas trade. *Economics and Politics,* 1, 119–144.

Bartsch, Hans, 1990, Accord on Euro Integration by Paris and Bonn. *German Tribune* May 6, 1. (First published in *Stuttgarter Nachrichten,* April 26, 1990.)

Bergsdorf, Wolfgang, 1990, Political and economic factors behind the resolution of the German question. *German Tribune,* January 28, 5. (First published in *Frankfurter Neue Presse,* January 13, 1990.)

Berlin, Tony Allen-Mills, 1991, Kohl's triumph stokes fires of neo-Nazi hate. *Times* (London, Sunday, December 15.)

Blackburn, Keith and Michael Christensen, 1989, Monetary policy and policy credibility: Theory and evidence. *Journal of Economic Literature,* 27, 1–45.

Buchan, David, 1989a, Delors stresses implications of expanding EC. *Financial Times,* December 1, 3.

——, 1989b, Parliament seeks strong new powers under EMU treaty. *Financial Times,* December 9, 3.

——, 1989c, Why Britain is fighting alone. *Financial Times,* December 6, 20.

——, 1989d, Delors urges E.C. to meet Eastern Europe challenge. *Financial Times,* October 18, 1.

Buchan, David, and Ian Davidson, 1989, EC sets a course for economic and monetary union. *Financial Times,* December 11, 3.

Buchan, David, and Tim Dickson, 1990, Tackling the democratic deficit. *Financial Times,* March 14, sec. 1, 22.

Buchan, David and David Marsh, 1991, Tiers on the road to an EC currency union. *Financial Times,* December 10, 2.

Bulmer, Simon and William Paterson, 1987, *The Federal Republic of Germany and the European Community* (Allen and Unwin, London).

Busche, Jürgen, 1992, Engholm stamps authority on the Social Democrats. *German Tribune,* March 20, 4. (First published in *Suddeutsche Zeitung,* March 11, 1992.)

Cameron, David R., 1992, The 1992 initiative: Causes and consequences, in: Alberta Sbragia, ed., *Europolitics: Institutions and policymaking in the "new" European Community* (Brookings Institute, Washington, D.C.).

Colchester, Nicholas and David Buchan, 1990, *Europower: The essential guide to Europe's economic transformation in 1992* (Random House, New York).

Deutsche Bundesbank, 1990, Statement on creating economic and monetary union in Europe. *Europe Daily Bulletin,* Document No. 1655, October 5. Statement originally released on September 19, 1990.

———, 1992, The Maastricht agreements on European economic and monetary union: Statement by the Central Bank Council. *Europe Daily Bulletin,* Document No. 1764, March 2. (Statement originally released in February 1992).

de Weck, Roger, 1991, The decisions have been taken, but the debate is only beginning. *German Tribune,* December 22, 3 (First published in *Die Zeit,* December 13, 1991).

Dickson, Tim, 1990, Delors makes his boldest pitch yet for EC political union. *Financial Times,* January 18, 2.

Dixit, Avenash and Barry Nalebuff, 1991, *Thinking strategically: The competitive edge in business, politics, and everyday life* (Norton, New York).

Hanrieder, Wolfram, 1989, *Germany, America, Europe: Forty years of German foreign policy* (Yale University Press, New Haven).

Hauser, Erich, 1991, The Länder step up own initiatives, hope for a council of regional states. *German Tribune,* August 4, 6. (First published in *General-Anzeiger,* July 22, 1991.)

Johnson, Boris, 1989, Two-tier Europe threat to Britain over EEC union. *Daily Telegraph,* November 23, 1.

———, 1990, Delors calls for East Germany to join Market, *Daily Telegraph,* January 18, 10.

Jukes, Stephen, 1989, Turmoil in East Europe prompts new move on EC single currency. *Reuters Library Report,* October 22, 3.

Kellaway, Lucy, 1989a, Delors calls for second special conference. *Financial Times,* December 13, 16.

———, 1989b, Delors seeks European reform: "Institutional change needed to cope with EMU." *Financial Times,* November 22, 2.

Koelle, Hans Martin, 1992, Fears about the new currency of Europe. *German Tribune,* February 28 (First published in *Rheinischer Merkur,* February 14, 1992).

Kirchner, Emil J., 1991, The Federal Republic of Germany and the European Community: Past, present and future, in: Eva Kolinsky, ed., *The Federal Republic of Germany: The end of an era* (Berg Publishers, New York).

Landrey, Wilbur G., 1991, European leaders take home the spoils of negotiations. *St. Petersburg Times,* December 13, 2A.

Lane, Jan-Erik, and Svante O. Ersson, 1991, *Politics and society in Western Europe* (Sage, London).

Ludlow, Peter, 1982, *The making of the European Monetary System: A case study of the politics of the European Community* (Butterworth Scientific, London).

Marsh, David, 1989, Bonn's balancing act: Foreign policy. *Financial Times,* October 30, German Survey sec. 2.

———, 1991a, Europe's honeymoon starts to sour. *Financial Times,* December 21, 7.

———, 1991b, Bundesbank decides to look after Number One. *Financial Times,* December 29, 2.

Marsh, David, and Kieran Cooke, 1990, Kohl resists push for EC monetary union. *Financial Times,* February 18, 2.

Moravcsik, Andrew, 1991, Negotiating the Single European Act: National interests and conventional statecraft in the European Community. *International Organization* 45 (Winter), 19–56.

Nelson, Mark M., 1990, Kohl champions early EC political-unity talks. *Wall Street Journal,* March 30, A8.

Nelson, Mark M., and Martin du Bois, 1990, West German officials set to disclose plans for economic, monetary union. *Wall Street Journal,* February 13, A19.

Nelson Mark M., and Philip Revzin, 1992, EC leaders strive for political union. *Wall Street Journal,* April 30, A9D.

Parkes, Christopher, 1991, Kohl tries to calm fears over summit. *Financial Times,* December 31, 2.

Peel, Quintin, 1991, German SPD threatens to block EC treaty. *Financial Times,* November 15, 2.

Pöhl, Karl-Otto, 1990, Plaidoyer pour une politique monétaire indépendente. *Le Monde,* January 18, 1.

Putnam, Robert, 1988, Diplomacy and domestic politics: The logic of two-level games. *International Organization* 42, 427–461.

Putnam, Robert D., and Nicholas Bayne, 1987, *Hanging together: Cooperation and conflict in the seven-power summits* (Harvard University Press, Cambridge, Mass.).

Roth, Terence, and Mark M. Nelson, 1990, Bundesbank's Pöhl fashions German position in Europe's drive for unified monetary system. *Wall Street Journal,* October 15, B11C.

Schelling, Thomas C., 1980, *The strategy of conflict,* 2d ed. (Harvard University Press, Cambridge, Mass.).

Schlesinger, Helmut, 1992, The challenges to German monetary policy. Address presented to the American Institute for Contemporary Studies, June 1.

Sturm, Roland, 1989, West Germany, in: Francis Jacobs, ed., *West European political parties* (Longman, Essex).

Trean, Claire, 1990a, L'adversaire du Chancelier Kohl reçu à l'Élysée; M. Lafontaine prône la concertation avec les voisins de l'Allemagne. *Le Monde,* March 16, 6.

Trean, Claire, 1990b, La relance de la construction communautaire: Le chancelier Kohl veut hâter l'union politique européenne. *Le Monde,* March 30.

Treverton, Gregory F., 1991, The new Europe. *Foreign Affairs,* December, 94–112.

Tsebelis, George, 1990, *Nested games: Rational choice in comparative politics* (University of California Press, Berkeley).

Tsoukalis, Lucas, 1977, *The politics and economics of European monetary integration* (Allen and Unwin, London).

Usborne, David, 1990, Delors calls for EC reform in response to East Europe. *The Independent* January 18, 1.

Vorkoetter, Uwe, 1991, Christian Democrats spell out broad aims in a wide-ranging policy document. *German Tribune,* November 3, 3. (First published in *Stuttgarter Zeitung,* October 21, 1991.)

Williams, Shirley, 1991, Sovereignty and accountability in the European Community, in: Robert O. Keohane and Stanley Hoffman, eds., *The new European Community* (Westview, Boulder, Colo.).

# 5

## INTERNATIONAL AND DOMESTIC INSTITUTIONS IN THE EMU PROCESS

### LISA L. MARTIN

European progress toward monetary union takes place within the highly institutionalized setting of the European Community (EC). This paper examines the ways in which formal institutions and decisionmaking procedures have constrained the Economic and Monetary Union (EMU) process. The EC's structure has both created demands for and facilitated cross-issue linkages, and these linkages characterize the successful bargaining on EMU. However, success also requires ratification. Domestic ratification procedures and changes in the EC's context of linkage have created challenges for the ratification of the Maastricht treaty. Ratification is also tied to concerns about democratic accountability, which arise from current legislative procedures and are the subject of ongoing institutional reform.

IN 1985, members of the European Community (EC) agreed in the Single European Act (SEA) to move rapidly toward completion of the internal market and to use qualified majority voting on questions relating to their commercial relations. In December 1991, in Maastricht, EC members extended the scope of supranational cooperation on economic and monetary issues.[1] The Maastricht Treaty on European Union modestly expands regional cooperation on social, foreign, and defense policy, but its centerpiece is a timetable for Economic and Monetary Union (EMU). The treaty specifies institutional procedures and substantive goals for moving to monetary union and presents a plan for the management of members' financial affairs through a European Central Bank (ECB).

The Maastricht treaty ran into trouble during the ratification process, and it is unlikely to be implemented precisely as envisioned by political leaders and the European Commission. Most analyses of the current troubled progress of EMU focus either on the alleged economic and efficiency problems of the Maastricht

I gratefully acknowledge the support of the Social Science Research Council's Advanced Foreign Policy Fellowship Program and the Hoover Institution's National Fellows Program. My thanks to Barry Eichengreen, Jeff Frieden, Robert Keohane, Peter Lange, Ron Rogowski, John Woolley, and participants in the workshop on the Political Economy of European Integration for their comments.

[1]The term "supranational" is used here to indicate situations in which policymaking authority has been delegated to a body that individual member governments cannot directly control. In practice, within the EC, supranational decisionmaking has consisted of giving up state veto power previously established in the Luxembourg Compromise through acceptance of qualified majority voting.

treaty or on the conflicts of interest among the most powerful member states.[2] I argue that a full understanding of the EMU process also requires careful attention to the institutional features of regional and domestic politics. I find that outcomes cannot be explained solely in terms of efficiency or by the interests of the most powerful states; they are in large part shaped by the opportunities and constraints created by institutional arrangements.

The institutionalized rules under which the EC operates, and through which member states make decisions about EC affairs, condition the outcomes of regional bargaining. EMU is embedded in a complex, institutionalized pattern of intermember cooperation on many issues. The bargains struck on EMU and the likelihood that they will be implemented are not dependent solely on state power and the potential economic benefits of EMU, but also on the ways in which decisionmaking on EMU is constrained by EC procedures. Foremost among these institutional constraints are the linkages between EMU and other EC issues, the ratification procedures for treaty revisions, and the need for accountability to domestic politicians. Each of these constraints is explored in this paper.

The first section argues that issue linkages enhanced by the EC's institutional structure are vital to an understanding of the bargains reached at Maastricht. This structure enhances the value of members' reputations for living up to agreements, allowing them to construct deals that would be more difficult to sustain if undertaken outside of the institutional context. Because the institutionalized framework of the EC offers members benefits in many issue areas, it decreases temptations to renege on agreements and thus increases the level of cooperation. Moreover, issue linkage creates possibilities for mutually beneficial deals that would not be available in single-issue bargaining. Members are able to gain cooperation on those issues of most vital interest to themselves – e.g., political unification for Germany – by making concessions on issues of lesser concern. Such deals would be unstable outside a formal institutional framework.

The second section turns to the ratification problem. I examine how domestic ratification procedures and the prospect of a multispeed Europe constrain states' decisions on the Maastricht treaty, focusing on Denmark as an illustrative case. Because the EC's rules require ratification of the Maastricht treaty by all members, the bargaining leverage of small states is enhanced relative to what we would expect in typical interstate bargaining. A relevant example is the disproportionate attention paid to satisfying Denmark's demands in late 1992 and early 1993, since its rejection of the treaty created additional questions about the future of EMU. While national representatives, in general, have incentives to construct cross-issue deals, domestic interests often prefer to separate issues from one another, thus threatening to undermine EC agreements, such as the Maastricht plan for EMU. These pressures come into play during the domestic ratification process, when the specific rules governing ratification determine

---

[2]Students of international relations will recognize these two approaches as neofunctionalism [Haas (1958)] and intergovernmentalism [Moravcsik (1991); Garrett (1992)].

whether domestic interests can reduce the level of cooperation to which government negotiators have agreed. Stringent ratification procedures, such as Denmark's, if not properly anticipated by negotiators, can lead to failure to carry out mutually beneficial deals. If anticipated, they can enhance an individual state's bargaining power. Both domestic rules and the changing context of international linkage constrain both the nature of EC bargains and the probability of successful ratification.

Ratification is also tied to correcting a perceived lack of democratic accountability, and in the third section, I analyze how the EC's regulatory structure has produced and is attempting to correct this deficit. Accountability problems are more severe in day-to-day EC business than in the treaty ratification process. Ratification requirements give domestic actors the opportunity to influence bargaining on treaty revisions. However, questions have arisen as to the ability of such actors to have a say in the normal EC legislative process. Such concerns are a central part of the debate over Maastricht and thus influence the future of EMU. Analysis of legislative procedures shows that concerns about accountability are valid and that changes in the role of the European Parliament (EP) can increase accountability, but also that such changes are predictably opposed by national parliaments. The future of EMU cannot be divorced from ongoing debates about how to correct the accountability deficit.


## ISSUE LINKAGE AND EMU

International institutions such as the EC play a powerful role through changing the incentives states face. States' incentives change because of stable linkages among issues created by institutions. The Maastricht agreement on the terms of monetary union was influenced and facilitated by a link between EMU and other issues within the EC. Such linkages are unstable and susceptible to reneging if done on an ad hoc basis, thus the EC's institutional framework explains why state leaders are willing to take the risk of committing themselves to such deals as the one reached in Maastricht [Weber and Wiesmeth (1991)]. In this way, the EC framework contributes to a network of political relationships, identified by Cohen (1993) as necessary for monetary union.

International organizations such as the EC facilitate stable linkages among issues that are not inseparably intertwined for functional reasons. As Robert Keohane put it, "Clustering of issues under a regime facilitates side-payments among these issues: more potential *quids* are available for the *quo*. Without international regimes linking clusters of issues to one another, side-payments and linkages would be difficult to arrange in world politics" (1984, p. 91). The EC has, indeed, linked clusters of issues: commercial policy, agricultural subsidies, social policies, occasional foreign policy initiatives, and so on. Members have been able, at times, to use institutionalized linkage to gain the support of other states on issues on which the latter have no other compelling interest. Since refusal to go along could jeopardize the broad array of benefits provided by the EC, linkages have increased incentives to cooperate.[3] For example, in 1982 Britain used the leverage created by linked issues to generate support from reluctant member states for economic sanctions against Argentina during the Falklands war [Martin (1992)]. Frieden (1992) cites the linkage between monetary and broader EC issues as a component of French and Italian decisions to join the EMS.

EC linkage incentives can be strong. Ireland, for example, receives EC aid equivalent to approximately 5 percent of its GDP, channeled through agricultural, social, and regional funds (*The Economist*, Dec. 7, 1991, 53). This financial windfall inclines Ireland and similarly positioned recipients to support further moves toward European union, even though such movement is likely to pose real challenges for their national economies and social structures. In the past, side-payments to poorer EC states have been essential to gaining their agreement on social policies that would threaten their competitive edge as low-cost producers [Marks (1992)] and their agreement to the SEA in 1985 [Moravcsik (1991, p. 25)]. Their acquiescence to the Maastricht social protocol and EMU was, according to some, explicitly linked to financial incentives, following this historical pattern [Lange (1993)].

In the bargaining over EMU, demands from poorer states for financial compensation in exchange for support of Franco-German plans were unusually explicit. Because EMU proposals implied austerity measures with high short-term economic costs and even higher political costs for the governments of the poor countries, they were unwilling to sign on to EMU without gaining something in return. In 1988, the "structural funds" that provide resources for structural reform to poorer members had been doubled, as anticipated in the SEA deal. In the bargaining over EMU, Spain led a group of the four poorest EC members (the other three were Portugal, Greece, and Ireland) in threatening to veto any treaty unless the group received increased transfers. Beyond increases in the structural funds, the group sought and achieved promises of a "cohesion fund", so that transfers would again double. These initiatives were not enshrined in the Maastricht treaty itself, but in a package known as Delors II, presented by European Commission president Jacques Delors immediately following the summit.

A number of institutional aspects of this deal are particularly intriguing. First is the decision of richer states, particularly Germany, to respond positively to Spanish demands. The German economy, under strain from the demands of unification, is not in a condition in which increases in transfers to poor EC members can be regarded as negligible. Although the increased resources of the cohesion fund represent only a small fraction of Germany's GDP, it is not obvious that Germany would have been willing to commit money for increased transfers

---

[3]While it is conceivable that states could use linkage to block attempts to cooperate, we instead observe frequent linking of issues to expand the set of agreements that are Pareto-superior to the status quo, consistent with the framework of Tollison and Willett (1979); see also Oye (1992, pp. 35–48) and Morrow (1992).

unless it saw clear benefits in doing so. From a purely intergovernmental perspective, relying on state power as the key explanatory variable, Germany's decision to increase transfers significantly is puzzling since it involves a significant concession by Germany to weaker states. As one formal analysis of linkage puts the puzzle, "Why offer concessions when you will prevail without them?" [Morrow (1992, p. 164)]. Considering the institutional setting in which bargaining took place provides insight. Because the Maastricht plan took the form of a treaty requiring ratification by all members, each state had veto power. A veto would have dealt a blow to Germany's efforts to make rapid progress on European integration, an especially urgent agenda since German reunification [Garrett (1993)]. EC rules that require unanimous approval of the treaty changed the bargaining dynamics from those we would expect in typical, noninstitutionalized interstate bargaining, increasing the leverage of smaller countries such as Spain.[4]

Institutional constraints – here, unanimity requirements – help us understand why Spain was successful in gaining targeted concessions for the four poorer EC members. However, questions remain on the other side of the ledger, in explaining the willingness of the four to sign the treaty while increases in structural funds were left to a separate budget package, on which Germany could, in principle, renege. Here, consideration of institutional factors provides guidance. Deals cut within an institution rather than outside one gain stability because members put increased value on their reputations for living up to agreements. If the richer states were to back down from the understandings reached in Maastricht, their reputations and ability to reach mutually beneficial cross-issue deals within the EC in the future would suffer. Thus, the four could rely on commitments by the other eight to increase transfers in spite of difficult economic conditions in the richer countries. In fact, at the Edinburgh summit in December 1992, after much debate, the rich countries formally committed themselves to budget provisions very close to those of the Delors II package. A focus on the EC's institutional structure provides insight into two related sets of questions about issue linkage: why it was necessary for the richer countries to make side-payments, and why the four poorest found such commitments credible.

The dependence of past patterns of EC cooperation on reliable issue linkages draws our attention to the *acquis communautaire*. New entrants to the EC have been required to accept the *acquis communautaire*, the accumulated set of norms, rules, and obligations developed by the EC. This concept makes explicit the linkages created by the EC, further solidifying them and thus enlarging the scope

---

[4]For development of a model in which small states acquire disproportionate power in international cooperative agreements, see Casella (1992). Decisionmaking procedures have consequences for the power of differently sized states. A unit-veto system, such as the one in place for treaty ratification, maximizes the power of small states, since they are weighted as heavily as large ones. Supermajority requirements, such as those embodied in the EC's qualified majority voting, also enhance small states' influence, but to a lesser extent. Some models of intermember bargaining, such as those adopted in intergovernmental studies of the SEA, assert that small states' influence is negligible, with major powers determining outcomes.

for jointly beneficial agreements [Tollison and Willett (1979); Sebenius (1983)].
Because the process of ratification is public and the terms of membership clear
and explicit, acceptance of the *acquis communautaire* has served as a signal of
members' intentions and linked their reputations to the EC in a way that informal
or ad hoc agreements could not [Lipson (1991)].

Overall, the characteristics of EC bargains, such as those embodied in the
Maastricht treaty, are as strongly influenced by the EC's formal structure as by
considerations of economic efficiency or state power. Two effects of the
institution are evident: the facilitation of stable linkages across issues, and
disproportionately large bargaining power of small states. These features have
resulted in a pattern of concessions and side-payments, allowing us to understand
the willingness of government leaders to agree to the Maastricht plan for EMU.
However, governmental agreement does not guarantee implementation of EMU;
the crucial step of formal ratification intervenes.

### RULES, WEAKENED LINKAGES, AND RATIFICATION

A focus on institutions helps clarify certain puzzles about the bargains struck
at the Maastricht summit, drawing our attention to issue linkages, which are
demanded by unanimity rules and facilitated by reputational effects. However,
such linkages are no guarantee of success, and the future of deals struck at
Maastricht remains in doubt, especially following Danish rejection of the treaty
in a June 1992 referendum, very narrow French approval, and a commitment
by Britain to delay consideration of ratification until a change in the Danish
decision. In this section, I consider the effect of domestic ratification requirements
on EC bargaining. I focus on Denmark to examine both the effect of domestic
institutions and the changing context of EC linkage politics.

One threat to cross-issue deals, such as that struck at Maastricht, arises from
the differing incentives facing negotiators and domestic interest groups. National
representatives in the Council, representing broad constituencies, generally strive
to realize aggregate gains arising from cross-issue deals and are thus willing to
compromise on some issues. However, those domestic groups whose interests
are "traded away" in a grand bargain can be expected to protest, attempting
to disaggregate such deals and avoid the compromises to which their national
representatives have committed their country, thereby threatening processes of
ratification. While national representatives appreciate large-scale bargains,
domestic actors with narrower interests may favor a multispeed Europe and/or
attempt to disrupt linkages. We find evidence of such a pattern in Germany,
where the Bundesbank argued in favor of a flexible approach to EMU that
Chancellor Helmut Kohl explicitly rejected, reflecting different valuations of a
one-speed, tightly linked EC. Domestic resistance to the Maastricht treaty suggests
that we turn our attention to problems of ratification.

The Danish case is illustrative of the impact of institutions on bargaining and
ratification. Studies of the EC have noted that Denmark does not behave as do

other small member countries. It behaves more as does Britain, being reluctant to surrender decisionmaking authority to supranational bodies, passing amendments to the original Rome treaties by small margins, and accepting EC decisions with reservations [Williams (1991, pp. 159–160)]. However, until the 1992 referendum, the Danish stance was seen more as a minor irritant than as a major impediment to EC cooperation. From an intergovernmental perspective on cooperation, it would not be possible for such a small country to exercise significant influence over the course of events.

The Danish political system makes it difficult for the government to commit to international agreements without working through stringent ratification procedures in the parliament and/or national referenda. Through these domestic institutional constraints, the Danes have succeeded in maintaining unusually tight control over the scope of EC agreements into which they enter, and over the actions of their representatives once treaties are ratified. Constitutionally, ratification of all treaties in the Folketing (the Danish parliament) requires a five-sixths vote, far exceeding the supermajority requirements of other liberal democracies. If the parliament supports a treaty by only a simple majority, it will be considered ratified only after passing a national referendum with participation of at least 30 percent of the electorate [Petersen and Elklit (1973, p. 198)].

In 1972, Denmark held a referendum on the decision to join the EC, which passed with 63.4 percent of the vote [Borre (1986, p. 191); Petersen and Elklit (1973)]. In 1986, because a parliamentary majority opposed ratification of the SEA, Prime Minister Poul Schlüter called for a "consultative" referendum. A decision to refuse to vote in favor of the SEA was in part a tactical parliamentary move by the opposition Social Democratic party, which wished to force a general election. The prime minister circumvented parliamentary opposition by calling for a referendum, as the Social Democrats would feel bound for electoral reasons to vote according to its results. Thus, when the SEA was approved by 56.2 percent of the voters in February 1986 the Folketing duly ratified the treaty [Worre (1988)]. Nevertheless, the referendum revealed a significant decline since 1972 in popular support for the terms of European integration. Rural areas voted in favor of the treaty, while opposition came primarily from the region around Copenhagen and other strongholds of left-leaning political parties [Borre (1986, pp. 191–193)]. In June 1992, support for the Maastricht treaty fell to 49.3 percent (*New York Times*, June 3, 1992, A1). This result means that just over 23,000 Danish voters – the difference necessary to have produced a majority yes vote – threw the future of EMU into question.

In addition to rules that give the national parliament and electorate the power to veto treaties, the Folketing attempts tightly to constrain activities of Danish ministers in the European Council. Because Denmark is characterized by frequent minority government, party line voting is not sufficient to guarantee a majority for government legislation and thus ensure implementation of agreements reached in the Council [Auken, Buksti, and Soerensen (1975, p. 16)]. The Folketing established a Market Relations Committee (MRC) to ensure that Danish ministers would not commit themselves to agreements that would not meet with parliamentary approval [Fitzmaurice (1976)]. The MRC, on which the parties in parliament are proportionally represented, requires that ministers confer with it regarding proposed negotiating positions prior to discussions in the Council [Moeller (1983)]. If the content of the subject under discussion in the Council changes significantly, ministers are to return for further instructions. Danish implementation of EC directives suggests the effectiveness of consultation and direction. While Danish representatives are obstinate in negotiations, by April 1992, Denmark had implemented nearly 140 of the 158 White Paper measures requiring national approval, the highest approval rate of any EC member (*The Economist*, July 11, 1992, Survey p. 10).

Recognizing the strategic advantages of not fully revealing a negotiating position in advance, instructions for Danish ministers are given orally; thus the MRC acts with significant autonomy from the rest of parliament [Fitzmaurice (1976, p. 283)]. The short leash on which the MRC keeps ministers creates conditions in which they can credibly threaten "involuntary defection" if EC agreements do not satisfy the demands of domestic politics [Putnam (1988)]. The pattern of delegation in Denmark enhances its bargaining power beyond what we would predict from a model that did not take institutional constraints into account. For example, Denmark has received concessions in the form of addenda to the Maastricht treaty as a condition of reconsidering ratification. In addition, British Prime Minister John Major has postponed parliamentary consideration of the treaty until after Danish ratification, leading to suggestions that British foreign policy is now being made in Copenhagen.

Other EC members follow different procedures for domestic control of EC business, and these procedures have effects on the ability of domestic politicians to control the activities of their representatives in the EC. The British House of Commons, like the Folketing, has expressed a great deal of interest in preventing the surrender of sovereign control over policy [Stevens (1976–1977); Kolinsky (1975)]. It has taken the unusual step of setting up a permanent EC Scrutiny Committee to study issues on the Council's agenda [Miller (1977)]. However, the Scrutiny Committee has not been as successful in tying the hands of ministers as has the Danish MRC. Because minority government is unusual in Britain, party discipline is a more effective guarantor of commitment than in the Danish system, reducing the demand for prior legislative mandates. The limited powers of the Commons Scrutiny Committee, which can express technical judgments on EC measures but has little power to bind the government, reflect this lower demand.

Denmark and Britain mark one end of a continuum of the extent to which national parliaments attempt to influence EC activities. France and Luxembourg represent the other extreme, with the government rather than parliament implementing the domestic obligations of EC membership [Gregory (1983, p. 80)]. The French system has been particularly centralized, with authority concentrated in the hands of the president and an executive agency concerned exclusively with European economic cooperation, leaving ministers and the parliament relatively uninvolved [Wallace (1973, pp. 19 and 37)]. Parliaments in the Netherlands, Italy, and Germany fall somewhere between these two extremes [Niblock (1971, p. 33)]. In Germany, the government appears more constrained by its federal structure and the role of the Länder (regions) than by the national parliament [Bulmer (1983, p. 361)]. While examining the effects of each of these structures is beyond the scope of this paper, the type of analysis used here would lead us to anticipate that variations in the constraints placed on government representatives by domestic procedures should lead to systematic differences in their bargaining leverage.

Turning to international institutions, we can consider how general EC benefits have contributed to ratification decisions, using the Danish case to further analyze the arguments developed above. The Danish pattern of decisionmaking on EC treaties suggests that discussion of the new concept of a flexible architecture may jeopardize past patterns of cooperation. The initial Danish decision to join the EC was a decision about EC benefits as a whole. In 1985, in the debate over the Single Act, proponents were again able credibly to argue that the referendum was not merely on the specific provisions of the SEA – particularly the acceptance of qualified majority voting on internal market issues – but also a referendum on continued participation in the EC [Borre (1986, p. 190)].

The argument that seemed to carry most weight with the electorate in 1985 was that Denmark's reputation within the EC, and thus its ability to secure the diverse benefits of membership, was at stake [Worre (1988, p. 372)]. The governing Liberal party proclaimed that "[a] Danish no to the package will be interpreted as a Danish no to further participation in Community co-operation. Thus, a Danish no to the EC package will start a development which will slowly lead to Denmark's withdrawal from the EC" [Worre (1988, pp. 372–373)]. That this message was accepted by the electorate is illustrated by the high percentage of yes votes coming from rural areas, which benefited from the Common Agricultural Policy (CAP).

However, by the time of the 1992 referendum, the nature of linkage had changed considerably. As the Maastricht treaty pushes the scope of anticipated supranational policymaking well beyond previous bounds, and as members calculate the consequences of enlarging the EC to include European Free Trade Area (EFTA) members and Eastern European countries, the notion that EC obligations must be accepted as a whole by all members is losing ground. As the scope (coverage of issues) and breadth (number of members) of the EC increase, so do conflicts of interest. Requiring unanimous approval of all policies under such conditions is a recipe for paralysis. To this extent, the decision to move toward greater use of qualified majority voting goes hand in hand with enlargement of the EC [Keohane and Hoffmann (1991)]. However, some states – particularly Britain and Denmark – have been reluctant to accept significant expansion of supranational decisionmaking. Confronted with such intransigence and dilemmas created by enlargement, analysts and politicians have begun considering a new, more flexible architecture for the EC.

The new architecture goes by a number of names: Europe a la carte, variable geometry, a multitiered, or multispeed, Europe, and so on. The core idea is that not all members of the EC would have to sign on to all its obligations, sacrificing the primacy of the *acquis communautaire*. Attention has focused on the benefits of such an architecture, which would allow rapid movement in those areas in which some subsets of members have strong common interests, or on the negative consequences of a multispeed Europe for those who would be "left behind" [Artis (1992, p. 305)]. Alesina and Grilli (1993) demonstrate another drawback of a multispeed process: its potential for finding an equilibrium that permanently excludes some states. At Maastricht, the multispeed concept was put into practice by allowing Britain to opt out of parts of the treaty (the social protocol and monetary union). Thus, while voters or legislators in eleven member states were asked to ratify the entire Maastricht treaty, the British government dealt with a smaller set of issues. Other examples of a flexible approach include a subset of eight members, the Schengen Group, which has created a passport-free zone, and the creation of a Franco-German military corps.

While flexibility may be unavoidable given the rapid increase of the EC's scope and breadth, if the idea of a flexible architecture supplants the idea of an *acquis communautaire*, the role of the EC in facilitating cross-issue deals will be significantly reduced. Rather than searching for mutually advantageous bargains across issues, members could choose to move forward independently with a few others who share common interests on narrowly defined topics. The threat of excluding members from the accumulated benefits of the EC if they do not sign on to new agreements loses its force under these conditions: the British example demonstrates how a country can retain the benefits it has received in the past without accepting the full range of new obligations.

Acceptance of a flexible architecture rendered those Danish pro-Maastricht claims that the vote on the treaty was indirectly a vote on EC membership less credible than they had been in 1985. The Danish vote on Maastricht became a vote on the specific provisions of the Maastricht treaty, not a sounding of opinion on whether it was better for Denmark to be in the EC than outside of it. Decoupling allowed those who appreciated EC membership but opposed specific elements of the treaty to vote no, creating a severe challenge for proponents of EMU.

Overall, the Danish ratification case illustrates the changing effects of issue linkage as well as a domestic institutional effect, enhanced bargaining power resulting from stringent ratification procedures. These procedures increase Denmark's leverage by raising the probability that EC bargains will be overturned on the domestic level unless they are widely acceptable to the Danish public. On the regional level, an additional threat to ratification has arisen through the likelihood that Denmark could choose to sign on to parts of the Maastricht deal while rejecting others, as a result of increasing acceptance of the notion of a multispeed Europe.

## DEMOCRATIC ACCOUNTABILITY

As the analysis of ratification suggests, the process of European union is conditioned by domestic political forces operating through institutionalized procedures. In this section, I consider the apparent upswing in concern about domestic control over EC business and potential solutions to the dilemmas created by lack of accountability. Such concern, argued here to be legitimate, threatens the Maastricht deal and thus EMU. Beyond the threats to ratification, demands for more rigorous procedures for accountability will condition the future of EMU. Formal legislative procedures have created concerns about accountability, and changes in these procedures may increase the control of directly elected representatives over EC business.

Most analyses of the EC have found that the effect of domestic politics on past deals has been slight. Some accounts claim that the process leading to the SEA was remarkably free of overt domestic interference, for example [Moravcsik (1991, p. 50)]. Politicians and academic observers often infer from such a pattern autonomy of the Commission and/or of government leaders. However, consideration of institutional constraints leads us to examine delegation of authority. Attention to delegation in the study of legislative-executive interaction in the United States, for example, shows that the apparent independence of agencies can be misleading [McCubbins, Noll, and Weingast (1989)]. The European Council and European Commission, like the agencies within the U.S. executive branch, act under delegation of authority from political actors. Analysts often infer from negotiating behavior that principals, such as national parliaments, have abdicated control over policymaking to their agents. One account concludes, for example, that in EC matters "national Parliaments . . . have no obvious part to play except to be compliant in the face of diminishing authority" [Niblock (1971, p. 34)]. However, because of the costs of exercising tight control over agents, an optimal structure of delegation may be one with little active oversight or overt interference in the negotiating process from principals. Agents rationally anticipate the responses of those they represent. The law of anticipated reactions suggests that we cannot infer a lack of political influence from a lack of observed oversight activity.

In the negotiations over the SEA and the Maastricht treaty, conditions for arm's-length influence of domestic political actors were probably met. Each state had a veto and formal ratification processes. There is little reason to believe that government leaders did not take these constraints into account when negotiating. However, in the day-to-day operations of the EC, the process moves away from such conditions to ones where national publics and legislatures cannot exercise effective constraints on their representatives in the Council. This has led to concern about a "democratic deficit", arising from the fact that the rules for EC legislation create the potential for significant agency slack. In contrast to treaty renegotiation, the day-to-day business of the EC often escapes domestic oversight.

The combination of three factors may create a democratic deficit as the EC continues along its present path: the direct effect of EC law in member states, qualified majority voting, and the closed nature of Council and Commission operations. The EC differs from most international organizations in the degree to which its legislation is binding on members. Once the process involving the Commission, Council, and European Parliament has been completed, legislation is immediately applicable in all member states, without explicit acceptance on their part [Garrett (1992, pp. 535–536)]. Direct effect does not apply to revisions of the Treaty of Rome, and there are some variations in how EC legislation is implemented on the national level. EC regulations are directly applicable without the need for national measures of implementation, while EC directives allow national parliaments to choose the form and method of implementation [Nugent (1991, pp. 168–171)]. Either method is sufficiently binding on states that it represents a significant surrender of the traditional lawmaking authority of national parliaments to the EC. Because EC legislation automatically comes into effect at the national level, without an opportunity for parliamentary veto or amendment, national-level politicians cannot directly influence its content.[5]

Extralegislative means of parliamentary control over EC legislation may in theory remain, operating through the law of anticipated reactions. In order for parliaments to retain significant control through indirect means, two conditions must be met: parliaments must have reliable information about what their ministers do in the European Council and the ability to reward or punish them on the basis of performance. The move toward qualified majority voting reduces the scope for national parliamentary influence, since ministers, who represent parliaments, can be outvoted in the Council. This creates a reduction in control by national political actors, but one that would exist with any majoritarian method of decisionmaking. A factor that undermines national parliamentary authority to an unusually high degree is the practice of Council secrecy. Council meetings take place in private, with no minutes kept [Nugent (1992, p. 314)]. No official record of voting patterns exists. Individual state votes on qualified majority voting issues are sometimes leaked, but in a haphazard and often distorted manner.[6]

Thus, national parliaments cannot count on having accurate information about the activities of their representatives in the Council. Without such information, and having sacrificed national veto power with the acceptance of qualified majority voting, parliaments cannot bind their representatives. The situation differs from that found on the domestic level in parliamentary systems in that the Council as a whole is not responsible to elected officials as the government

---

[5]Enforcement of EC legislation takes place through domestic courts and the European Court of Justice.

[6]In response to concerns about secrecy, the Council has drafted a "transparency plan" for making public some debates and the record of formal votes (*Financial Times*, Dec. 5, 1992, 2). The fate and scope of this plan remain in doubt.

is on the domestic level [Bogdanor (1989)].[7] While the Luxembourg Compromise held, allowing states to veto policies of "vital national interest", parliaments had some reliable information about ministers' activities, as they knew when ministers had refused to exercise a veto. Thus, the effects of secrecy on accountability were less significant as long as the other two conditions did not hold. But the conjunction of EC legislation, qualified majority voting, and secrecy of Council proceedings has severely restricted parliamentary control over the day-to-day proceedings of the EC.

In the aftermath of the Danish and French referenda, attempts to correct this democratic deficit have taken on new urgency. Jacques Delors, for example, has become a convert to the concept of "subsidiarity": the view that the EC should commit itself to deal only with issues on a supranational level that involve significant international externalities. Most attempts to find an institutional solution to the democratic deficit have concentrated on increasing the powers of the EP. The German and Italian governments have promoted the EP most vigorously, with the British resisting [Laursen (1992, p. 233)]. Because members of the EP are directly elected, granting legislative powers to it would in part satisfy demands for democratic accountability. The following discussion examines changes in the rules under which the EP has a role in policymaking, in order to determine whether they are likely to have any impact on problems of democratic accountability. Since EMU is linked to other EC issues in the Maastricht treaty, a failure to solve apparently separate accountability problems would have fundamental implications for EMU.

Before 1985, the EP had little role beyond that of consultation in the EC policymaking process. The SEA for the first time gave the EP a formal role in approving legislation, through the "cooperation" procedure [Fitzmaurice (1988)]. The cooperation procedure applied to the internal market, most significantly, under the terms of the SEA. The Maastricht treaty specifies use of the cooperation procedure in areas such as development cooperation, transportation, and the Social Fund. The procedure is shown in Figure 1. As shown, the Commission has a potentially powerful role in that it has gatekeeping power. The status quo remains in place unless the Commission decides to introduce a proposal to the Council. The Commission's ability to maintain the status quo allows it significantly to influence outcomes without having its influence perceived as overt bargaining activity. After the Commission presents a proposal, the Council adopts a position by qualified majority voting. The EP acts on this common position, accepting it, rejecting it, or making amendments. If the EP rejects the Council's position, it can be adopted only by unanimity in the Council. If the EP makes amendments, they are referred back to the Commission. If the Commission accepts the amendments, the Council can adopt

---

[7]The distinction between EC and national-level accountability rests on the assumption that national parliaments constrain government activities, a point with which some would disagree. For contrasting views, see Wallace (1975) and Waltz (1967).

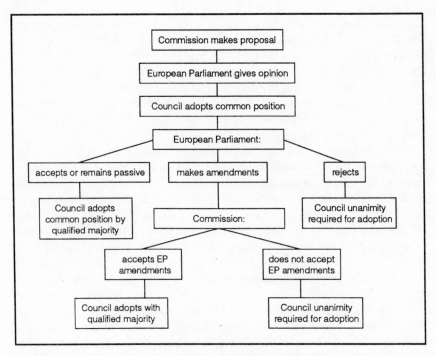

Figure 1.   The Cooperation Procedure: Decisionmaking under Article 189c.

them by a qualified majority vote; otherwise, the Council must act unanimously to change the status quo. Thus, if the EP and Commission have similar preferences, they can move outcomes away from the Council's common position. The EP also has veto power unless the Council unanimously prefers its common position to the status quo, i.e., unless the Council finds its common position Pareto-superior to the status quo, an outcome not guaranteed under qualified majority voting [see Tsebelis (1992)].

Article 189b of the Maastricht treaty enhances the EP's ability to influence legislation. The Article 189b procedure is commonly referred to as the "codecision" procedure, although British objections kept this terminology out of the treaty. The codecision procedure, shown in Figure 2, applies to the internal market and free movement of workers.

A straightforward way to understand the implications of codecision is to contrast it to the cooperation procedure. First, a major change is that if the EP rejects the Council's common position, the EP's decision cannot be overridden. Second, any amendments made by the EP go directly back to the Council, without being screened by the Commission. These two changes reduce the number of cases in which the EP can be overridden. The third major innovation is the creation of so-called Conciliation Committees. These committees come into play when the Council rejects EP amendments; they can be understood as analogous

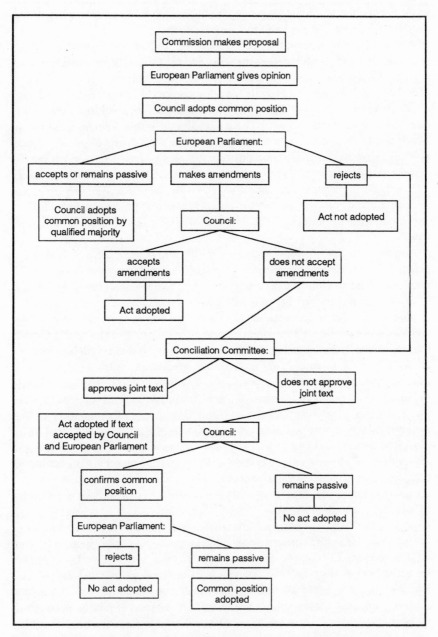

Figure 2.   The Codecision Procedure: Decisionmaking under Article 189b. A Conciliation Committee comprises the Council, twelve European Parliament members, and a Commission representative. A Conciliation Committee may be convened following Parliamentary rejection of the Council's common position, and is always convened if the Council rejects amendments made by the Parliament.

to the Conference Committees that resolve differences between Senate and House versions of legislation in the U.S. Congress.

A Conciliation Committee, consisting of twelve representatives from the Council and twelve from the EP and a Commission representative, searches for compromise legislation acceptable to a majority of the EP and a qualified majority of the Council. If such a compromise is found, it goes into effect. If the Conciliation Committee cannot find such a solution, the ball is back in the Council's court. The Council can either remain passive, in which case the status quo remains in place, or can reaffirm its original common position. However, this common position can now go into effect only if the EP accepts it on a closed vote, so under codecision, the EP has effective veto power over qualified majority decisions of the Council. The EP therefore has increased influence over outcomes, but only when it prefers to live with the status quo rather than accept the outcome of qualified majority voting on the Council.

Although the codecision procedure remedies the democratic deficit to some extent by increasing the influence of directly elected representatives on EC legislation,[8] the scope of the procedure is limited to a few issue areas. Moreover, a major impediment remains to relying on the procedure for further satisfying popular demands for accountability: national parliaments. As the scope of EP codecision is extended, national parliaments lose control over issues over which they traditionally have had legislative authority. Since treaty revisions necessary to extend the EP's powers pass through national parliaments, they may block this path toward democratic accountability. The Danish and British parliaments, in particular, demand an alternative mechanism in which national parliaments would have a greater say in day-to-day EC activities. Examination of the institutional constraints on European unification suggests that advocates of EMU would be unwise to believe that they can circumvent the claims of national legislatures. While efficiency may dictate the transfer of powers to organizations that can most effectively exercise them, existing constitutions and procedures create impediments to transfer of authority, leading to a process constrained by existing institutions.

Beyond the claims of narrowly defined interests, progress toward the EMU is threatened by public concern about accountability and opposition to further increments in the EP's power. The EMU is tied to other issues on the EC's agenda, since the Maastricht plan for the EMU is based on a set of cross-issue deals. For this reason, concern about a democratic deficit has direct implications for monetary union. Unless solutions are found, the progress of EMU will continue to be plagued by more general fears of a lack of accountability.

---

[8]Successful exercise of the EP's formal powers will require further development of political parties there. Such development, and incentives for ambitious politicians to develop careers in the EP, depend on rules that give the EP a potentially significant role in EC business.

## CONCLUSION

The issue linkages created by existing institutions and the formal procedures they use provide insight into the pattern of deals reached in the Maastricht treaty as well as the roadblocks now confronting EMU. In international politics, one of the primary functions of institutions is to solidify and make credible linkages among issues, allowing states to reach mutually beneficial deals by raising the costs of reneging. Within the EC, linkage among issues has allowed construction of many such deals, which may be threatened in the future by acceptance of the idea of a multispeed Europe. Because EC membership has implied cooperation in many different issue areas, it has decreased incentives for states to renege on particular deals they find distasteful. Such behavior would jeopardize a member's reputation and thus the benefits of EC membership on other issues, those valued highly by an individual state. The EC has thus facilitated mutually beneficial cross-issue deals, such as that on EMU.

Institutions not only provide opportunities; their procedures also impose constraints on decisionmaking and cause outcomes to diverge from predictions based purely on efficiency or national power considerations. The disproportionate influence of smaller actors, such as Spain and Denmark, depends on institutionalized decisionmaking, particularly the rule requiring unanimous approval of changes to the Treaty of Rome. The Maastricht agreement on EMU reflects concessions and side-payments that would not have been necessary or credible in an uninstitutionalized environment.

Similarly, domestic ratification requirements allow some national actors to bargain more effectively than state size would lead us to expect. In Denmark, stringent ratification procedures and tight control over EC representatives' activities allow that country to achieve concessions unusual for a small actor in interstate bargaining. Ratification problems in Denmark also illustrate the changing effects of issue linkage; the anticipated availability of opt-out clauses scuttled the treaty in Denmark's 1992 referendum.

A tie between EMU and other EC issues means that concern about a democratic deficit threatens progress on EMU. Analysis of decisionmaking rules in the EC substantiates this concern. While domestic interests have the opportunity to express themselves during treaty ratification, the existing pattern of delegation for daily EC business allows the Council and Commission to escape accountability to such interests. While the current pattern may have allowed rapid movement toward integration, those most concerned about accountability are now demanding changes as a condition of ratifying Maastricht. Proposed changes in the role of the EP would increase accountability, but predictably meet opposition from national parliaments.

Attention to institutions leads to several speculations about the future path of monetary union. First, problems with ratification of the Maastricht treaty support the notion that the apparent freedom of the Council from domestic political constraints is an illusion. The Council has been operating under delegated authority and cannot neglect the constraints of domestic politics when attempting to make progress in controversial areas, such as monetary union, particularly when such progress requires treaty revisions and formal ratification. Second, the process of European integration is at a key decision point. Up to now, tight linkages among sets of issues have allowed and required mutually beneficial package deals. However, if movement toward a flexible architecture gains momentum, the pattern of EC cooperation is likely to move closer to a purely intergovernmental one, where cooperation is based on narrowly defined state interests and tends to neglect the interests of less powerful members. A Europe in which cooperation occurred only among those states with an immediate interest in its results would see fewer transfers from rich states to poor, fewer concessions from powerful states on the form of cooperation, and, as a result, perhaps less stability in the face of economic and political shocks.

## REFERENCES

Alesina, A., and V. Grilli, 1994, On the feasibility of a one-speed or multispeed European Monetary Union. This volume.

Artis, M. J., 1992, The Maastricht road to monetary union. *Journal of Common Market Studies* 30, 299–309.

Auken, S., J. Buksti, and C. L. Soerensen, 1975, Denmark joins Europe: Patterns of adaptation in the Danish political and administrative processes as a result of membership of the European Communities. *Journal of Common Market Studies* 14, 1–36.

Bogdanor, V., 1989, The June 1989 European elections and the institutions of the Community. *Government and Opposition* 24, 199–214.

Borre, O., 1986, The Danish referendum on the EC Common Act. *Electoral Studies* 5, 189–193.

Bulmer, S., 1983, Domestic politics and European Community policy-making. *Journal of Common Market Studies* 21, 349–363.

Casella, A., 1992, Participation in a currency union. *American Economic Review* 82, 847–863.

Cohen, B. J., 1994, Beyond EMU: The problem of sustainability. This volume.

Fitzmaurice, J., 1976, National parliaments and European policy-making: The case of Denmark. *Parliamentary Affairs* 29, 281–292.

——, 1988, An analysis of the European Community's co-operation procedure. *Journal of Common Market Studies* 26, 389–400.

Frieden, J. A., 1992, European Monetary Union: A political economy perspective. Paper presented at the SSRC Conference on the Foreign Policy Consequences of Economic and Political Liberalization, Ballyvaughan, Ireland.

Garrett, G., 1992, International cooperation and institutional choice: The European Community's internal market. *International Organization* 46, 533–560.

———, 1994, The politics of Maastricht. This volume.

Gregory, F. E. C., 1983, *Dilemmas of government: Britain and the European Community* (Martin Robertson, Oxford).

Haas, E. B., 1958, The uniting of Europe: Political, social and economic forces, 1950–57 (Stevens & Sons, London).

Keohane, R. O., 1984, After hegemony: Cooperation and discord in the world political economy (Princeton University Press, Princeton, N.J.).

Keohane, R. O., and S. Hoffmann, 1991, Institutional change in Europe in the 1980s, in: R. O. Keohane and S. Hoffmann (eds.), *The New European Community* (Westview, Boulder, Colo.), 1–39.

Kolinsky, M., 1975, Parliamentary scrutiny of European legislation. *Government and Opposition* 10, 46–69.

Lange, P., 1993, Maastricht and the social protocol: Why did they do it? *Politics and Society* 21, 5–36.

Laursen, F., 1992, Explaining the intergovernmental conference on political union, in: F. Laursen and S. Vanhoonacker (eds.), *The intergovernmental conference on political union: Institutional reforms, new policies and international identity of the European Community* (European Institute of Public Administration, Maastricht), 229–248.

Lipson, C., 1991, Why are some international agreements informal? *International Organization* 45, 495–538.

Marks, G., 1992, Structural policy in the European Community, in: A. M. Sbragia (ed.), *Euro-Politics: Institutions and policymaking in the "new" European Community* (Brookings Institution, Washington, D.C.), 191–224.

Martin, L. L., 1992, Institutions and cooperation: Sanctions during the Falkland Islands conflict. *International Security* 16, 143–178.

McCubbins, M., R. Noll, and B. Weingast, 1989, Structure and process, politics and policy: Administrative arrangements and the political control of agencies. *Virginia Law Review* 75, 431–482.

Miller, H. N., 1977, The influence of British parliamentary committees on European Community legislation. *Legislative Studies Quarterly* 2, 45–75.

Moeller, J. O., 1983, Danish EC decision-making: An insider's view. *Journal of Common Market Studies* 21, 245–260.

Moravcsik, A., 1991, Negotiating the Single European Act: National interests and conventional statecraft in the European Community. *International Organization* 45, 19–56.

Morrow, J. D., 1992, Signaling difficulties with linkage in crisis bargaining. *International Studies Quarterly* 36, 153–172.

Niblock, M., 1971, *The EEC: National parliaments in Community decision-making* (Chatham House, London).

Nugent, N., 1991, *The government and politics of the European Community*, 2d ed. (Duke University Press, Durham, N.C.).

———, 1992, The deepening and widening of the European Community: Recent evolution, Maastricht, and beyond. *Journal of Common Market Studies* 30, 311–328.

Oye, K. A., 1992, *Economic discrimination and political exchange: World political economy in the 1930s and 1980s* (Princeton University Press, Princeton, N.J.).

Petersen, N., and J. Elklit, 1973, Denmark enters the European Communities. *Scandinavian Political Studies* 8, 198–213.

Putnam, R. D., 1988, Diplomacy and domestic politics: The logic of two-level games. *International Organization* 42, 427–460.

Sebenius, J. K., 1983, Negotiation arithmetic: Adding and subtracting issues and parties. *International Organization* 37, 281–316.

Stevens, A., 1976–1977, Problems of parliamentary control of European Community policy. *Millennium: Journal of International Studies* 5, 269–281.

Tollison, R. D., and T. D. Willett, 1979, An economic theory of mutually advantageous issue linkage in international negotiations. *International Organization* 33, 425–449.

Tsebelis, G., 1992, The European Parliament under the cooperation procedure: The power of the conditional agenda setter. Paper presented at the Annual Meeting of the American Political Science Association, Chicago.

Wallace, H., 1973, *National governments and the European Communities* (Chatham House, London).

Wallace, W., 1975, *The foreign policy process in Britain* (Royal Institute of International Affairs, London).

Waltz, K., 1967, *Foreign policy and democratic politics: The American and British experience* (Little, Brown, Boston).

Weber, S., and H. Wiesmeth, 1991, Issue linkage in the European Community. *Journal of Common Market Studies* 29, 255–267.

Williams, S., 1991, Sovereignty and accountability in the European Community, in: R. O. Keohane and S. Hoffmann (eds.) The new European Community. *Decisionmaking and institutional change* (Westview, Boulder, Colo.), 155–176.

Worre, T., 1988, Denmark at the crossroads: The Danish referendum of 28 February 1986 on the EC reform package. *Journal of Common Market Studies* 26, 361–388.

# 6

## ON THE FEASIBILITY OF A ONE-SPEED OR MULTISPEED EUROPEAN MONETARY UNION

### Alberto Alesina and Vittorio Grilli

This paper addresses two questions: (1) Is a twelve-country monetary union in Europe feasible? (2) Can monetary union be achieved at multispeed, i.e., with a small group of countries going first, and later admitting the others? After examining several politico-economic arguments concerning problems of feasibility of the union, we conclude with a fair amount of skepticism concerning the multispeed idea. We show that the final result of the process of monetary integration is dependent upon the number of countries that initiate it. Our discussion of feasibility sheds some light on the political economy of the recent (Fall 1992) turmoil in the monetary system of Europe.

THE RECENT turmoil in the European Monetary System, the Danish rejection of the Maastricht agreement, and the close vote on the agreement in France have again posed two key questions for the next decade of Europe: (1) Is a twelve-country single-currency area feasible? (2) Should European integration proceed at multispeed, i.e., should a given group of countries go ahead first, and create a single-currency subarea, while waiting for the other countries "to straighten up their act"?

This paper addresses both questions. First, we identify conditions that make a one-speed Europe (simultaneous monetary integration of all twelve EC members) feasible and discuss what allocation of control over European monetary policy is consistent with it. One specific issue we focus upon is "how to keep Germany in". One of the most commonly heard arguments for European monetary integration is the gain in credibility of low-inflation policies [e.g., Giavazzi and Giovannini (1989)]. The question left open, however, is why the lowest-inflation, most credible country would agree to help the others gain credibility. We argue that the low-inflation countries have a lot of bargaining power in the union; if the latter is to survive, the European Central Bank may have to be handed to the lowest-inflation country.[1] This discussion of feasibility issues also sheds light on the current turmoil in European exchange markets and, in our view, provides the key to explaining them.

Prepared for the University of California at Berkeley Group on the Political Economy of European Integration. We thank Barry Eichengreen and Jeffrey Frieden for useful comments.

[1]On this point, see also the discussion by Fratianni and von Hagen (1990).

We then examine the issue of a multispeed Europe, and we conclude with a good deal of skepticism about this idea.[2] We consider a situation in which a one-speed, twelve-country Europe is feasible, that is, a situation such that every country is better off with the union than without it. Suppose that a group of, say, three countries goes first, and subsequently decides, by majority rule, whether to admit a fourth, fifth, sixth, etc., member. It is perfectly possible – in fact, quite likely – that even at parameter values at which a one-speed Europe is feasible, a multispeed Europe will stop at the first group of countries: the first three countries will never choose to admit the fourth. Therefore, proceeding at "two speeds" or more will jeopardize the achievement of complete integration. We also discuss which features make it more or less likely for this problem to emerge. For instance, if there are two clusters of countries very similar to each other within each group but sizable differences across groups, then it is very likely that a two-speed Europe will never lead to a complete Europe. In more general terms, the final outcome of European monetary integration is path dependent.

The paper is organized as follows. First, we present the simple model that we use to make our points; this model draws upon Alesina and Grilli (1992). Next, we address the issue of the feasibility of a one-speed Europe, and then construct an example, which shows that a multispeed Europe may not be feasible even when a one-speed Europe is. In the last two sections, we discuss these results in light of the provisions of the Maastricht agreement and the current debate and set forth our conclusions.

## THE MODEL

Like Alesina and Grilli (1992), we focus on the trade-off between credible policies with low inflation and the need to stabilize exogenous shocks with monetary policy. Therefore, we focus exclusively on the trade-off between average inflation and variance of output, which is a key issue for the agreement over a common monetary policy in Europe.[3] A second important issue is the financing of government deficits and the lack of convergence of fiscal policies. For reasons of tractability, the fiscal argument is not explicitly formalized here, but our general point concerning the feasibility of a one-speed or multispeed Europe goes well beyond our specific model.

Consider five countries that have to decide whether to form a monetary union. For reasons that will become clear later, five is the smallest number of countries necessary to make our point in the simplest possible way, but there is not loss of generality in this choice. For the moment, suppose that these countries are of equal size. The generic country $i$ is characterized by the following loss function:

---

[2]*The Economist* (October 2–9, 1992) has recently taken the opposite view.

[3]The recent events that led to the devaluation of the pound and its exit from the ERM are an exemplary illustration.

$$L^i = \frac{1}{2}E\{\pi^2 + \beta_i(x - \bar{x})^2\}, \tag{1}$$

where $\pi$ is inflation, $x$ is output, $\bar{x} > 0$ is the targeted level of output, and $E(\cdot)$ is the expectation operator. This loss function states that policymakers in the generic country, $i$, will attempt to stabilize inflation around the target value of zero, and output around the target value of $\bar{x}$. The parameter $\beta_i$, which is the key for our analysis, represents the weight attributed to the output target relative to the inflation target. The higher is $\beta_i$, the more country $i$ cares about output relative to inflation. Output is determined according to the standard expectation-adjusted Phillips curve relation,

$$x = (\pi - \pi^e) + \mu_i, \tag{2}$$

where $\pi^e$ is the expected inflation and $\mu_i$ is a random shock with mean zero and variance equal to $\sigma^2_{\mu_i}$. Equation (2) implies that output increases (decreases) when inflation is higher (lower) than anticipated. When expectations are correct, output has an expected value of zero, while its actual value depends upon the realization of the shock $\mu_i$. Therefore, we have assumed, without loss of generality, that the "natural" level of output is zero, and we have set equal to one the partial derivative of output with respect to unexpected inflation.

The loss function given in equation (1) is adopted by the Central Bank of country $i$ ($CB_i$) and reflects the country's preferences, which can be thought of as those of the median voter, or of the political party in office. These preferences imply that $CB_i$ has a target of output, $\bar{x}$, that is greater than what would be achieved, on average, by the market without any unexpected inflationary shocks. This wedge between the market-generated, "natural" level of output (i.e., zero) and the target level, $\bar{x}$, can be justified by the existence of various distortions in the labor market, such as income taxation or labor unions. These distortions keep employment and output below the levels that would be achieved in an undistorted economy. Thus, the policymakers have an incentive to circumvent these distortions by generating unexpected inflation, which increases the level of economic activity.[4]

The countries considered may differ in two dimensions: their preferences summarized by the loss function, (1) and the nature of their output shocks, $\mu_i$. The difference in preferences is captured by the parameter $\beta_i$. A low $\beta$ country is one that cares relatively more about inflation and relatively less about output stabilization. The parameter $\beta$s are ranked in an increasing order: $\beta_i < \beta_j$ if $i < j$. The second difference involves the variance of $\mu_i$, which may vary across countries. Furthermore, the degree of correlation between $\mu_i$ and the other country shocks is an important difference between countries, as shown in Alesina and Grilli (1992).

---

[4]See Persson and Tabellini (1990) and Cukierman (1992) for more discussion on this point.

Without a monetary union, each country sets its monetary policy (i.e., $\pi$) independently. We assume that the monetary authority directly controls inflation. This shortcut involves no loss of generality: at the cost of more notation and algebra, one could close the model with a demand and supply for money. No insights for our purposes are gained by complicating the model this way; therefore we keep matters as simple as possible. We assume that without a monetary union, each country is completely isolated, thus we do not have to worry about the complexities of the preunion exchange regime. This is, of course, a gross simplification but it is somewhat orthogonal to the thrust of our analysis and should not affect the nature of our results.

The timing of events in this model is as follows: at the beginning of each period, wage contracts are set and, more generally, expectations about inflation are formed. Then, the shock, $\mu_i$, is realized and observed by the $CB_i$, which sets the inflation rate on the basis of this information. By assumption, wage contracts cannot be contingent on the realization of the shock, nor can they be indexed. The time-consistent inflation policy in this setup is given by

$$\pi = \beta_i \bar{x} - \frac{\beta_i}{1 + \beta_i} \mu_i, \tag{3}$$

and the corresponding output level is

$$x = \frac{1}{1 + \beta_i} \mu_i. \tag{4}$$

Equation (3) is obtained by substituting (2) into (1), taking the first-order conditions with respect to $\pi$ and then imposing the condition of rationality of expectations, namely, $\pi^e = E(\pi)$. Equation (4) is obtained by substituting (3) into (2). From (4), it immediately follows that the variance of output, $\sigma_{x_i}^2$, is given by

$$\sigma_{x_i}^2 = \frac{\sigma_{\mu_i}^2}{(1 + \beta_i)^2}. \tag{5}$$

This equation shows that monetary policy reduces the variance of output relative to the variance of the shock: $\sigma_{x_i}^2 < \sigma_{\mu_i}^2$. The higher is $\beta_i$, i.e., the more the $CB_i$ cares about output relative to inflation, the lower is the output variance.

Equations (3), (4), and (5) highlight a well-known time inconsistency problem: the term $\beta_i \bar{x}$ in equation (3) implies that the average inflation rate is above zero – its target value according to (1) – without any benefits in terms of average or variance of output. In other words, suppose that the $CB_i$ could commit to the following policy:

$$\pi = -\frac{\beta_i}{1+\beta_i}\mu_i.$$
(3a)

With (3a), instead of (3), the average inflation would be zero, its target value; the average output would be zero; and the variance of output would be as in equation (5). Thus, the policy (3a) is superior to (3) because it improves on the inflation front, without affecting output. However, the policy (3a) is time inconsistent. If the public expects this policy, the policymaker has an incentive to revert to policy (3). In doing so, the policymaker creates a one-shot inflation surprise, which increases output. Thus, the policy rule (3a) would not be believed if announced, and the credible policy is (3). This policy incorporates an "inflation bias" equal to $\beta_i$. Note a key trade-off: a high $\beta_i$ implies a high inflation bias, but a low output variance.

As discussed at length in the vast literature on the subject [see Cukierman (1992) for a recent survey], the inflation bias problem can be eliminated or reduced in two ways. One way is for policymakers to commit themselves to the first best policy, given in (3a). However, for well-known reasons,[5] the optimal policy is not credible. For several theoretical and empirical reasons, the assumption that irrevocable commitments are feasible is rather uninteresting, and we exclude this possibility henceforth.

The second way of reducing the inflation bias is to appoint an independent and "conservative" Central Banker [Rogoff (1985); Lohmann (1992); Alesina and Grilli (1992)]. By varying $\beta_i$, one can choose different points on the continuum of the trade-off between average inflation and output variance. A lower $\beta$ implies lower average inflation and more output variance. Rogoff (1985) shows that "society" [or the "median voter", as shown by Alesina and Grilli (1992)] would be made better off by appointing an independent Central Banker with a lower $\beta$ than that of society itself. This arrangement reduces the inflation bias and allows a better choice on the trade-off between inflation and output variance.[6]

For the most part, we assume away this possibility, which is not our focus. Some discussion of "conservative" Central Bankers in the context of the European Monetary Union appears in the next section of this paper. For now, we proceed under the assumption that each country operates with the objective function given in (1).

A Monetary Union is defined as a situation in which the inflation rate (i.e., monetary policy) is the same for every country, and it is decided by a European Central Bank (ECB). The ECB has the following loss function, where the subscript *eu* indicates European variables:

---

[5]See Kydland and Prescott (1977); Barro and Gordon (1983); and Cukierman (1992).
[6]For further discussion of this point see Lohmann (1992).

$$L_{eu} = \frac{1}{2}E\{\pi_{eu}^2 + b(x_{eu} - \bar{x}_{eu})^2\}, \tag{6}$$

where European output, $x_{eu}$, is given by

$$x_{eu} = \pi_{eu} - \pi_{eu}^e + \varepsilon. \tag{7}$$

The loss function of the ECB is identical to the one discussed above for the individual country, except that the ECB targets "European" variables. The parameter $b$ reflects the relative weight attributed to output relative to inflation in the ECB's objective function: the selection of $b$ is the key for our discussion of the feasibility of the union. The shock, $\varepsilon$, with mean zero and variance $\sigma_\varepsilon^2$, is the European output disturbance. As above, we impose $\bar{x}_{eu} > 0$. This parameter is the European analog of $\bar{x}$ in (1): if we interpret output in per capita terms, then $\bar{x} = \bar{x}_{eu}$. In other words, the ECB targets a level of European per capita output, $\bar{x}_{eu}$, which is above the "natural" market level of zero. We will proceed under this assumption.

The ECB minimizes (6), given (7) exactly as above, in the case of country $i$. Therefore we obtain

$$\pi_{eu} = b\bar{x}_{eu} - \frac{b}{1+b}\varepsilon, \tag{8}$$

and

$$x_{eu} = \frac{1}{1+b}\varepsilon, \tag{9}$$

with

$$\sigma_{x_{eu}}^2 = \frac{\sigma_\varepsilon^2}{(1+b)^2}. \tag{10}$$

The derivation and interpretation of these equations is exactly as above, for the case of a single country.

The crucial question for the feasibility of a European union is whether the generic country $i$ is better off with or without the union. In order to answer this question we need to compare the loss with and without the union for country $i$. The loss of country $i$ without the union, $(L^i)$ is obtained by substituting (3) and (4) into (1) and by computing expectations. The loss of country $i$ with the union $(L_{eu})$ can be computed by substituting (8) and (9) into (1). After some algebra [described in more detail in Alesina and Grilli (1992)], one obtains

$$L^i - L^i_{eu} = \frac{1}{2}\left\{ -\bar{x}^2(b^2 - \beta_i^2) + (1 + \beta_i)\left[\left(\frac{\beta_i}{1 + \beta_i}\right)^2 \sigma^2_{\mu_i} - \left(\frac{b}{1 + b}\right)^2 \sigma^2_{\varepsilon}\right]\right.$$

$$\left. + 2\beta_i\left[\left(\frac{b}{1 + b}\right)\sigma_{\varepsilon\mu_i} - \left(\frac{\beta_i}{1 + \beta_i}\right)\sigma_{\mu_i}\right]\right\}. \tag{11}$$

Equation (11) represents the net gain of joining the union, and $\sigma_{\varepsilon\mu_i}$ is the covariance between $\mu_i$ and $\varepsilon$. This expression highlights two distinct components of the difference in welfare with and without a monetary union. The first one is due to differences in preferences, as represented by differences between $b$ and $\beta_i$. The second component depends upon economic dissimilarities, summarized by $\sigma^2_{\varepsilon}$, $\sigma^2_{\mu_i}$ and $\sigma_{\varepsilon\mu_i}$.

Consider first the differences in preferences. To better focus upon them, let us eliminate the economic difference by assuming $\mu_i = \varepsilon$ in all states of the world, so that $\sigma^2_{\mu_i} = \sigma^2_{\varepsilon} = \sigma_{\varepsilon\mu_i} \equiv \sigma^2$. Then (11) becomes

$$L^i - L^i_{eu} = \frac{1}{2}\left[ -\bar{x}^2(b^2 - \beta_i^2) + \sigma^2\left(\frac{\beta_i}{1 + \beta_i} - \frac{b}{1 + b}\right)\left(\frac{1 + \beta_i}{1 + b}b - \beta_i\right)\right]. \tag{12}$$

Equation (12) is critical to the development of our argument. Let us define the gains of the union for country $i$, $G^i$, as the following gain function:

$$G^i(b, \beta_i) = L^i - L^i_{eu}. \tag{13}$$

The function $G^i(b, \beta_i)$ is rather complex, but several observations can be made before proceeding to a complete study of it. First of all, the gains are zero when the ECB adopts the same $\beta_i$ parameter as that of country $i$, namely,

$$G^i(\beta_i, \beta_i) = 0. \tag{14}$$

In fact, if $b = \beta_i$, it makes no difference whether country $i$ is in the union or not (remember that all the countries are identical in terms of their economic shocks). It is also interesting to check whether country $i$ gains or loses when the ECB stabilizes inflation, without worrying at all about output. In other words, we look at what happens if $b = 0$:

$$G(0, \beta_i) \gtreqless 0 \quad \text{if} \quad \bar{x}^2(1 + \beta_i) \gtreqless \sigma^2_{\varepsilon}. \tag{15}$$

Equation (15) implies that if the output variance is low and $\beta_i$ is high, country $i$ benefits from the union even if the ECB does not stabilize output at all, i.e., if $b = 0$. This is the extreme version of the "credibility gains" of the union: country $i$ benefits because the gain in credibility, which ensures a zero inflation rate, more than compensates for the complete lack of output stabilization. Clearly, this

114

a)

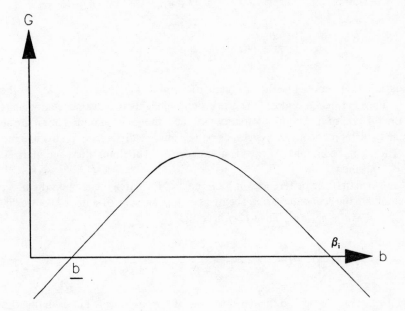

b)

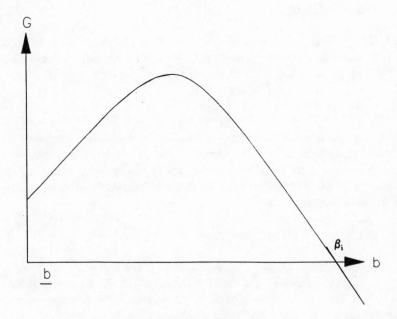

Figure 1.    The $G(b, \beta_i)$ Curve.

is more likely to happen when the variance of output is low, and thus the costs of not stabilizing are low.

Computer simulation shows that the function $G(b,\beta_i)$ has the parabolalike shape displayed in Figure 1. Details about the simulation procedure are available upon request. The important features are that this function is single-peaked and crosses the horizontal axis twice: one intersection is at $\beta_i = b$, and the other is at $\underline{b} \gtreqless 0$, depending upon the inequality in (15). Obviously, from an economic perspective, negative values of $b$ are uninteresting and can be ignored. Figure 1a represents the case in which is $\bar{x}^2(1 + \beta_i) < \sigma_\varepsilon^2$, and Figure 1b represents the opposite case. In Figure 1a, if $b > \beta_i$, country $i$ is worse off with the union: the ECB is even less credible than the CB$_i$. If $b < \underline{b}$, country $i$ loses from the union because the ECB is "too conservative" and does not stabilize enough. The loss in terms of output variance more than compensates for the gains in reduced inflation. If $b \in (\underline{b},\beta_i)$, country $i$ is strictly better off with the union. Within this range of parameter values, the gains in credibility from a low-inflation policy more than compensate for the reduced stabilization. The optimal choice of $b$ for country $i$ is $b_i^*$.

Let us now briefly discuss how economic differences (i.e. in the shocks) influence the position of the curve $G^i(b,\beta_i)$. Suppose that $\beta_i = b$ for every $i$, and that the shocks are perfectly correlated, but $\sigma_{\varepsilon_i}^2 \neq \sigma_\mu^2$. Manipulations of (11) readily establish the following:

$$G(b,b) = \frac{1}{2}\left[\frac{b^2}{1+b}(\sigma_\varepsilon^2 - \sigma_\mu^2)^2\right]. \qquad (16)$$

Therefore, if there are differences between the variance of national and European output, the welfare of the country will be lower in a monetary union, with $\beta_i = b$. The intuition is clear; if $\sigma_\varepsilon^2 < \sigma_\mu^2$, for instance, the ECB will not be stabilizing enough. Given (16), it is clear what happens to the curve shown in Figure 1a if country $i$ has a variance higher than $\sigma_\varepsilon^2$. The curve $G(\beta_i,b)$ shifts, as in Figure 2. The range of values of $b$ for which country $i$ would join the monetary union shifts up: stabilization is now more valuable, since the variance of output is higher.

Finally, consider the case where the variances of the shocks are all identical, all the $\beta$s are the same, but the national shocks are not perfectly correlated, i.e., $\rho_i \neq 1$, where $\rho_i$ is the correlation coefficient between $\mu_i$ and $\varepsilon$. Simple manipulations of (11) readily establish the following:

$$G(b,b) = -\frac{1}{2}\left[\frac{b^2}{1+b}\sigma_\varepsilon^2(1-\rho_i)\right]. \qquad (17)$$

Therefore, the smaller is the correlation between $\mu_i$ and $\varepsilon$, the worse off country $i$ is made by its participation in the monetary union. In fact, if $\rho_i$ is low, the

116

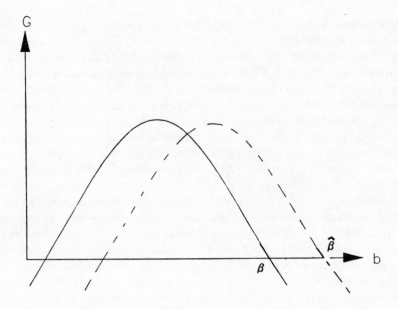

Figure 2. The Case of $\beta_i = b$; $\sigma_{\mu i}^2 > \sigma_\varepsilon^2$. ----- curve with $\sigma_{\mu i}^2 > \sigma_\varepsilon^2$.

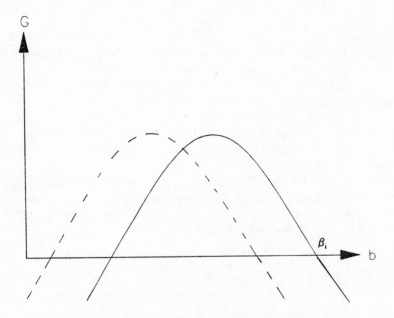

Figure 3. The Case of $\rho_i < 1$. ----- curve with $\rho_i < 1$.

ECB will constantly stabilize, either too much or not enough from the point of view of country $i$. For example, in the extreme case of perfect negative correlation, the ECB contracts when country $i$ experiences a recession, and expands when country $i$ experiences an expansion. From equation (17), it follows that if $\rho_i < 1$, the curve shown in Figure 1a shifts, as in Figure 3. If $\rho_i < 1$, the range of values of the parameter $b$, which makes country $i$ better off in the union, decreases. In fact, the benefits of stabilization are downplayed by country $i$, given that the ECB reacts to a shock that is only imperfectly correlated with country $i$'s disturbance.

### THE FEASIBILITY OF THE MONETARY UNION

We define as "feasible" a monetary union in which all the participant countries are not worse off with the union than without it. In our framework, the problem of "feasibility" is whether one can find a range of values for the parameter $b$ that makes every country not worse off with the union.

Consider Figure 4, which plots the $G^i$ curves for three countries, with identical shocks but different $\beta$s. Let us call country 1 Germany, country 2 France, and country 3 Italy, recalling that $\beta_1 < \beta_2 < \beta_3$. This figure represents a case in which one can find a range of parameter values at which the union is feasible. This range is given by $b \in [\underline{b}_3, \beta_1]$, where $\underline{b}_3$ represents the lowest feasible $b$ for country 3, Italy.

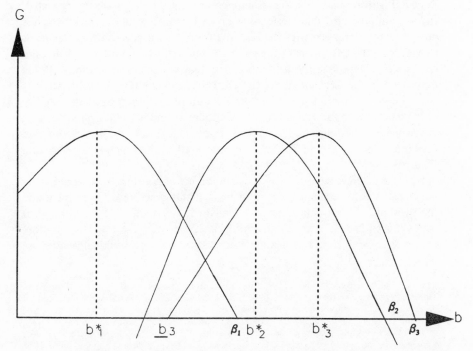

Figure 4.   Three-Country Feasible Union. The feasible set is expressed by $b = [\underline{b}_3; \beta_1]$.

Suppose that the three countries decide by majority vote on the choice of $b$, i.e., on the appointment of a Central Banker, who cannot be removed from office.[7] The functions displayed in Figure 4 show that France and Italy would vote against any feasible $b$ smaller than $\beta_1$. Thus, the choice of the ECB implies $b = \beta_1$, even though for both France and Italy, $\beta_1$ is lower than the optimal choice ($b_1^*$ and $b_2^*$, respectively). The message is clear: in order to "keep Germany in", the ECB has to be handed to this country because Germany would never join a union with $b > \beta_1$.

Note that Germany would be better off with an even more inflation-averse ECB, namely, with $b < \beta_1$; that is, Germany would like to appoint a ECB even more antiinflationary than its own preferences, if this arrangement were possible. However, France and Italy would vote against any $b$ lower than $\beta_1$.[8] In fact, in the discussion that follows, we disregard the possibility of appointing a Central Banker more antiinflationary than the most inflation-averse country, i.e., Germany. More generally, this assumption implies that each country can gain antiinflation credibility by joining the union, but each country alone cannot appoint a governor of the Central Bank with preferences different from its own.

This example illuminates an element of fragility in the union: Germany is indifferent as to whether it joins the union or not. The consequences of this fragility are highlighted by the following example, which may capture some elements of the recent (September 1992) turmoil in the European Monetary System. Figure 4 is based on the assumption of identical, i.e., perfectly correlated, shocks. Suppose now that Germany is hit by a "new" kind of shock, which is not perfectly correlated with the rest of Europe. As argued before, this leads to a shift to the left of the $G$ curve for Germany, as in Figure 3. This implies that $b = \beta_1$ is not feasible any more: the feasible set of $b$s shrinks. If the movement in the German curve, $G(b, \beta)$, is large enough, the feasible set may easily become empty. The German unification can be interpreted as a change in the nature of the shocks hitting the Germany economy, requiring increasing government borrowing and high interest rates. This shock has, in fact, imposed the kinds of strain on the ERM that are captured by the functions displayed in Figure 3.

Figure 5 displays a case in which the union is not feasible; Italy would never hand the ECB to Germany because if $b \leqslant \beta_1$, Italy is worse off with the union than without it. The important question, then, is whether in this situation, it is possible to form a union by an appropriate "compensation" of one or more of the three countries. The two most interesting ways of thinking about these

---

[7]If the Central Banker could be removed from office, his or her appointment would not be credible. This is one of the arguments in favor of Central Bank independence. For a discussion in the context of the European Monetary Union, see Alesina and Grilli (1992). For evidence on the benefits of Central Bank independence, see Grilli, Masciandaro, and Tabellini (1991) and Alesina and Summers (1993).

[8]Note that this is not always the case. Suppose that $b_2^* < \beta_1$, that is, that the optimal $b$ for France were below $\beta_1$, so that $b_1^* < b_2^* < \beta_1$. In this case, France and Germany would prefer $b_2^*$ to $\beta_1$. If $b_2^*$ were feasible, Italy would stay in the union with $b_2^*$.

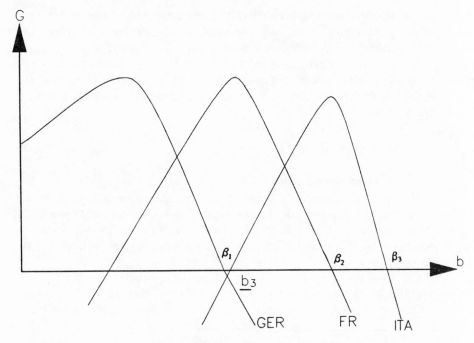

Figure 5.   A Nonfeasible Union.

compensations are in terms of (1) the benefits of participating in the union, beyond the credibility gains, and (2) differential treatment for low inflation countries. Let us examine these two issues in more detail.

1. *The benefits of the union.* The more enthusiastic supporters of monetary integration have argued that the gains in credibility are only one of the many benefits of the monetary union. Amongst the most cited additional economic benefits are the elimination of exchange volatility, the reduction of transaction costs, and the international currency role of the (ECU). Like the credibility gains of a monetary union, these other benefits are very difficult to quantify. Nonetheless, the European Commission, in its effort to support the process toward the Economic and Monetary Union (EMU), has provided some estimates, albeit rough and probably overoptimistic. It has been argued [see, e.g., Emerson and Huhne (1991)] that a reduction of just one-half of a percentage point in real interest rates, following the elimination of exchange rate risk premiums, could lead to an increase in European Community (EC) income of about 5–10 percent in the long run. Savings in transaction costs, deriving from the abolishment of cross-currency conversions, would amount to over 15 billion ECUs per year (about 0.5 percent of the EC's total GDP). Moreover, if because of EMU, the ECU were to develop into a major international reserve currency, this could imply a once and for all seigniorage revenue of about 28 billion ECUs. A different type of benefit is political. Monetary union is a necessary step toward political

integration [Alesina and Grilli (1992)]. If the latter is viewed as desirable for several economic and noneconomic reasons, the benefits of political integration must be included in the calculation of costs and benefits of the monetary union.

Define as $H_{in}$ the net additional benefits of joining the union for country $i$ when $n$ countries participate. For example, in our three-country example, $H_{13}$ is the benefit for Germany of belonging to a three-country union. Thus, for Germany we have

$$\hat{G}^1(b,\beta_1) = G^1(b,\beta_1) + H_{13}, \qquad (18)$$

where the expression for $G^1(b,\beta_1)$ is the same as above in equation (13). $H_{13}$ shifts up the gain curve for Germany, and analogous arguments hold for the other countries. The curves displayed in Figure 6 show that because of these shifts, relative to the functions displayed in Figure 5, we can now identify a feasible range, $b \in [\underline{b}_3, \overline{b}_1]$, for the union. In this example, France and Italy strictly prefer $\overline{b}^1$ to any other feasible $b$; thus $\overline{b}_1$ prevails by majority rule.

For these parameter values, the European monetary policy is less antiinflationary than German preferences. It follows that the ECB should not be handed to Germany: the three countries should share control of the ECB.

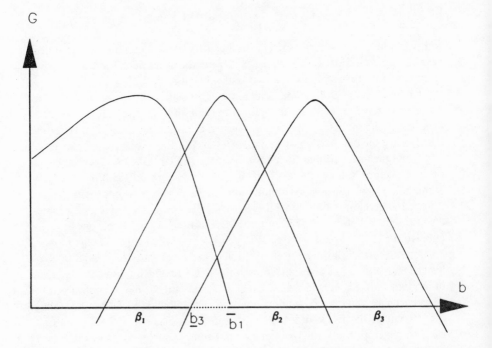

Figure 6.   A Feasible Union with $H_{ij} > 0$. The feasible set is expressed by $b = [\underline{b}_3; \overline{b}_1]$.

One important caveat, however, is that we have assumed that all the costs and benefits of the union, $H_{ij}$, are observable. If they were not, Germany, for instance, would have an incentive to underreport its true $H_{13}$, claim that the shift in its curve is less than that displayed in Figure 6, and argue that the feasible set of $b$s is smaller than that shown in Figure 6. In particular, Germany could claim that the only feasible point is $b = \underline{b}_3$, which is the most desirable point for Germany in the original feasible set.

The problem of revelation of true costs and benefits from joining the union is, we believe, quite important. Each country has an incentive to underreport benefits from joining, in order to achieve a stronger position at the bargaining table. Given the nature of these benefits, often hard to pinpoint in theory and even harder to nail down in practice, it is quite clear that there is much uncertainty about the magnitude of these $H_{ij}$. In principle, the same argument could be made about the $\beta$s in the national loss function. However, one may argue that by observing the monetary system of each individual country before the union is created, these parameters can be estimated.[9] Obviously, the same argument does not apply to the $H_{ij}$.

2. *Differential treatment.* Consider now the case in which the three countries not only differ in their preferences (i.e., the $\beta$s) but also have imperfectly correlated shocks with different variances. This case is displayed in Figure 7. The feasible set is empty: since the German shock is not perfectly correlated with the others, Germany would join a union only if $b < \beta_1$. Thus, even though Italy would accept $b = \beta_1$, Germany would not. In fact, Germany needs a gain in credibility to delegate monetary policy to a ECB that does not target the German output fluctuations only.

Suppose now that France and Italy agree to hand the ECB to Germany, letting the bank adopt the $\beta_1$ parameter and letting it stabilize the German shock; that is, the ECB not only adopts the German perferences ($\beta_1$) but reacts to the fluctuations of the German economy only, rather than to "European" shocks. Then $b = \beta_1$ becomes feasible, since Germany is indifferent as to whether it joins the union or not, and the two other countries may still benefit because of the gains in credibility, even though, from their joint of view, the ECB is stabilizing the "wrong" shock. This mechanism is obviously more likely to work if the correlation between shocks is not too low. The idea is clear: the other European countries "buy" German credibility in exchange for a special treatment of this country in terms of output stabilization.

This arrangement, however, exposes another element of fragility in the union. Suppose that while the ECB stabilizes the German economy, the latter is hit by a very large idiosyncratic shock. Then, at least in the short run, monetary policy is completely inadequate and possibly very costly for the other countries. Even though, for the reasons given above, in the long run, it is in everybody's

---

[9]For an interesting attempt to estimate these parameters for several EC countries, see Collins and Giavazzi (1993).

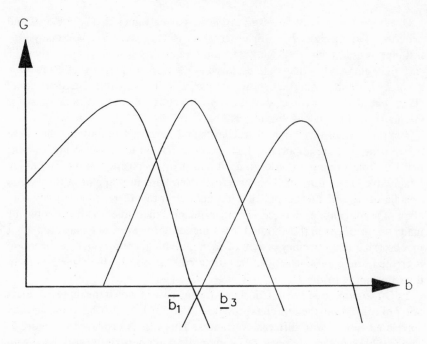

Figure 7. A Nonfeasible Union with Uncorrelated Shocks. In this model, $\underline{b}_1 < \underline{b}_3$: highest $b$ for country 1 is lower than lowest $b$ for country 3 ⇒ union not feasible.

interest to suffer through the German shock, in the short run, the other countries may have to bear large costs. This argument is even stronger if other countries are hit by shocks while the ECB is stabilizing Germany. Various political or electoral reasons may make the short-run performance of the economy extremely important; for instance, it may turn out to be extremely painful for a government to have its hands tied and have to sit through a recession with an ECB interested only in the fate of the German economy. We leave it to the judgment of the reader whether this hypothetical example bears some resemblance to the recent English-German clash over monetary policy. We think it does.[10]

In summary, this section has provided an answer to a question often heard in the debate over a European Monetary Union: if the benefits of the union are mainly gains in credibility, why would the most credible country want to join? In addressing this question, we have highlighted an element of fragility in the union: to "keep Germany in", concessions have to be made to this country, which can make the most credible threat of leaving the union. These concessions may

---

[10]One aspect of the September 1992 events that this story does not capture is the alleged clash between the German government and the Bundesbank. The bank was apparently "tougher" than the government about the policy of not lowering interest rates. This aspect of the story (if at all real) can be easily explained if we view the Bundesbank as the "conservative" Central Bank of Germany discussed above, that is, as a tool for ensuring credible low inflation policies. [For more on this topic, see Geoffrey Garrett, "The Politics of Maastricht", in this issue. – Eds.]

become hard to bear for the other countries, especially in hard times. In the next section we continue our analysis of feasibility by considering the multispeed argument.

### THE FEASIBILITY OF A MULTISPEED EUROPE

Suppose that a five-country union is feasible, as shown in Figure 8, which is drawn for simplicity, with no loss of generality for the case in which $H_{i5} \geqslant 0$ but all the shocks are perfectly correlated and have the same variance. There is no loss of generality in these assumptions: the argument that follows could be easily extended to the more general case. Remember that we are always assuming – for simplicity and, again, with no loss of generality – that all the countries are of equal size. Thus a one country, one vote rule and a vote weighted by size are equivalent. Let us designate countries 4 and 5 Portugal and Spain, respectively ($\beta_4 < \beta_5$). The range of feasible $b$s is $b \in [\underline{b}_5, \overline{b}_1]$, where $\underline{b}_5$ is the smallest acceptable $b$ for Spain (i.e., the lowest interception of the $G$ curve of Spain with the horizontal axis) and $\overline{b}_1$ is the highest acceptable $b$ for Germany. If the five countries decide, by majority vote, which $b$ should be adopted, $b_3^*$ will prevail. This is the $b$ preferred by the median country (i.e., Italy), and it is in the feasible set.[11]

Suppose that, instead, we proceed with a multispeed union. For instance, suppose that France and Germany go ahead and unify their monetary systems first. The feasible set for a Franco-German union is $b \in [\underline{b}_2, \overline{b}_1]$, where $\underline{b}_2$ is the lowest acceptable $b$ for France. As is shown in Figure 8, $b_2^*$ is in the feasible set of the Franco-German union. Both countries prefer this point to any point above it. Thus, regardless of how the bargaining process between France and Germany is resolved, the chosen $b$ is between $\underline{b}_2$ and $b_2^*$. In this example, both France and Germany are better off with any choice of $b$ between $\underline{b}_2$ and $b_2^*$ than with $b_3^*$, which would be the equilibrium choice in a five-country union. Thus, France and Germany will never admit the other three countries as a group.

It is even possible that Germany and France will not want to admit Italy alone, particularly if Germany takes an aggressive position about it. If Italy alone enters, France becomes the median voter in the union. If $b_2^*$ (the optimal $b$ for France) is feasible, then France will be better off in the three-country union. If, however, $b_2^*$ is not feasible, then $\overline{b}_1$ will prevail in a three-country union. If in the

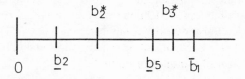

Figure 8.   A Five-Country Feasible Union. The $G$ curves are not displayed. Union is feasible because $\underline{b}_5 < \overline{b}_1$. The feasible range $b = [\underline{b}_5, \overline{b}_1]$.

[11]If $b_3^* > \overline{b}_1$, that is, it is not feasible, then $\overline{b}_1$ is chosen in equilibrium, if $b_3^* < \underline{b}_5$, that is, it is not feasible, then $\underline{b}_5$ is chosen in equilibrium.

Franco-German union, the chosen $b$ is smaller than $\underline{b}_1$, Germany will oppose the admission of Italy, since $\bar{b}_2$ is below the feasible set for the three countries. If the admission of a new member requires unanimity of members, Italy will not be admitted.

Even if Italy were admitted, the union would stop there. In fact, suppose that Italy is in, and $b_2^*$ is feasible and prevails (see Figure 8). France will never want any new members because it cannot do any better than $b_2^*$. Germany will also be against new members: new members can only increase the chosen $b$, which is already above the optimal one for Germany. Thus, there is a two–one majority against new members: the union stops at three.

This example shows that the number of speeds with which a European Monetary Union is constructed matters a great deal. Our example suggests that even though a five-country union is feasible, integration may stop at two or three countries. The idea is simple. The first group of countries anticipates the political equilibrium that would prevail if the union were extended. It may easily be the case that a majority of the first group of countries would be worse off in the new political equilibrium. In our example, France and Germany are better off alone or, at most, with Italy than with Spain and Portugal.

It is also apparent that the most credible, low-inflation countries should be the most vocal in favor of a multispeed union. They cannot lose from it: either the other countries change their behavior and/or preferences (i.e., drop their high $\beta$s, perhaps with a political change) and therefore their admission to the union is costless, or the union will stop at the first group.

An interesting question is whether it would be in the interest of the countries left out from the "first speed" to form their own union. In the example above, for instance, Spain and Portugal, if left out, could form their own union. As for Italy, it is not clear a priori whether it would be in its interest to join the Franco-German union or the other one. In the first case, Italy would gain in credibility and lose on the stabilization front; in the second case, the opposite would occur.

In principle, different coalitions could form. One thing that can be said in general is that all the possible coalitions have to include "adjacent" countries, in terms of the $G$ curves. In other words, if country 3 is better off joining countries 4 and 5, instead of countries 1 and 2, then it cannot be the case that country 4 is better off joining countries 1 and 2, rather than countries 3, 4, and 5.

Enlarging the possibilities for coalition formation by considering the possibility of multiple unions in Europe clearly complicates the analysis. However, the key insight emphasized above remains: it does matter how and at how many speeds Europe proceeds toward a monetary union.

## DISCUSSION

The previous two sections help clarify current events in the process of European monetary integration and its future prospects. First of all, while we focused on differences in preferences across countries, the same arguments would apply if the countries differed in their economic problems and environment. As we discussed, different preferences over monetary policy may derive from different shocks; they may also derive from different levels of public debt and deficit. Even though we cast our discussion in terms of the $\beta$s, we could have told a similar story in which high-$\beta$ countries are high-debt countries. The incentives to use monetary policy actively, for instance, to control interest rates, are increased by a sizable outstanding stock of government debt.

Second, the probability of stopping at the first stage is increasing if the countries are not of equal size and the largest country has the most extreme preferences, which seems to be the case of Germany. If you go back to the French-German union, if Germany had more than half of the weight, Italy would never be admitted, while if France had more than half of the vote, Italy would be admitted by a majority vote (see Figure 8). Clearly, the country with the weakest interest in expanding the union to countries with higher $\beta$s is the country with the lowest one. If this country is the largest, we have a problem.

Third, it is less likely that a multispeed Europe will ever be completed if the countries cluster in two easily distinguishable groups. For instance, if $\beta_3$, $\beta_4$, and $\beta_5$ are much higher than $\beta_2$, a move from a three- to a five-country union implies a large increase in the chosen $b$, because country 3 is now the median voter and $\beta_3$ is much larger than $\beta_1$ and $\beta_2$. The same argument applies to the interpretation of these differences in terms of economic conditions rather than preferences. In this case, as briefly discussed above, one outcome could be the creation of two monetary unions.

Fourth, even though we cast our analysis in terms of the median voter theorem (i.e., the decisive voter is median), our results are much more general. In fact, our basic point applies to any voting mechanism adopted within the union. The crucial point is that the first group of countries can anticipate the political equilibrium that would be generated by the next entrants to the union.

The supporters of multispeed Europe claim that this process allows "weaker" countries to "put their houses in order" before joining the union. The Maastricht agreement in some sense follows this approach by setting certain targets which have to be met before joining the union. If these targets are reached, then new members can automatically join the first group of countries, without requiring a new vote. If this were, in fact, the case, then the problems highlighted in the preceding section would disappear: in fact the first group of countries could not vote against the entry of additional members satisfying the preset criteria.

The problem with this argument is that the formulation of a target may leave a fair amount of room for different interpretations; in addition, one may reasonably argue that evolving economic conditions require revisions of such targets. For instance, in the Maastricht agreement, the fiscal targets are so unrealistic for certain countries that their admission to the union is either left to the discretion of the "first speed" countries, or it will not materialize in the foreseeable future. The point is that with sufficiently vague, unrealistic, perhaps contingent targets, any agreement leaves a large amount of discretion, which can be used by the "first speed" countries to never admit the second group. Sufficiently "loose" targets may boil down to essentially a discretionary decision of the first group of countries to admit the others.

On the other hand, the imposition of prespecified targets may, in fact, help the more fiscally irresponsible countries to stabilize their budgets. However, an expectation that, because of the problems highlighted above, the first group of countries will never admit the second, may in fact undermine the credibility of the targets themselves.

## CONCLUSION

Two questions are often asked by the observers of the process of European Monetary Union: (1) What is in it for Germany? (2) Is a multispeed Europe a good idea?

This paper has provided answers that raise some concerns over both issues. First, we argue that unless Germany obtains a disproportionate degree of control over the monetary policy of the union, it will not have much interest in joining. This creates tensions, particularly in hard times. If the European monetary policy follows German preferences, other countries are likely to have to endure the "wrong" monetary policy in times of need. For instance, the British might have to suffer through a lengthy recession without lowering interest rates. If they are not willing to do so, there is no hope for the union, since Germany cannot be asked to agree to change its policies. In more colorful terms, one cannot ask Germany to sell "credibility" for free.

On the idea of a multispeed union, the paper expresses some skepticism. We argue that it is quite likely that once the first group of countries forms a restricted union, those countries will never agree to enlarge the union. This may happen even if every country would be better off with full-scale integration than with no integration at all. Therefore, if the monetary union proceeded at "one speed" it would be feasible. Instead, with a multispeed process, the union would stop at a smaller group of countries.

Similar arguments apply to the extension of the union beyond the current twelve potential members. Whether new members would or would not be admitted depends very much on their preferences (and economic conditions) relative to the "median" of the twelve country union. For instance, suppose that a potential new member has exactly the same preferences as the median of the twelve countries. Then, if the "median voter" is decisive in policy formation, European policy does not change. The original members would not oppose the new member, since they might benefit by the enlarged community without any change in policy.

The opposite case is one in which the new entrant has "extreme" preferences so that the "median" may change substantially. In this case, it is much more likely that a majority of the members would oppose the new entrant, because the benefits of the new entry might be more than offset by the loss due to the change in the political equilibrium of the enlarged union.

## REFERENCES

Alesina, A., and V. Grilli, 1992, The European Central Bank: Reshaping monetary politics in Europe, in: Matthew Canzoneri, Vittorio Grilli, and Paul Masson, eds., *The creation of a Central Bank* (Cambridge University Press and CEPR, Cambridge).

——, and L. Summers, 1993, Central Bank independence and economic performance: Some comparative evidence. *Journal of Money, Credit and Banking*, forthcoming.

Barro, R., and D. Gordon, 1983, Rules, discretion and reputation in a model of monetary policy. *Journal of Monetary Economics* 12, 101–122.

Casella, Alessandra, 1991, The impact of monetary unification on the composition of markets (unpublished).

Collins, S., and F. Giavazzi, 1993, Attitudes toward inflation and the viability of fixed exchange rates: Evidence from the EMS, in: M. Bordo and B. Eichengreen, eds., *A retrospective on the Bretton Woods system* (University of Chicago Press and NBER, Chicago).

Cukierman, A., 1992, *Central Bank strategy: Credibility and independence* (M.I.T. Press, Cambridge, Mass.).

Emerson, M., and C. Huhne, 1991, *The ECU report*, (Pan Books, London).

Fratianni, M., and J. von Hagen, 1990, Credibility and asymmetries in the EMS, in: V. Argy and P. de Grauwe, eds., *Choosing an exchange rate regime: The challenge for smaller industrial countries* (International Monetary Fund, Washington, D.C.).

Giavazzi, F., and A. Giovannini, 1989, *Limiting exchange rate flexibility: The European Monetary System* (MIT Press, Cambridge, Mass.).

Grilli, V., D. Masciandaro, and G. Tabellini, 1991, Political and monetary institutions and public finance policies in the industrial democracies. *Economic Policy* 13, 101–153.

Krugman, P., 1989, Policy problems of a monetary union (unpublished).

Kydland, F., and E. Prescott, 1977, Rules rather than discretion: The inconsistency of optimal plans. *Journal of Political Economy* 85, 473–490.

Lohmann, S., 1992, Optimal commitment in monetary policy: Credibility vs. flexibility. *American Economic Review*, 82, 273–286.

Persson, T., and G. Tabellini, 1990, *Macroeconomic policy, credibility and politics* (Harwood Academic Publishers, London).

Rogoff, K., 1985, The optimal degree of commitment to an intermediate monetary target. *Quarterly Journal of Economics* 100, 1169–1190.

# 7

## THE TRANSITION TO EUROPEAN MONETARY UNION AND THE EUROPEAN MONETARY INSTITUTE

### Jürgen von Hagen and Michele Fratianni

The European Monetary Institute (EMI) will prepare a framework for European Monetary Union (EMU) monetary policy during the transition to the EMU. This involves a trade-off between deepening financial market integration and harmonizing central bank instruments, a choice between centralized and decentralized monetary strategies with significant welfare implications, and a trade-off between expected welfare and certainty of policy outcomes. As a result of being dominated by national central bankers and of the conflict between the core and the periphery of the European Community (EC), the EMI is biased toward an inefficient solution. Enlargement of the EC by the European Free Trade Area (EFTA) group would raise the probability of a more efficient, two-track EMU, which initially would involve only the core group.

THE REVISION of the Treaty of Rome as proposed in the December 1991 Maastricht agreement foresees the creation of a European Monetary Union (EMU) in three stages. Currently, in Stage One, things are essentially as they were in the late 1980s, with nine European currencies bound together by the Exchange Rate Mechanism (ERM). Stage Two, which began January 1, 1994, will proceed further with liberalization of capital markets in the European Community (EC) and will replace the current Council of Central Bank Governors with a new institution, the European Monetary Institute (EMI). Stage Three, scheduled to begin no later than January 1, 1999, will begin with the dissolution of the EMI and the introduction of the EMU and the European System of Central Banks (ESCB). Until then, the national central banks will remain responsible for monetary policy in Europe, and the national governments will remain responsible for exchange rate realignments in the ERM.

Recent turmoil in the financial markets and the bumps in the political ratification process have called the future of the Maastricht agreement into question. Still, the history of European monetary integration [Fratianni and von Hagen (1992)] teaches that we should expect future attempts at EMU to rest on a multistage approach, including an institutional transition as envisaged in the EMI. Thus, even if the Maastricht agreement fails, a consideration of the specific problems of its transition strategy remains relevant for future European monetary arrangements.

In this paper, we focus on the EC's task of devising a framework for the EMU monetary policy. The notion of EMU is compatible with many different financial market environments in Europe. However, EC decisions on how to organize EMU monetary policy will impose regulatory provisions and barriers to market integration with important welfare implications for the future EMU. Preparing a framework for monetary policy compatible with the largest possible economic benefits from EMU will be an important task during the transition.

During Stage Two, the EMI will assume the administration of the ERM. Beyond that, its mandate is to strengthen central bank cooperation in the EC and to prepare monetary control techniques and operating procedures for the ESCB. The Maastricht agreement does not actually vest the EMI with any decisionmaking power in these areas. The EMI will submit a proposal on the operation of the ESCB to the European Central Bank (ECB) council at the start of EMU, thus setting the initial agenda for the council's vote on operating procedures and control techniques. In the meantime, the EMI may publish opinions on the progress of European monetary integration and educate the public and policymakers about critical issues in the wake of EMU left open in the Maastricht agreement.

The Maastricht agreement contains only vague stipulations or none at all with regard to important aspects of the financial markets environment and the implementation of monetary policy in the EMU. Among these are the choice between a multiple-currency and a single-currency EMU, the degree of money market integration, the extent to which central bank operations and the regulation of the banking industry are centralized and harmonized, and the formulation of monetary policy objectives in the EMU. A casual look at the EC today reveals that there are no "natural" choices in these matters given the large degree of diversity among the current, national arrangements.

Nonetheless, the preparation of the EMU requires policymakers to reach decisions on these issues. The purpose of this paper is to outline the critical choices EC decisionmakers will face before the start of the EMU and to discuss the politico-economic forces that will come into play in the relevant decisionmaking processes.

Our paper proceeds as follows. First, we lay out a menu of choices facing the EC, organized around two dimensions: the financial markets environment and the decisionmaking structures of monetary policy. We show that there is a trade-off between deepening financial market integration and the harmonization and coordination of central bank instruments. Furthermore, we argue that the adoption of a decentralized EMU monetary strategy would preempt the achievement of a high degree of financial market integration. Next, we pick three likely scenarios from this menu and consider their welfare implications. We show that there is a trade-off between expected welfare and initial certainty about the performance of EMU monetary policy. We then discuss the political economy of the transition process with regard to these choices, examining the role of the national central bankers and the EMI and the importance of a possible enlargement of the EC before 1999. In the final section, we summarize our main conclusions.

DIMENSIONS IN THE IMPLEMENTATION OF THE EMU

*The Financial Markets Environment: Integration, Harmonization, and Regulation*

To illustrate the arguments that follow, consider a monetary union (MU) consisting of two regions, $A$ and $B$, with two regional central banks, $CB_A$ and $CB_B$, supplying reserves to commercial banks in the two regions. Let the total MU money supply denominated in a common accounting standard be

$$D = D_A + D_B, \tag{1}$$

and the total supply of central bank reserves be

$$R = R_A + R_B, \tag{2}$$

where, $R_i$, $i = A, B$, denotes reserves held at the central bank in country $i$.

Commercial banks hold reserves to hedge against unexpected liquidity outflows and to meet reserve requirements. The desired reserve ratio is the reserve ratio that banks wish to apply against deposits given their liquidity risk and the opportunity cost of holding reserves. We assume that nonbank behavior is homogeneous across regions, so that, other things being equal, desired reserve ratios do not differ across regions. This requires the absence of regulatory barriers dividing the MU artificially into regions of high and low liquidity risk.[1] The demand for central bank reserves depends negatively on the short-term MU interest rate, $r$, and positively on the relevant required reserve ratio, $rr$. Furthermore, since the access to short-term central bank credit is the main substitute for reserves as a hedge against liquidity risk, the demand for reserves depends on the central banks' lending conditions. For simplicity, we represent effective lending conditions by a summary statistic, $z_i$, which includes the interest rate applied and nonpecuniary elements, such as maturity and provisions for early repayment and collateral.[2] Thus,

$$R = R_A(D_A, D_B, r, z_A, z_B, rr_A, rr_B) + R_B(D_A, D_B, r, z_B, z_A, rr_B, rr_A). \tag{3}$$

---

[1] For example, in the U.S., regulatory barriers to cross-state and even cross-county banking prevent deposit markets from integrating, with the result that banks cannot pool liquidity risk between regions.

[2] For example, discount credit in Germany is granted at the discount rate and requires eligible trade bills as collateral. A discount loan must be held to the maturity of the bill used as collateral. In contrast, discount loans in Italy can be repaid before expiration. Given these liquidity differences, discount loans at the Bundesbank and the Bank of Italy are not perfect substitutes and hence can have different discount rates in equilibrium.

In the absence of money market frictions, the opportunity cost of holding money should not depend on where money balances are held within a currency area. In view of this, we propose to assess MU money market efficiency by the extent to which changes in the local composition of money balances, leaving the total MU money supply the same, affect the MU interest rate. In a perfectly efficient MU, such changes have no consequences for the demand for bank reserves and, therefore, the interest rate. Thus, they do not affect monetary policy outcomes or send misleading signals about the stance of MU monetary policy. The larger the interest rate effect of such changes, the lower the efficiency of the money markets.

The MU money market is perfectly efficient, if

$$\frac{dR}{dD_A}\Bigg|_{dD_A = -dD_B} = \left[\frac{dR_A}{dD_A} - \frac{dR_B}{dD_B}\right] + \left[\frac{dR_B}{dD_A} - \frac{dR_A}{dD_B}\right] = 0. \tag{4}$$

If banks can hold reserves against deposits irrespective of the location of the deposit, condition (4) becomes:

$$\frac{d(R_A + R_B)}{dD_A} = \frac{d(R_A + R_B)}{dD_B}. \tag{5}$$

The decline in total reserves held against deposits in $A$ is just offset by the increase in total reserves held against deposits in $B$. This would be true if the reserve ratios held against deposits in $A$ or $B$ are the same.

In the absence of reserve requirements, condition (5) holds if banks are indifferent about where they hold reserves against their deposits. Banks must then be able to draw on their reserve accounts at both central banks to meet their payments obligations in either region, i.e., there must be no artificial impediments to cross-border payments and transaction costs must be similar to the cost of intraregional payments. Furthermore, since interregional deposit flows may involve flows between different banks, banks must have the same desired reserve ratio regardless of their location. To ensure that all banks in the MU have the same borrowing opportunities at the central banks, this requires either that no central bank lend money to commerical banks or that all central banks conduct lending operations with commercial banks regardless of their location or that each central bank lend only to banks located in its own region at terms equal to those of all other central banks. Since central banks will lend to banks from other regions only if they are sure about their creditworthiness, the second option requires that the standards of prudential supervision and regulation of banks be sufficiently harmonized across the MU. In fact, these standards would have to be uniformly strict enough to satisfy the most risk-averse central bank. In contrast, such harmonization is not necessary in the third case.

Condition (5) does not imply that required reserve ratios be the same in both regions. For example, if central banks impose reserve requirements on deposits banks have in their region and reserves can be counted against the requirement regardless of where they are held, condition (5) may be met even if the central banks apply different ratios, provided that the resulting reserve requirement for the total deposit volume in the MU is not binding, i.e., is less than the desired reserves. In particular, some central banks may impose reserve requirements while others do not. Only when total reserve requirements are binding, does condition (5) demand equalization of required reserve ratios.

If the demand for reserves at the central bank in $A$ is independent of the deposits at banks in $B$ and vice versa, such that

$$\frac{dR_A}{dD_B} = \frac{dR_B}{dD_A} = 0, \tag{6}$$

then condition (4) requires that the change in reserves held at $CB_A$ match the change of reserves held at $CB_B$, such that

$$\frac{dR_A}{dD_A} = \frac{dR_B}{dD_B}. \tag{7}$$

Restriction (6) could be the result of significant barriers to cross-border payments in the union. Alternatively, banks may be obliged to hold reserves against deposits in $A$ at $CB_A$ and similarly for deposits in $B$. Money markets are then less integrated, and a flow of deposits from $A$ to $B$ requires a flow of reserves in the same direction. Under such circumstances, desired reserves will be the same only if the two central banks harmonize borrowing terms tightly, i.e., $z_A = z_B$, regardless of the degree of harmonization of regulatory standards. Furthermore, if reserve requirements are binding in at least one region, they must be the same throughout the union.

In conclusion, a given degree of efficiency can be achieved either by harmonizing lending conditions and reserve requirements at central banks in disintegrated money markets or by harmonizing prudential and regulatory standards in perfectly integrated money markets.

*One vs. Multiple Currencies: Credibility and Financial Stability*

In a completely credible MU, perfect money market efficiency does not require the adoption of a common currency. It is compatible with having different currencies in the two regions and even with restricting legal-tender laws to regional currency. If the exchange rate between the two currencies is credibly fixed, and the national central banks swap assets through a common balance sheet operation [Kenen (1992)], the distinction between $A$ money and $B$ money, as regards the operation of monetary policy, is equivalent to the distinction between bills of large and small denomination. The asset swap between the central banks implies that payments between them involve merely bookkeeping operations and require no trading of assets in the financial markets. However, the least efficient setup of an MU is a multiple-currency one. When the participating central banks refuse to swap their assets and use interventions in the foreign exchange market to peg their rates, exchange rate fixity requires interest rate parity between assets denominated in different currencies and traded in disintegrated markets. Condition (4) then demands an extremely high degree of policy coordination, since changes in regional demand for reserves must be precisely offset by changes in the regional supply of reserves. Very detailed rules for coordinating central bank interventions would be necessary to achieve this, which are unlikely to be implementable in practice.

The choice between a single-currency and a multiple-currency monetary union becomes an important issue, however, when the MU suffers from imperfect credibility: a multiple-currency MU will exhibit more financial instability than will a single-currency MU and impede full market integration.[3] To see the point, consider a bank located in $A$ holding loans and deposits denominated in both $A$ and $B$ currencies. For simplicity, assume that the bank holds no reserves at $CB_B$. Let $L$ be the market value of the bank's loan portfolio, and let $F$ be its total deposits, both including interest accruals; let $n$ be the bank's ratio of nonborrowed reserves to deposits; let $p$ be the perceived probability of a breakdown of the MU; and let $e$ be the post-MU exchange rate between $A$ currency and $B$ currency. Normalizing the MU exchange rate to one and assuming that $A$ currency appreciates after the breakdown implies that $e < 1$. Finally, let $g = L_B/L$ express the share of assets denominated in $B$ currency in the bank's portfolio; let $f = F_B/F$ express the ratio of $B$ currency deposits at the bank; and assume that $f < g(1 - n)$, i.e., that deposits at banks in $A$ are predominantly denominated in $A$ currency.

We assume that depositors have knowledge of the bank's balance sheet, including the relevant currency denomination of all assets and liabilities. However, depositors cannot infer the location of the bank's depositors and borrowers from that data. Therefore, depositors in a multiple-currency MU can assess the actual ratios $g$ and $f$ and, hence, the post-MU value of the bank's portfolio. In contrast, depositors in a single-currency MU have no information about the post-MU currency composition of the bank's balance sheet; hence they cannot make decisions depending on the expected post-EMU value of the bank.

Depositors will run on a bank when they perceive that the market value of its assets is insufficient to cover their deposits. In a multiple-currency MU, a run occurs if

---

[3] It is often argued that the multiple-currency MU is per se less credible than the single-currency MU, since the former entails a lower cost of seceding from the union than does the latter. Cohen (1993) argues that this claim is not supported by the historical experience with monetary unions.

$$k^* = E\left[\frac{1-p(1-e)g}{1-n-p(1-e)f} \cdot \frac{L}{F}\right] < 1, \tag{8}$$

where the expectation $E$ is with respect to the stochastic variables $L$ and $F$, i.e., where the expectation incorporates the loan and the liquidity risks of the bank. In contrast, in a single-currency MU, the condition for a run on the bank is

$$k = E\left[\frac{1}{1-n} \cdot \frac{L}{F}\right] < 1. \tag{9}$$

Several things are noteworthy. First, the fact that $A$ currency deposit holders care about the bank's ability to cover their deposits in $A$ currency means that a run occurs at larger ratios of assets to deposits than with a single currency. The multiple-currency MU thus produces greater financial instability. Second, the bank's exposure to runs depends on the share of deposits in $B$ currency relative to total deposits. This means that banks have an incentive to price-discriminate against $B$ currency deposits: the credibility problem creates an inefficiency in the deposit market of a multiple-currency MU. Third, given $L$, $F$, and $f$, $k^*$ decreases as the share of loans denominated in $B$ currency increases, as the post-MU exchange rate falls, and as the credibility of the MU deteriorates. The vulnerability of banks in country $A$ is the greater, the more $A$'s currency is expected to appreciate after the breakdown and the larger the share of $B$-denominated loans in their portfolios. This implies that countries enjoying persistent current account surpluses in a multiple-currency MU face a rising risk of bank runs. Furthermore, banks have an incentive to discriminate against $B$ currency assets, so the credibility problem also results in a loan market distortion.

As a result, given the loan and liquidity risks of the banking industry, a multiple-currency MU has more need of lender-of-last-resort interventions, especially in those countries whose currencies are deemed strong after the breakdown of the union and which have lasting current account surpluses. Furthermore, the central banks in a multiple-currency MU have an incentive to introduce regulations forcing banks to curtail their maximum exposure to loans denominated in other currencies. Thus, a lack of credibility limits the degree of financial markets integration a MU can achieve.

### STRUCTURING POLICY DECISIONS: MONETARY STRATEGIES IN THE EMU

Once its operation has begun, the ECB must formulate and implement a monetary strategy, that is, a set of policy objectives and ways to achieve them. One way to define monetary policy objectives for the EMU is to adopt EC-wide aggregates of prices and income as the target variables for monetary policy. For example, the ECB objective of "price stability" could be defined as a zero or small increase in the European price level, i.e., the cost of a European commodity basket.

Alternatively, the ECB could set targets for the individual national aggregates and derive the EMU objective by simply adding these up to an EC average.

The difference between these two approaches becomes important when real shocks to the EMU demand relative price adjustments. Continuing our example, let $\pi_U$ be the union inflation rate, $\pi_A$ the change in the price level in $A$, and $q_B$ the change in the ratio of $B$'s to $A$'s output prices, so that

$$\pi_U = \pi_A + \alpha q_B, \tag{10}$$

where $\alpha > 0$ is $B$'s relative weight in the union price level. If MU monetary policy aims at controlling $\pi_U$, prices may adjust freely in $A$ and $B$ to accommodate relative price changes. With $q_B = 0$, this is equivalent to pursuing two identical national target rates of inflation. Otherwise, a decentralized objective requires more information to predict the relative price changes.

More important, the two approaches have different political economy implications. A decentralized approach creates inflation differentials in the MU; consequently, the distribution of the adjustment cost to a relative price change becomes an explicit policy choice. Consider a real shock demanding a relative price adjustment of $q_B = 4$ percent. To achieve price stability in Europe, say, $\pi_U = 1$ percent, prices must change in $A$ by $\pi_A = 1 - 4\alpha$ percent, which is negative for $\alpha > 0.25$. With a decentralized objective, this requires that $CB_A$ announce a deliberately deflationary policy to ensure EMU price stability, while $CB_B$ is "allowed" to inflate by $\pi_B = 5 - 4\alpha$ percent. One may reasonably expect that the public and the government in $A$ will perceive that country $A$ bears a larger burden of adjustment in such a situation and will put political pressure on $CB_A$ for a higher price increase. Even a central bank largely independent from government will find it hard to resist such pressures.

The September 1992 ERM shakeup illustrates this point. Adjustment to German union required a real appreciation of the deutschmark [von Hagen (1993)]. However, the Bundesbank was not willing to accept the German price level increase implied by fixed exchange rates and moderate inflation in the other ERM countries. At the same time, the U.K. and Italy did not accept the deflation required by a fixed deutschmark exchange rate and low German inflation. In the end, therefore, those two countries decided to leave the system.

Thus, monetary authorities will find it hard to accept national inflation targets of zero or below in the bargaining process leading up to a set of policy objectives for the EMU. In any case, to make EMU inflation consistent with inflation differentials, the decentralized approach is likely to produce higher MU inflation than would the centralized one. Alternatively, the central banks may try to enforce equal rates of price change in all parts of the union, that is, to force the economies to adjust through quantity changes rather than relative price changes. The real performance of the MU will be worse, therefore, with decentralized than with centralized policy objectives.

A similar choice between centralization and decentralization arises for the regional structure of central bank operations in the MU. In a centralized setting, all monetary operations are delegated to a single institution, such as the Federal Reserve Bank of New York, which executes all open market operations for the Federal Reserve System. In a decentralized setting, in contrast, monetary operations are conducted by different central banks. If decentralized operations are oriented to a single union operating target, such as a short-term interest rate or a common reserve aggregate, close coordination and continuous mutual information sharing among the central banks is necessary to avoid policy errors. In contrast, coordination and mutual information sharing are less important if a sufficient degree of market segmentation ensures a stable link between national central bank actions and national operating targets and limits policy spillovers into other markets, requiring only that national operating targets be derived from an overall union target in a consistent way. Thus, a decentralized operating structure would be easier to implement with a limited degree of market integration; the adoption of such a setup would raise the probability that the EMU would preserve significant market distortions.

Furthermore, while a centralized policy objective can be pursued with centralized or decentralized operations, decentralized objectives require decentralized operations and therefore a minimum degree of market segmentation. Finally, a multiple-currency MU seems a more natural setting for decentralized objectives. To ensure a reliable link between national monetary aggregates and policy targets, this also would require a minimum degree of segmentation in the deposit markets to limit currency substitution.

To summarize, a broad menu of choices in two dimensions – the financial market environment and decisionmaking structures – is available to the EC in setting up the EMU. These choices are characterized by important interdependencies. Suppose that the EC decides to adopt a set of national policy objectives. Monetary policy operations will then likely be decentralized, since this is more consistent with the assignment of responsibilities of national objectives to national authorities than centralized operations, and the single currency will no longer be a relevant choice. The degree of market integration must then be low – all the more so, the less the use of the national instruments is coordinated. Finally, regulatory standards must be relatively high to preserve financial stability, but require little coordination.

If the EC adopts a union policy objective instead, there are more choices and possibilities left in the other dimensions. Here, a choice between a single-currency and a multiple-currency union is possible. Decentralized operations in a multiple-currency setting require some regulatory barriers, however, leading to a lower degree of money market integration. A high degree of market integration requires close coordination of regulatory arrangements, but leaves a choice of close or loose coordination of policy instruments. In sum, the decision for or against a union approach to policy objectives and monetary operations is critical, since

TABLE 1   DEGREE OF USE OF MONETARY POLICY INSTRUMENTS

| | Belgium | Denmark | Germany | Greece | Spain | France | Ireland | Italy | Netherlands | Portugal | U.K. |
|---|---|---|---|---|---|---|---|---|---|---|---|
| Operations with individual intermediaries in domestic market | H | H | H | L | H | H | H | I | H | L | L |
| Central bank discretion over quantity | I | I | I | N | H | H | H | I | I | H | H |
| Central bank discretion over borrowing cost | H | H | H | N | H | H | H | I | I | H | H |
| Operations in domestic market | H | L | H | N | L | L | I | H | I | H | H |
| Central bank discretion over quantity | I | L | L | L | I | I | I | H | I | H | H |
| Central bank discretion over cost of liquidity | H | H | H | H | H | H | H | L | L | N | N |
| Forward foreign exchange operations | N | L | L | L | I | L | L | N | H | H | H |
| Degree of sterilization | L | L | L | L | I | I | L | N | L | N | I |
| Operations with treasury (volume) | L | L | L | L | I | I | L | H | L | I | N |
| Limits of treasury access to overdraft | I | H | H | H | L | L | H | L | I | I | H |
| Operations in government securities at issue | N | N | N | H | H | N | H | H | H | H | H |
| Open market operations in government securities | I | N | L | L | H | H | H | H | N | H | H |
| Reserve requirements | N | N | I | I | L | L | I | H | N | H | N |

*Sources:* Padoa-Schioppa and Saccomanni (1992); Neumann and von Hagen (1992).
*Note:* H: high; I: intermediate; L: low; N: none.

it will determine subsequent decisions with regard to the financial markets environment in Europe.

Agreement on a common union policy objective and centralized operations would be facilitated if the national central banks already followed similar strategies to pursue similar objectives today. However, this is far from true. As is shown in Table 1, with regard to their monetary policy instruments, EC central banks today are variations of two basic models. The Bank of England model is a central bank conducting mostly outright purchases and sales in the domestic open market and almost no direct transactions with domestic banks. The Bundesbank model is a central bank engaged almost exclusively in lending and other operations with domestic banks.[4] The central banks of France, Denmark, Belgium, Spain, and the Netherlands are closer to the latter, while the central banks of Italy, Portugal, and Ireland are closer to the former model. Reserve requirements are of varying significance. The central banks of Belgium, Denmark, the Netherlands, and the U.K. do not use them at all any more. Where reserve requirements are large, central banks pay interest on them. While some central bankers regard reserve requirements as critical for monetary control [Schlesinger (1992a, 1992b)], others stress their adverse implications for the competitiveness of the banking system [Leigh-Pemburton (1992)]. Most central banks use their instruments to target some money market interest rate in their daily operations.[5]

As is shown in Table 2, central bank involvement in banking regulation also varies considerably. Only the Danish central bank has no regulatory functions at all. In contrast, the central banks of Greece, Spain, Ireland, Italy, and Portugal all have broad regulatory responsibilities, mainly in the sense of limiting banking activities.

The central banks' role in deposit protection is limited in all EC countries.[6] Garber and Weisbrod (1990) and Folkerts-Landau and Garber (1992) point to the importance of the central bank's lender-of-last-resort function in financial markets with high degrees of securitization. The need for a lender of last resort varies substantially in the EC, since the U.K. today has a high degree of securitization, Germany maintains a low degree, and France and Italy have recently moved toward more securitization.

In sum, current arrangements in the EC do not point to a "natural" choice of a policy framework or regulatory environment.

---

[4]Note that we classify repurchase agreements according to their economic function, i.e., loans to domestic banks collateralized with securities.

[5]See Kneeshaw and van den Bergh (1989), Batten et al. (1990), and Artis and Lewis (1991) for the U.K.; see Melitz (1992) for France, and Neumann and von Hagen (1992) for Germany.

[6]The Maastricht agreement limits the ECB's role in this area to a purely executive and advisory one. A widely shared view holds that central banks should be involved actively in regulation [e.g., Folkerts-Landau and Garber (1992); Padoa-Schioppa and Saccomanni (1992)], because serving as lenders of last resort, they should be able to control their own exposure to payments crises. The main counterargument is that financial regulation should be clearly separated from monetary policy functions to avoid the temptation to use the former for short-run policy goals.

TABLE 2  CENTRAL BANK INVOLVEMENT IN BANKING SUPERVISION

|  | Belgium | Denmark | Germany | Greece | Spain | France | Ireland | Italy | Netherlands | Portugal | U.K. |
|---|---|---|---|---|---|---|---|---|---|---|---|
| Regulation | L | N | I | E | E | I | E | E | E | E | E |
| Authorization | N | N | N | E | E | I | E | E | E | E | E |
| Prudential supervision | N | N | I | E | E | E | E | E | E | E | E |
| On-site control | L | N | L | E | E | E | E | E | E | E | I |
| Sanctions | N | N | N | E | E | E | E | E | E | E | E |
| Deposit protection | I | N | N | N | N | N | E | I | E | N | I |
| Memo: Nonbank supervision | N | N | I | I | E | E | E | E | E | E | N |

*Source:* Padoa-Schioppa and Saccomanni (1992).
*Note:* E: extensive; I: intermediate; L: low; N: none.

## WELFARE IMPLICATIONS OF ALTERNATIVE SCENARIOS OF EMU

Table 3 singles out three basic scenarios. The first is characterized by a union policy objective, centralized operations, a single currency and a high degree of money market integration. Regulatory standards would be uniform in the EMU but could be set relatively low. The second scenario is characterized by a union policy objective, decentralized central bank operations, multiple currencies and a medium degree of money market integration. It resembles the proposal of the Delors Report (1989). Neither the use of national policy instruments nor banking regulation requires intense coordination. In the third scenario, national policy objectives prevail, with decentralized central bank operations, multiple currencies, and a minimal degree of money market integration. This is just a tighter version of the "New EMS" [Giavazzi and Spaventa (1990)] that lasted until September 1992. Therefore, it largely preserves the status quo: national central banks would remain almost intact and maintain their traditional ways of monetary policy.

The first scenario maximizes the achievable degree of market integration and minimizes the need for money and capital market distortions. In this sense, it maximizes EMU market efficiency and, among the three scenarios, is best in an expected-welfare sense. However, it also maximizes uncertainty in the early phase of the EMU. Monetary policymaking would require reliable information about the empirical links between central bank instruments and operating targets and between operating targets and union policy objectives. Recent research [Kremers and Lane (1990, 1992); Barr (1992); Artis (1992)] notwithstanding, little will be known initially about these issues. Thus, the first scenario pairs high expected welfare with high variance of outcomes.

TABLE 3   THREE SCENARIOS OF EUROPEAN MONETARY UNION

|  | Scenario 1 | Scenario 2 | Scenario 3 |
|---|---|---|---|
| Definition of policy objective | Union | Union | National |
| Monetary policy operations | Centralized | Decentralized | Decentralized |
| Currency arrangement | One | Many | Many |
| Degree of money market integration | High | Medium | Low |
| Regulation | Uniform but low standards of regulation | Heterogeneous, closely coordinated central bank instruments; heterogeneous, high and coordinated regulatory standards | Heterogeneous, closely coordinated central bank instruments; heterogeneous, uncoordinated regulatory standards |

The second scenario implies a lower degree of market integration and therefore produces a lower expected welfare level than that of the first scenario. But it also yields less uncertainty, since the existing links between central bank instruments and operating targets remain largely intact. The main additional source of uncertainty is the link between operating targets and the union policy objective. The third scenario yields the lowest expected welfare level, but minimizes uncertainty relative to the status quo.

One might suggest that in order to reduce initial monetary policy uncertainty in the EMU, the EC should initially adopt an arrangement like the third scenario and later proceed to the most efficient one. However, the third scenario would yield little guidance for the transition to the first, since it would preserve market segmentation and therefore impede the very learning processes necessary to discover the empirical link among a single European currency, the central bank instruments for its control, and a union policy objective. Such a transition would therefore do little to reduce the uncertainty involved in the final step to a single currency and a unified monetary strategy. Instead, the inefficiencies of the third scenario would only keep the public from enjoying the benefits of a fully integrated currency area and thus diminish the political support for the EMU in its early phase.

Facilitating the immediate introduction of the first scenario would require successful reputation-building of the ECB in the early phase of the EMU. Since policy outcomes are uncertain, the ECB would have to convince the public of its firm commitment to price stability if the initial annual rates of price change were above the target rates because of policy errors. Successful reputation-building would be facilitated by clear institutional arrangements that left no doubt about the independence of the ECB, nonpartisan appointments to the ECB council to guarantee the personal independence of the council members, and a transparent operative structure to allow the public to monitor and understand ECB monetary strategies.

In view of these requirements, the role of the EMI becomes critical. In commenting on pre-EMU monetary policy, the EMI would have to educate the public about the future policy objectives and the importance of central bank independence to achieve a high performance. In the preparation of operating procedures, the EMI would have to minimize the need for experimenting with new procedures after the start of the EMU.

The comparison of these three scenarios indicates that a welfare ranking of alternative EMU arrangements depends critically on the degree of risk aversion assumed. Clearly, a risk-neutral decisionmaker would adopt the first scenario, and the most risk-averse decisionmaker would adopt the third scenario.

POLITICAL ECONOMY ISSUES IN THE TRANSITION TO THE EMU

The preceding argument suggests that "conservative" decisionmakers would most likely prefer the third scenario. Here, again, the role of the EMI is critical, since it will be dominated by central bankers, who will tend to favor conservative, status quo–based solutions. Thus, Jean-Jacques Ray, the chairman of the council of central bank vice presidents, affirmed the intention of the EMI not to establish a union policy objective before EMU: "The EMI has no ambition to set a joint monetary target for the EC as a whole during the second stage of EMU" [VWD (1992)]. Helmut Schlesinger, the current Bundesbank president, described the task of the EMI as follows:

> Now already – in the Committee of Central Bank Governors and the more so in the EMI – the coordination of monetary policy is being and will be implemented through the orientation at national monetary targets. This is a good exercise for the ECB to come. ...
> The single European currency – whatever its name will be – must earn its credibility right from the beginning. Therefore, it will be good to let a greater period of time pass by between stage IIIA (12 currencies) and stage IIIB (a single currency). [Schlesinger (1992b)]

Schlesinger's statements clearly show a bias against the first scenario and in favor of preserving national money markets and policy targets.

In the political debate leading up to the Maastricht agreement, the Bundesbank's fierce opposition prevented any transitional arrangement that would transfer monetary policy authority from the national central banks to new EC institutions before the start of the EMU.[7] The specific transition path devised in Maastricht, including the setup of the EMI and the assurance that it would be dominated by national central bankers, may be regarded as a compromise between the political leaders, who were interested in the EMU primarily as a first step toward a European political union, and the central bankers, led by the Bundesbank, who were interested in maintaining as much of the current system for as long as possible. This suggests that the EMI's bias in favor of a relatively inefficient, undesirable EMU was a price the political leaders were willing to pay to allay the Bundesbank's opposition to the EMU.

The EMI's choice of a particular scenario for the EMU will depend heavily on the solution to the membership question that the Maastricht agreement left open. A core group of central banks in the EC – those of Belgium, Germany, Luxembourg, the Netherlands, and since the mid-1980s, France – have built up reputations as central banks committed to price stability in the past. They will be reluctant to give up their brand names entirely and join in a first-scenario EMU if it includes less reputable central banks in Europe. As long as the membership question is unsolved and the latter have a reasonable chance to join, this core group will prefer a solution that allows them to retain a maximum degree of autonomy and the option to dissolve the EMU at a relatively low cost – i.e., an arrangement with decentralized objectives and operations, multiple currencies, and a low degree of market integration. Thus, the likelihood of winding up with the most efficient EMU may depend on restricting membership to the core group.

---

[7]Such possibilities had still been envisioned, for example, in the Delors Report (1989, e.g., para. 57).

One way to achieve this would be to adopt a "two-speed" approach, allowing the core countries to form the EMU as soon as technically possible. Obviously, the noncore members of the EMI will not accept such a solution readily, since they stand to gain relatively more from a fully integrated EMU including all EC members. It seems unlikely that those members could override the opposition of the core group to this solution in the EMI council. However, it is equally unlikely that the core group could muster a majority in favor of a small EMU through the EMI council, either. As a result, the core group will settle for an all-EC EMU, as characterized by the third scenario. Unless the membership of the EMI council is changed during the transition to allow for a core EMU, the conflict of interest between the core group and the remaining countries reinforces the EMI's bias toward advocating an inefficient EMU.

In view of this, the possibility of an EC enlargement during the transition to the EMU becomes relevant. So far, four of the six European Free Trade Area (EFTA) countries – Austria, Finland, Switzerland, and Sweden – have applied for EC membership.[8] Norway is expected to apply soon. These candidates are today close to satisfying the entry conditions for the EMU laid out in the Maastricht agreement. Austria would come in as an immediate member of the core group, while the others would be closer to this group than to the periphery members.

Assuming that Denmark and the U.K. ratify the Maastricht agreement but are exempted from the EMU, the number of countries in the current EC necessary to form a majority for EMU purposes is six (of ten), one more than the core group. If the EC is enlarged before 1997, however, the required majority will be eight (of fifteen with Switzerland or fourteen without Switzerland). The core group plus Austria and two new members could form such a majority. Thus, EC enlargement would raise the probability of an early EMU.[9]

In view of this, the incentives to support enlargement differ among the current EC members. Those expected to meet the convergence criteria and preferring an early, core group EMU will favor enlargement before 1997. Others will opposite it, fearing that an early EMU would relegate them to a second-tier status and would rob them of bargaining power vis-à-vis the core countries. Indeed, once the core group EMU is formed, it could maintain a low-inflation policy without concern about the effect on the slow-track countries.[10]

In such a scenario, the EC enlargement would raise the requirement of policy adjustment for the "periphery", delaying the entry of these countries to Stage Three of the EMU. Consequently, these countries will vote against the enlargement

---

[8]The Swiss application has been called into question by the referendum rejecting Swiss membership in the EC-EFTA association on December 6, 1992. However, the Swiss government, which favors membership, decided not to revoke the application in order to keep all options open (*Frankfurter Allgemeine Zeitung*, Dec. 6, 1992).

[9]See also Qvigstad (1992, p. 22); and CEPR (1992, p. 33).

[10]Alesina and Grilli (1994) argue that this would, indeed, be the equilibrium result of ECB council decisions in a two-track EMU.

unless they receive adequate compensation. It is important to note, therefore, that the applicant countries would be net contributors to the EC budget because of their above-average per-capita incomes, their high degree of agricultural protection, and the absence of severe regional problems in these countries. Italy, Spain, Portugal, Ireland, and Greece, on the other hand, would be the main beneficiaries of an increased EC budget. Thus, it is possible to compensate the peripheral countries for accepting an enlargement and the subsequent core group EMU by creating additional structural and regional funds paid for by additional receipts of the EC from the new members. Such was essentially the deal struck at the December 1992 Edinburgh summit: the peripheral countries consented to the opening of membership negotiations with the new applicants after the core countries had agreed to an increase in the ratio of the EC budget to EC GNP of about 12 percent after 1994.

The advantages of such bargains between the core and the periphery are twofold. First, they facilitate the implementation of an EMU corresponding to the first scenario. Since this scenario maximizes the expected welfare from the EMU, it would raise the probability of success of Stage Three. Second, before entering a stability-oriented EMU, monetary and fiscal policies in the peripheral countries could concentrate on achieving sufficient price stability and fiscal stability. In the meantime, the core group would gain experience in the implementation of a unified EMU monetary policy. To the extent that this experience could be brought to bear when the peripheral countries joined the EMU, the two-speed approach would reduce information costs to these countries.

Alesina and Grilli (1994) fear that under a two-speed approach, the core group would never agree to enlarge for EMU later on. The EC would then be stuck with an incomplete EMU for a long time. This risk can be reduced by lowering the power the EMU members would have to keep the gates closed. One way to do that would be to introduce more realistic and specific entry conditions for EMU than the current criteria, which leave ample room for discretion and interpretation and hence for the core group to defend their exclusive EMU. Institutionally, the ECB's General Council, which will comprise both participants and nonparticipants in the EMU, will ensure that the latter have a voice in EMU matters even with a two-speed approach.

The main political opposition against a two-speed EMU, including that from the German government, stems from the fear that it might lead to the design of a "Europe à la carte, with different obligations for different members" (Martin 1994). For example, the Danish government won four opt-out clauses at Edinburgh, allowing it to opt out of EMU and the common European policies in matters of defense, the interior, and law. In this broader context, the choice of a particular EMU scenario could be the result of a deal involving other areas of EC policies. Such a deal may be desirable to overcome opposition against a fully integrated EMU by making concessions in other policy fields and to enable the EC to adopt the efficient solution; it may be undesirable if the deal involves accepting an inefficient EMU.

Such deals, however, require that EC governments be able to make agreements involving the design of the EMU, which is impossible under the Maastricht agreement since the agreement grants the EMI the same independence as that accorded to the ECB. Thus, the main point of EMI independence may be to prevent such deals. One may speculate that in the negotiations leading up the Maastricht agreement, the core central banks insisted on EMI independence to prevent deals forcing them to accept a highly integrated EMU that included countries less committed to price stability. However, the impossibility of "buying off" the opposition against an efficient, core group EMU also lowers the chances that Europe will get the best possible EMU in the foreseeable future.

## CONCLUSIONS

The Maastricht agreement leaves many options to design the monetary and financial market institutions of the EMU. The institutional choices at hand carry important implications for the welfare of the future EMU. There is a hierarchy of decisions to be made, starting with the structure of policy objectives, followed by the structure of operating regimes, the choice of a single-currency or a multiple-currency EMU, and the degree of market integration. The best EMU would come with a union policy objective, centralized operations, a single currency, and perfect money market integration. However, the characteristics of the EMI and the political forces in the transition process create a bias toward an inefficient EMU with decentralized policy objectives and operating procedures, multiple currencies, and little market integration. In a revision of the Maastricht agreement, the EC should consider an institutional alternative to the EMI that would be more conducive to efficient outcomes.

Proponents of the EMU have long regarded monetary integration as a vehicle for political integration. Our discussion points to an internal contradiction of this view: as long as political integration has not been established, EC-wide objectives of monetary policy will be hard to communicate to the public in the various member nations and will be unlikely to be condoned by them. Accepting hardship at home to pursue European price stability requires solidarity among EMU citizens and their identification with a common cause. Lacking political integration to back a common monetary policy, the EMU risks settling for merely a set of tightly coordinated, yet essentially national monetary strategies. Public dismay with the resulting inefficiencies may well become an obstacle to the political integration of Europe.

## REFERENCES

Alesina, Alberto, and Vittorio Grilli, 1994, On the feasibility of a one-speed or multispeed European Monetary Union. This volume.

Artis, Michael, 1992, Monetary policy in Stage Two of EMU (CEPR discussion paper).

Artis, Michael, and Mervyn Lewis, 1991, *Money in Britain: Monetary policy, Innovation and Europe* (Philip Allan, London).

Barr, David, 1992, The demand for money in Europe: Comment on Kremers and Lane. IMF *Staff Papers* 39, 718–729.

Batten, Dallas, Michael Blackwell, In-Su Kim, Simon E. Nocera, and Yuruzu Ozeki, 1990, *The conduct of monetary policy in the major industrial countries: Instruments and operating procedures.* IMF Occasional Paper. no. 70 (International Monetary Fund, Washington, D.C.).

Buttiglione, Luigi, and Alessandro Prati, 1990, La scelta del meccanismo di collocamento dei titoli di Stato: analisi teorica e valutazione dell'esperienza italiana. *Contributi all'analisi economica del Servizio Studi,* no. 6 (Banca d'Italia, Rome).

CEPR, 1992, *Is bigger better? The economics of the EC enlargement* (Center for Economic Policy Research, London).

Cohen, Benjamin J., 1994, Beyond EMU: The problem of sustainability. This volume.

Delors Report, 1989, Report on Economic and Monetary Union in the European Community. *Report of the Committee for the Study of Economic and Monetary Union in the European Community* (EC, Luxembourg).

Folkerts-Landau, David F. I., and Peter M. Garber, 1992, The European Central Bank: a bank or a monetary policy rule? NBER Working Paper no. 4016 (National Bureau of Economic Research, Cambridge, Mass.).

Fratianni, Michele, and Jürgen von Hagen, 1992, *The European Monetary System and European Monetary Union* (Westview, Boulder, Colo.).

Garber, Peter, and Steven Weisbrod, 1990, Banks in the market for liquidity. NBER Working Paper no. 3381 (National Bureau of Economic Research, Cambridge, Mass.).

Giavazzi, Francesco, and Luigi Spaventa, 1990, The new EMS, in: Paul de Grauwe and Lucas Papdemos, eds., *The European Monetary System in the 1990s* (Longman, London).

Kenan, Peter, 1992, *EMU after Maastricht* (Group of 30, Washington, D.C.).

Kneeshaw, J. T., and P. van den Bergh, 1989, Changes in central bank money market operating procedures in the 1980s. BIS *Economic Papers* 23 (Bank of International Settlements, Basel).

Kremers, Jeroen J. M., and Timothy D. Lane, 1990, Economic and monetary integration and the aggregate demand for money in the EMS. IMF *Staff Papers* 37, 777–805.

———, 1992, The demand for money in Europe: Reply to Barr. IMF *Staff Papers* 39, 730–737.

Leigh-Pemberton, Robin, 1992, Monetary aspects of European integration. *Auszüge aus Presseartikeln* 14, 4–9.

Martin, Lisa L., 1994, International and domestic institutions in the EMU process. This volume.

Melitz, Jazques, 1992, France, in: Michele Fratianni and Dominick Salvatore, eds., *Monetary policy in developed economies* (Greenwood, Westport, Conn.).

Neumann, Manfred, and Jürgen von Hagen, 1992, Monetary policy in Germany, in: Michele Fratianni and Dominick Salvatore, eds., *Monetary policy in developed economies* (Greenwood, Westport, Conn.).

Padoa-Schioppa, Tommaso, and Fabrizio Saccomanni, 1992, Agenda for Stage Two: Preparing the monetary platform. CEPR Occasional Paper no. 7 (Center for European Policy Research, London).

Qvigstad, Jan Fredrik, 1992, Economic and Monetary Union (EMU): A survey of the EMU and empirical evidence on convergence for the EC and the EFTA countries. Occasional paper no. 36 (European Free Trade Association, Geneva).

Santomero, Anthony, 1990, European banking post-1992: Lessons from the United States, in: Jean Dermine, ed., *European banking in the 1990s* (Basil Blackwell, Cambridge, Mass.).

Schlesinger, Helmut, 1992a, Stabilität unserer Währung heute und in einer Europäischen Währungsunion. *Auszüge aus Presseartikeln* 35, 1–5.

———, 1992b, Auf dem Weg zur Europäischen Währungsunion: Die Rolle des Europäischen Währungsinstituts. *Auszüge aus Presseartikeln* 38, 1–4.

von Hagen, Jürgen, 1993, Monetary union, money demand and money supply: A review of the German monetary union. *European Economic Review* forthcoming.

VWD, 1992, Pressekonferenz anläßlich der Vorstellung des ersten Jahrasberichts des Ausschusses der Präsidenten der Zentralbanken der EC-Mitgliedstaaten am 14. April 1992 in Basel. *Auszüge aus Presseartikeln* 30, 1–2.

# 8

## BEYOND EMU: THE PROBLEM OF SUSTAINABILITY

### Benjamin J. Cohen

A common currency, as envisioned in the Maastricht treaty, is thought to be the surest way to "lock in" commitments to monetary cooperation among sovereign states. But historical evidence suggests otherwise. Comparative analysis of six currency unions demonstrates that while economic and organizational factors are influential in determining the sustainability of monetary cooperation, interstate politics matters most. Compliance with commitments is greatest in the presence of either a locally dominant state, willing and able to use its influence to sustain monetary cooperation, or a broad network of institutional linkages sufficient to make the loss of monetary autonomy tolerable to each partner.

STUDENTS of international monetary relations have long understood that in a world of high capital mobility and separate national currencies, governments are perennially confronted with a problematic trade-off between the goal of exchange rate stability and a desire for monetary policy autonomy. For both economic and political reasons, stability of exchange rates is frequently sacrificed for the presumed benefits of policy autonomy. Even among countries formally committed to monetary cooperation, joint interests are often compromised by the pursuit of independent national objectives. Can otherwise unreliable commitments to international monetary cooperation be reliably "locked in" in some way? Logically, the surest solution would seem to be a common currency (or its equivalent, a formally irrevocable freezing of exchange rates), where individual monetary sovereignty is – in principle – permanently surrendered by each partner government. For the members of the European Community (EC), this is the strategy envisioned in the now-troubled Maastricht treaty for Economic and Monetary Union (EMU). At the start of Stage Three, supposedly to begin no later than January 1, 1999, exchange rates among participating countries' currencies are to be inalterably fixed "and the ECU will become a currency in its own right" (Article 109), formally abrogating monetary policy autonomy at the national level.

Historical evidence, however, suggests that not even a common currency or formal exchange rate union may suffice to lock in the gains of monetary cooperation. The nineteenth and twentieth centuries have seen a number of examples of currency integration among nominally sovereign governments. But

This article has benefited from the constructive comments and suggestions of Barry Eichengreen, Jeffry Frieden, John Woolley, and an anonymous reader. The research assistance of Kelley Hwang and Stephen Reti is also gratefully acknowledged.

not all these schemes, however firm their members' commitments in principle, have ultimately proved to be sustainable in practice. Europeans have no assurance that EMU, if ever enacted, would indeed be genuinely irreversible. Even should they get to Stage Three, they will not be able to breathe easily. The risk would still remain, so long as member states retain political independence, that one or another government might eventually choose to reassert its monetary autonomy. Getting to Stage Three, therefore, is only half the battle. Even beyond Stage Three, care would have to be taken to ensure that joint interests were not once again jeopardized by unilateralist impulses.

The purpose of this paper is to explore some of the key conditions that may be influential in determining the sustainability of interstate commitments to monetary cooperation.[1] The discussion is based on a comparative analysis of six historical examples of formal currency unions among sovereign national governments,[2] including three that still exist (the Belgium-Luxembourg Economic Union, the CFA Franc Zone, and the East Caribbean Currency Area) and three that ultimately failed (the East African Community, the Latin Monetary Union, and the Scandanavian Monetary Union). Although the circumstances of the six cases obviously correspond most closely to the ambitions of EMU beyond Stage Three, the experiences involved arguably are of more general relevance, providing insight into the challenges facing EC members in their efforts to achieve monetary integration even short of full implementation of the Maastricht treaty. Three separate sets of variables are considered: economic, organizational, and political. Systematic evaluation of the six cases demonstrates the disproportionate importance of political factors in determining the durability of commitments to monetary cooperation. Economic and organizational factors matter, but interstate politics appears to matter most of all.

The discussion begins with a brief outline of the analytical approach to be followed and a short factual description of each of the six historical cases. Comparative analysis of the six cases follows, with the principal implications of the discussion summarized in the concluding section.

### THE ANALYTICAL APPROACH

The central analytical issue, the problem of sustainability, stems directly from the persistent risk of time-inconsistency inherent in the familiar trade-off between exchange rate stability and monetary policy autonomy: the possibility that so long as governments attach importance to monetary independence, they may be

---

[1]For the purposes of this article, sustainability – the dependent variable in my analysis – is defined solely in terms of longevity. Other possible criteria by which to judge the "success" or "failure" of commitments to monetary cooperation (e.g., impacts on price stability, employment, or economic growth) are not directly considered.

[2]In this article the terms "currency union" and "monetary union" will be used interchangeably and are defined to encompass both forms of currency integration – common currencies as well as their equivalent, formal exchange-rate unions.

tempted to renege on prior commitments to policy cooperation. Such risks are omnipresent, of course, in relations between sovereign states, where compliance mechanisms are by definition normally weak or nonexistent. The challenge is to find some compliance mechanism that will actually work – some institutional arrangement that will truly deter governments from breaking bargains that turn out to be inconvenient. Logically, the surest solution would seem to be a common currency or its equivalent, since in principle such policy commitments are supposed to be permanent and irrevocable. But not even the most formal currency union may prove to be sustainable in practice. The question thus is, What are the key conditions that determine the sustainability of commitments to monetary integration among sovereign national governments?

Neither economists nor political scientists have directly addressed this question.[3] The voluminous literature by economists on the theory of "optimum currency areas" clearly does involve issues of international monetary integration. Most of the work in this area, however, focuses on factors thought to be decisive in a government's selection of an exchange rate policy at a particular point in time – ordinarily posed as a binary choice between the two extremes of independent floating or absolute pegging – rather than on conditions that ensure the durability of exchange rate commitments, once made, over time. The voluminous literature by political scientists on "international regimes" – more or less formally institutionalized agreements to promote cooperation between nations – might also be thought to have applications to the question at hand. But in fact relatively little has been written specifically about the particular type of regime represented by a monetary or currency union.

For the purposes of this paper, therefore, an alternative, more historical approach is taken, drawing in part on the separate literatures on optimum currency areas and international regimes, but relying mainly on a methodology of comparative case study analysis. My discussion focuses on six relatively recent examples of formal currency unions among sovereign governments: the Belgium-Luxembourg Economic Union (BLEU), CFA Franc Zone (CFA), the East African Community (EAC), the East Caribbean Currency Area (ECCA), the Latin Monetary Union (LMU), and the Scandinavian Monetary Union (SMU). Though this sample of a half-dozen currency unions is by no means exhaustive,[4] it does illustrate a wide range of relevant experience, including three unions that have been successfully sustained as well as three that, ultimately, were not; three among

---

[3]For a rare exception, see Graboyes (1990).

[4]Other examples could be cited, including a number of smaller states that have long relied on a foreign government's money for domestic legal tender, such as Liberia and Panama (which use the U.S. dollar), Liechstenstein (the Swiss franc), Kiribati (the Australian dollar), and Namibia (the South African rand), as well as currency areas encompassing political federations that are currently in a state of dissolution, such as Yugoslavia and the former Soviet Union. There are also additional examples in the nineteenth century, e.g., the Austro-German Monetary Union established in 1857 by Austria and the members of the German Zollverein, which lasted until the Austrian-Prussian War of 1866. None of these cases, however, seem as relevant to the case of EMU as the six selected for the purpose of this article.

industrial nations as well as three among less developed economies; two that have featured a common currency, at least for a time, as well as four that have relied exclusively on formally linked national or regional currencies; and two from the nineteenth century as well as four from the twentieth. None of the six cases replicates EMU's circumstances precisely, of course. But collectively, the sample does provide instructive lessons for the EC as it tries to maintain the momentum of monetary integration.

The discussion is structured in terms of three sets of possible explanatory variables: economic, organizational, and political. The economic factors considered are drawn directly from optimum currency area theory and include such characteristics as wage and price flexibility, factor mobility, geographic trade patterns, the openness of economies, and the nature and source of potential payments disturbances. Organizational factors include legal provisions concerning the issuing of currency and monetary management: Are national currencies replaced by a single common currency? Are national central banks replaced by a single monetary authority? Political factors, which for purposes of brevity are limited here to considerations of interstate politics, include the presence or absence of either a locally dominant state (a "hegemon") or a sufficiently dense network of institutional linkages to successfully preserve a currency union over time. Although in a short article analysis can be impressionistic at best, the evidence does seem clearly to suggest that political conditions are most instrumental in determining the sustainability of monetary cooperation among sovereign governments.

## THE SAMPLE

The basic facts of the six cases are summarized in the appendix.[5] The two nineteenth-century examples, the Latin Monetary Union and Scandinavian Monetary Union, both originated at a time when national currencies were still largely based on metallic monetary standards; their subsequent histories were largely conditioned by the broader evolution of money systems at the time, from bimetallism to the gold standard and from full-bodied metal coinage to various forms of paper currency. Each was built on a standardized monetary unit (respectively, the franc and the krone) issued by nominally autonomous central banks; and each was successfully sustained as a distinct currency area, despite recurrent difficulties in the case of the LMU, until effectively terminated with the outbreak of World War I.

The immediate purpose of the Latin Monetary Union, formed by Belgium, France, Italy, and Switzerland in 1865, was to standardize existing gold and silver

---

[5]Comprehensive sources on these cases are not easy to come by. The best available introductions are as follows: for the Latin Monetary Union and Scandinavian Monetary Union, Nielsen (1933) and Bartel (1974); for the Belgium-Luxembourg Economic Union, Meade (1956); for the CFA Franc Zone, Boughton (1993); for the East African Community, Letiche (1974); and for the East Caribbean Currency Area, McClean (1975).

coinages. (Greece adhered to the terms of the LMU in 1868, though it did not become a formal member until 1876.) A de facto regional monetary bloc had already begun to coalesce earlier as a result of independent decisions by Belgium, Greece, Italy, and Switzerland to adopt currency systems modeled on that of France, with the franc (equivalently, the lira in Italy and the drachma in Greece) as their basic monetary unit. Starting in the 1850s, however, serious Gresham's law-type problems developed as a result of differences in the weight and fineness of silver coins circulating in each country. The LMU established uniform standards for national coinages, and by making each member's money legal tender throughout the union, it effectively created a wider area for the circulation of a harmonized supply of metal coins. LMU members as a group were distinguished from other countries by the reciprocal obligation of their central banks to accept one another's currencies without limit. Although subsequently subjected to considerable strain by the global depreciation of silver beginning in the late 1860s, which led eventually to a suspension of silver coinage by all the partners (effectively transforming the LMU from a bimetallic standard into what came to be called a "limping gold standard"), the union managed to hold together until the generalized breakdown of monetary relations during World War I. Following Switzerland's decision to withdraw in 1926, the LMU was formally dissolved in 1927.

The Scandinavian Monetary Union, too, was designed to standardize existing coinages, although, unlike the LMU, the SMU was based from the start on a monometallic gold standard. Formed in 1873 by Sweden and Denmark, and joined by Norway two years later, the SMU established the krone (crown) as its uniform monetary unit, with national currencies permitted full legal circulation in all three countries. As in the LMU, members as a group were distinguished from others by the reciprocal obligation to accept one another's currencies without limit; also as in the LMU, mutual acceptability was initially limited to gold and silver coins only. In 1885, however, the three members went further, agreeing to accept one another's bank notes and drafts as well, thus facilitating free intercirculation of all paper currency and resulting eventually in the total disappearance of exchange rate quotations among the three moneys. By the turn of the century, the SMU had come to function, in effect, as a single region for all payments purposes, until relations were disrupted by the suspension of convertibility and floating of individual currencies at the start of World War I. Despite subsequent efforts during and after the war to restore at least some elements of the union, particularly after the members' return to the gold standard in the mid-1920s, the agreement was finally abandoned, following the global financial crisis of 1931.

The third European case is the Belgium-Luxembourg Economic Union, which, unlike the Latin and Scandinavian Unions, still remains in force more than seven decades after its inception in 1922. Following severance of its traditional ties with the German Zollverein after World War I, Luxembourg elected to link itself commercially and financially with Belgium, agreeing to a comprehensive economic union including a merger of their separate money systems. Reflecting the partners' considerable disparity of size (Belgium's population is roughly thirty times that of Luxembourg), Belgian francs under BLEU form the largest part of the money stock in Luxembourg as well as in Belgium, and alone enjoy full status as legal tender in both countries. Only Belgium, moreover, has a full scale central bank. The Luxembourg franc is issued by a more modest institution, the Luxembourg Monetary Institute; is fixed in supply; and serves as legal tender only within Luxembourg itself. Despite the existence of formal joint decisionmaking bodies, Luxembourg in effect exists as an appendage of the Belgian monetary system.

The three remaining examples all involve developing countries, and all had their origins in earlier colonial arrangements. In the case of Francophone Africa, the roots of today's CFA Franc Zone go back to 1945, when the French government decided to consolidate the diverse currencies of its various African dependencies into one money, "le franc des Colonies Françaises d'Afrique" (CFA francs). Subsequently, in the early 1960s, as independence came to France's African empire, the old colonial franc was replaced by two new regional currencies, each conveniently named to preserve the CFA franc appellation: for the seven members of the West African Monetary Union,[6] "le franc de la Communauté Financière Africaine", issued by the Central Bank of West African States; and for the six members of the Customs and Economic Union of Central Africa, "le franc de la Coopération financière en Afrique centrale", issued by the Bank of Central African States.[7] Though each of the two currencies is legal tender only within its own region, the two are equivalently defined and are jointly managed, in cooperation with the Bank of France, as integral parts of a single monetary union.

The roots of the remaining two examples, both involving former dependencies of the United Kingdom, go back to the British tradition of using administrative currency boards to manage colonial financial affairs. In the Caribbean, Britain's monetary legacy has proved remarkably successful. The British Caribbean Currency Board, first created in 1950, evolved first into the East Caribbean Currency Authority, in 1965, and then into the East Caribbean Central Bank, in 1983, issuing one currency, the East Caribbean dollar, to serve as legal tender for all seven participating states. Embedded in a broadening network of related agreements among the same governments, such as the East Caribbean Common Market and the Organization of Eastern Caribbean States, the East Caribbean Currency Area has functioned without serious difficulty since its establishment in 1965.

---

[6]Benin, Burkina Faso, Côte d'Ivoire, Mali, Niger, Senegal, and Togo. The West African Monetary Union was formally established in 1962.

[7]The six members of UDEAC are Cameroon, the Central African Republic, Chad, Congo, Equatorial Guinea (a former Spanish colony), and Gabon. Although UDEAC was not formally established until 1964. BEAC had already been created earlier, in 1959. In the central region BEAC issues an identifiable currency for each member, although all these currencies are similar in appearance, carry the same name ("franc de la Coopération financière en Afrique centrale"), and are legal tender throughout the region. This is in contrast to the western region, where BCEAO issues a single currency that circulates freely in all seven UMOA states.

In East Africa, on the other hand, Britain's colonial legacy ultimately failed, despite creation of an East African Currency Board as early as 1919 to administer a single money, the East African shilling, for the territories of Kenya, Tanganyika (later Tanzania), and Uganda. The three colonies also inherited a customs union, dating from 1923, as well as a variety of other common services for railways, harbors, air transport, and the like. However, once independence arrived in the region (for Tanganyika in 1961, for Uganda in 1962, and for Kenya in 1963), joint institutions, including the common currency, quickly began to break apart; and by the middle of the decade, all three countries had decided to install central banks and national currencies of their own to replace the East African shilling. In 1967 a fresh attempt was made to preserve some semblance of monetary union in the context of the newly established East African Community and Common Market, which specifically provided for free exchange among the separate national currencies at par. Unfortunately, although the EAC provided, for the first time, a formal legal basis for the integration of the three economies, regional cooperation continued to disintegrate; and by the mid-1970s, all vestiges of the economic community had completely disappeared. The final nail in the monetary union's coffin came in 1977, when all three governments extended existing exchange controls to one another's currencies.

## ECONOMIC FACTORS

Manifestly, the historical record is varied. Three of the six unions in my sample (BLEU, CFA, and ECCA) may fairly be described as successful, having been sustained, apparently without undue strain, for decades. One other (EAC) disintegrated almost as soon as its members gained political independence and can only be judged a failure. And the remaining two (LMU and SMU) elicit a mixed verdict: each functioned more or less effectively for up to half a century (a not inconsiderable achievement), yet ultimately proved unsustainable. What might explain these strikingly contrasting experiences?

To begin, we might consider some of the factors that have come to figure centrally in the literature on optimum currency areas.[8] The standard approach of this branch of theory is to identify criteria that seem most likely to influence a government's choice of a currency regime, emphasizing in particular conditions affecting the costs of balance-of-payments adjustment with either a pegged or a floating exchange rate. Most prominently, these variables are thought to include wage and price flexibility, resource mobility, geographic trade patterns, the openness of economies, and the nature and source of potential payments disturbances. Countries are expected to prefer mutually fixed exchange rates to the extent that prices and wages are flexible, factors of production are mobile, trade interdependence is high, economies are open, and shocks tend to be

---

[8]For recent surveys, see Kawai (1987), Masson and Taylor (1992), esp. pp. 43–50, and Tavlas (1992).

synchronized rather than asymmetric. Might these characteristics be key ones in determining the sustainability of mutually fixed rates as well?

A firm answer to this question is precluded by inadequate statistics and knotty measurement problems. Little evidence appears to exist in our six cases, however, to suggest a decisive role for any of the economic factors cited, either singly or in combination. Wage and price flexibility, for instance, might help to explain why the Latin and Scandinavian unions were able to last as long as they did, before being effectively dismantled at the start of World War I. Certainly we know that costs and prices were far less "sticky" in the nineteenth century than they have tended to become in the twentieth. But nothing in the available data indicates that wages or prices are any less flexible in East Africa, where currency integration failed, then in Francophone Africa or the East Caribbean, where it has so far succeeded. Likewise, factors of production, particularly capital, were undoubtedly fairly mobile in the two nineteenth-century unions, as well as in BLEU since its inception; but there seems no reason to suppose that resources were any less mobile in East Africa before the breakup of the EAC than in either the CFA Franc Zone or ECCA.

Trade patterns are particularly unhelpful, indicating no systematic relationship at all with the outcomes of our six cases. Only in two instances, LMU and BLEU, has trade interdependence been comparatively high. In both cases, however, the pattern has been distinctly asymmetrical, reflecting primarily the economic importance of the dominant member (respectively, France and Belgium).[9] In the SMU, the volume of reciprocal trade was not particularly small but was greatly overshadowed by relations with two outside powers, Britain and Germany.[10] And in the three cases involving developing countries, intragroup trade has barely existed at all. In typical postcolonial fashion, most of the African and Caribbean states do far more business with industrial countries than they do with each other [Masson and Taylor (1992, p. 46)].

Nor are the remaining variables any more helpful. All of the members of the CFA Franc Zone and ECCA, for instance, have relatively open economies, a characteristic that is supposed to favor exchange rate pegging rather than floating; and the same may be said of the two members of BLEU as compared with their immediate trading partners. Among these three successful unions, however, only in the East Caribbean do balance-of-payments disturbances tend, for the most part, to be synchronous (owing to the members' common reliance on the same narrow range of exports, mainly sugar and bananas). In both Francophone Africa

[9]In the case of the Latin Monetary Union, according to early estimates by Mulhall (1899), France accounted for 34 percent of the aggregate foreign trade of Italy during the 1880s; 25 percent of Belgium's; and 22 percent of Switzerland's. France's biggest trading partners, on the other hand, were Great Britain and Germany rather than the other LMU members. Similarly, while Belgium accounts for as much as one-third of Luxembourg's foreign trade, Luxembourg is too small to provide an important market or source of supply for Belgium.

[10]While reciprocal trade within SMU, according to Mulhall's (1899) estimates for the 1880s, amounted on average to less than 15 percent of members' aggregate foreign trade, Britain and Germany each accounted for as much as one-third of the total.

and BLEU, production structures are rather more diverse, causing external shocks to affect regional partners in quite different ways, a characteristic that is supposed to favor floating rather than pegging. The three former members of the East African Community had open economies and a history of relatively symmetrical payments shocks, yet ultimately chose to go their separate ways. This stands in sharp contrast to the Latin and Scandinavian unions, which for several decades managed effectively to stay together, despite the fact that by the standards of the nineteenth century, most of their members had relatively diversified economies and were subject to rather more differentiated external disturbances.

In short, for every one of the characteristics conventionally stressed in the literature on optimum currency areas, contradictory examples exist – some cases conform to the expectations of theory, and others do not.[11] No factor seems sufficient to explain the outcomes in our sample. This is not to suggest that economic factors are therefore unimportant. Clearly they do matter insofar as they tend, through their impact on adjustment costs, to ease or exacerbate the challenge of monetary cooperation. But, equally clearly, more was going on in each of the six cases than can be accounted for by such variables alone. Other things matter too.

### ORGANIZATIONAL FACTORS

Some of those other things might have been organizational in nature. It is evident that formal legal provisions concerning the issuing of currency and monetary management have differed sharply in the six cases. Only in two cases have members relied exclusively on a common currency – in the East Caribbean and, before the mid-1960s, in East Africa. In all the others, including EAC after 1967, arrangements have featured national or regional currencies, with varying degrees of formal linkage. Monetary institutions have also varied, involving a single central authority in two cases (once again, ECCA and EAC before the mid-1960s), two regional authorities in one case (CFA), and separate national agencies in all the others (BLEU, EAC after 1967, LMU, SMU). Might these organizational differences explain the contrasting experiences in our sample?

In principle, organizational differences should matter insofar as they affect the net costs of compliance or defection. Recent theoretical literature on transaction costs and institutions emphasizes the key role that organizational design can play in promoting credible commitments by structuring arrangements to match anticipated incentive problems [North (1990)]. From this perspective,

---

[11]These results should not come as any surprise, since it is well known that the characteristics themselves are often inherently contradictory. (For example, should a small open economy subject to severe external shocks prefer a fixed exchange rate because of its openness or a flexible rate to insulate itself from outside disturbance?) Moreover, empirical tests of the determinants of exchange rate choices by individual governments persistently find that in many instances, variables that are supposed to matter in theory often fail to do so in practice. For a recent survey, see Edison and Melvin (1990).

creation of a single currency would appear to be superior to a formal linkage of national currencies because of the higher barriers to exit involved: the greater cost of reintroducing an independent currency and monetary authority.[12] This is also the conclusion of recent policy discussions of alternative strategies for EMU, which have directly addressed the relative merits of full currency integration versus a formal multicurrency union in the EC [Gros and Thygesen (1992, pp. 230–233); von Hagen and Fratianni (1994)]. Most analysts have expressed doubt that a system retaining existing currencies and central banks, however solemn the political commitments involved, would be as credible as a genuine common currency, precisely because the risk of reversibility would presumably be greater. The implication, in effect, is that compliance mechanisms are likely to be weaker to the extent that national governments continue to exercise any control at all over either the price or the quantity of their currency. Hence, one might expect to find in the historical evidence a direct correlation between the degree of centralization of a currency union and its practical sustainability over time.

For Griffiths (1992), this is the key reason why the Latin Monetary Union ultimately could not be sustained. Many of the recurrent difficulties experienced by the LMU in the decades before World War I were directly attributable to the bloc's decentralized structure, which permitted each country's central bank to continue to pursue its own domestic policy objectives. Once the global depreciation of silver began in the late 1860s, several members (in particular, Italy) succumbed to the temptation to increase the amount and circulation of their silver coinage, in effect attempting to extract additional seigniorage gains at the expense of their partners (especially France, where many of the silver coins ended up). To hold the union together, the members first restricted and finally, in 1878, suspended all silver coinage (other than token money), transforming the LMU into a "limping gold standard"; in 1885, at the behest of France, they also added a liquidation clause requiring any state wishing to leave the group to redeem all of its silver held by other member governments in gold or convertible paper. Even before the financial disruptions of World War I, it was clear that little sense of common interest remained among the union members, other than a mutual desire to avoid a potentially costly dissolution. In Griffiths's words: "This demonstrates the rather obvious point that a monetary union based on independent central banks is potentially unstable" (1992, p. 88).[13]

But what, then, of the Scandinavian Monetary Union, which was also based on independent central banks, yet managed to function far more smoothly than did the LMU in the decades before World War I? Or the Belgium-Luxembourg

---

[12]The same point is also suggested by a companion theoretical literature on the economics of investment under uncertainty, which stresses the importance of "sunk costs" as a barrier to exit: the greater the cost of starting up again in the future, the lower is the incentive to abandon an unprofitable investment in the present. See, e.g., Dixit (1992).

[13]Graboyes (1990, p. 9) concurs, arguing that the fatal flaw of LMU was that it "decreed a common monetary policy but left each central bank to police its own compliance".

Economic Union and CFA Franc Zone, both of which are still sustained successfully despite the absence of either a common currency or a single central institution? Or the East African Community, where neither a common currency nor a central authority proved an effective barrier to disintegration? Once again, contradictory examples abound. And while, once again, this is not to suggest that such factors are therefore unimportant – clearly, the degree of organizational centralization does matter insofar as it influences the potential cost of exit – it is equally clear that there is still something else at work here. That something, of course, is politics.

## POLITICAL FACTORS

From the perspective of interstate politics, two characteristics seem to stand out as crucial to the outcomes in my sample. One, suggested by traditional "realist" approaches to the analysis of international relations, is the presence or absence of a dominant state willing and able to use its influence to keep a currency union functioning effectively. The other, suggested by an "institutional" approach of the sort stressed by Martin (1994), is the presence or absence of a broader constellation of related ties and commitments sufficient to make the loss of monetary autonomy, whatever the magnitude of prospective adjustment costs, seem basically acceptable to each partner. The first calls for a local hegemon and is a direct reflection of the distribution of power among states.[14] The second calls for a well developed set of institutional linkages and reflects, more amorphously, the extent to which a genuine sense of solidarity and community exists among all the countries involved – what Keohane and Hoffmann (1991, p. 13) call a "network" form of organization, in which individual units are defined not by themselves but in relation to one another. Judging from my six cases, it seems clear that one or the other of these two factors is necessary for the sustainability of currency integration among sovereign states. Where both are present, they constitute a sufficient condition for success. Where neither is present, currency unions tend to fail.

Consider, for example, the Belgium-Luxembourg Economic Union, by far the most durable among the six cases. Both of these necessary political characteristics have long been evident in BLEU. As indicated earlier, Belgium from the beginning has been the acknowledged dominant partner, in effect making all important monetary decisions for both countries. While the two states officially retain separate national agencies to issue currency, de facto there is just one central authority. In the words of Donald Hodgman: "Luxembourg . . . has no capacity for an independent monetary policy . . . . Through mutual agreement these powers

---

[14]On a broader global scale, the role of a hegemonic power in promoting and enforcing monetary cooperation has been frequently explored. Notable recent contributions include Eichengreen (1990, ch. 11); Walter (1991); and Frieden (1992).

are exercised by the Belgian authorities'' (1974, p. 23).[15] In part, the success of the arrangement reflects Belgium's willingness as well as ability to shoulder the responsibility of managing the partners' joint affairs. And in part it reflects the broader constellation of reciprocal ties shared by the two countries, in BLEU itself, as well as in related regional groupings, such as Benelux and the EC. These states clearly share both a network of institutional linkages and a sense of common interest sufficient to make a permanent commitment to monetary cooperation attractive, or at least not intolerable, to both sides.

At the opposite extreme lies the East African Community, the least durable among the six cases. Here, neither of the necessary political characteristics was ever in much evidence. Certainly, there seems to have been little feeling of solidarity among the three countries, despite a legacy of common colonial services and institutions. Much more influential was a pervasive sensitivity to any threat of encroachment on newly won national sovereignty. Once independent, each of the three new governments eagerly chose to concentrate more on building state identity than on preserving regional unity; a hardening of national priorities and interests, compounded by sharp divergences of ideology and political style, quickly eroded any commitment to continued economic cooperation [Rothchild (1974); Ravenhill (1979)]. Nor was there any locally dominant power willing and able to use its influence to counteract these disintergrative forces. Within the EAC, Kenya was the most advanced in terms of industrial development but was still too poor to act the role of hegemon. Instead of using its leading position in intraregional trade to promote community ties, Kenya was understandably tempted instead to exploit its privileged position for its own ends, thus aggravating rather than moderating strains and tensions among the members (Mugomba, 1978; Mbogoro, 1985). Beyond the EAC, Britain, as the former colonial ruler, might have continued to provide support to regional institutions – but burdened by its own economic difficulties, it chose instead to distance itself from its former East African dependencies. The dismantling of the sterling area in the early 1970s removed the last barrier to pursuit of independent monetary policies by each government [Graboyes (1990, p. 10)]. Given these inauspicious political circumstances, it is hardly surprising that the EAC failed as totally as it did.

The importance of a local hegemon is demonstrated by two other cases in addition to BLEU, namely, the CFA Franc Zone and the Latin Monetary Union – ironically, both involving France. The durability of CFA, most sources agree, is clearly attributable to the pivotal role played by the Bank of France in underwriting (in effect, subsidizing) Francophone Africa's joint currency arrangements [Boughton (1993)]. Although not formally a member of the CFA,

[15]Only once has the Luxembourg government attempted to assert its own will. In 1935, following a 28 percent devaluation of the Belgian franc, Luxembourg also devalued, but by only 10 percent, unilaterally changing the partners' bilateral exchange rate from par to a ratio of 1.25 Belgian francs per Luxembourg franc [Meade (1956, pp. 14–16)]. Over the long haul, however, that solitary episode has proved to be the exception rather than the rule. Since restoration of parity during World War II, Luxembourg has willingly followed Belgium's lead on all monetary matters.

France exercises a decisive influence through the so-called operations accounts maintained by CFA's two regional central banks at the French Treasury, into which each is obliged to deposit the bulk of its foreign exchange reserves. In return, France enhances the credibility of the CFA franc by guaranteeing its convertibility at a fixed price. Monetary discipline is implemented through rules affecting access to credit from the Bank of France as well as through the firm peg of the CFA franc to the French franc, which has remained at a ratio of 50:1 for more than four decades. CFA countries also share some sense of community, of course, reflecting their common language and colonial experience and institutionalized in a network of related regional agreements. But there seems little doubt that, for better or worse,[16] the role of France is paramount.

The local hegemony of France was decisive also in the Latin Monetary Union, albeit in rather less benign form. In this case, the power of the dominant state was used in a much more narrowly self-interested fashion, first to promote French monetary leadership and later to prevent a costly dissolution, rather than in any more positive sense to underwrite relations, as in CFA (or to manage relations collegially, as Belgium does in BLEU). As Griffiths (1992) has written, "Throughout its evolution the influence of France remained ever-present, extracting concessions from its fellow members. Although only one country out of four [sic], France remained dominant, reflecting the realities of its economic and political power". Even before LMU was formally established, France's influence (based mainly on its dominating position in regional trade) was evident in the willing adaptation to its currency system by its smaller trading partners. French influence was further evident in the bloc's initial decision to base LMU on a bimetallic standard despite the objections of France's partners, all of whom would have preferred a monometallic gold standard instead [Bartel (1974, pp. 695-696)]. And it was certainly evident after the LMU was transformed into a "limping gold standard", when France resorted to a threat of penalities – formalized in the liquidation clause added at its behest in 1885 – to discourage member withdrawals that would have left the French with large holdings of irredeemable silver coins. But for this pressure from France, the LMU might have broken up well before the financial disruptions of World War I.

The importance of an institutionalized sense of community is also demonstrated by two other cases in addition to BLEU, namely, the East Caribbean Currency Area and the Scandinavian Monetary Union. Neither the ECCA nor the SMU could in any way be described as a hegemonic system. In the ECCA, the partners are all island microstates, comparably small and poor, and as in East Africa, they have been left more or less on their own by their former colonial master. In the SMU, Sweden may have been "first among equals", but it exercised nothing like the power that France enjoyed in the LMU. Nonetheless, both unions

---

[16]While for some authors [e.g., Boughton (1993)] the impact of France's role is, on balance, positive, promoting monetary discipline and stability, for others, the effect is clearly for the worse insofar as it perpetuates dependency, retards economic development, and reinforces income inequality. See, e.g., Yansane (1978–1979); Martin (1986); van de Walle (1991).

have managed to function reasonably effectively for long periods of time (the SMU until World War I; the ECCA, since its members' independence) for reasons that seem to be most directly related to the genuine feeling of solidarity shared by the members of each. In the East Caribbean, in contrast to East Africa, there has never been much value placed on separate sovereignties: identities have always been defined more in regional than in national terms, institutionalized in a whole network of related economic and political agreements. The ECCA, as one observer has noted, is just one part of a much broader effort by which these seven governments "have pooled their resources in a symbolic, symbiotic and substantive way with the aim of furthering their development" [Jones-Hendrickson (1989, p. 71)]. Likewise, the Scandinavian nations, unlike the members of the LMU, have long had a tradition of cooperation based on a common cultural and political background. In the words of Wendt, "Language, social life, administration, legislation, judiciary, poetry and literature, science, and many other aspects of life created bonds between these peoples who had been intimately linked for such a long and important period" (1981, p. 17). Given the density of existing ties, creation of a common currency system seemed not only natural but almost inevitable.

## IMPLICATIONS

What are the implications of all this for the sustainability of EC monetary cooperation under the Maastricht treaty? My analysis suggests that studies of currency integration that principally emphasize either economic variables [e.g., Masson and Taylor (1992)] or organizational characteristics [e.g. Griffiths (1992)] miss the main point. The issue is only secondarily whether the members of a monetary union meet the traditional criteria identified in the theory of optimum currency areas or whether monetary management and the issuing of currency happen to be centralized or decentralized. The primary question is whether there is likely to be either a local hegemon or a fabric of related ties with sufficient influence to neutralize the risk of time-inconsistency. Sovereign governments require incentives to stick to bargains that turn out to be inconvenient. The evidence from my historical sample suggests that these incentives may derive either from side-payments or sanctions supplied by a single powerful state or from the constraints and opportunities posed by a broad network of institutional linkages. One or the other of these political factors must be present to serve as an effective compliance mechanism.

More than two decades ago, economist Norman Mintz wrote:

> It has often been argued that the conditions under which monetary integration might reasonably be expected to succeed are very restrictive. In fact, these conditions appear no more restrictive than the conditions for the establishment of a successful common market. The major, and perhaps only, real condition for the institution of either is the *political will* to integrate on the part of prospective members. (1970, p. 33; emphasis added).

At one level, this conclusion might appear naive – yet another example of the economist's propensity to compress all the complexities of political process into the simple notion of political will. But at another level, Mintz shows profound insight, if "political will" is understood to refer to either the motivations of a local hegemon or the value attached to a common endeavor. These are in fact the main conditions necessary for success.

## REFERENCES

Bartel, Robert J., 1974, International monetary unions: The XIXth century experience. *Journal of European Economic History* 3, 689–704.

Boughton, James M., 1993, The CFA Franc Zone: Currency union and monetary standard, in: Anthony S. Courakis and George S. Tavlas, eds., *Monetary and financial integration* (Cambridge University Press, Cambridge).

Dixit, Avinash, 1992, Investment and hysteresis. *Journal of Economic Perspectives* 6, 107–132.

Edison, Hali J., and Michael Melvin, 1990, The determinants and implications of the choice of an exchange rate system, in: William S. Haraf and Thomas D. Willett, eds., *Monetary policy for a volatile global economy* (AEI Press, Washington, D.C.).

Eichengreen, Barry, 1990, Elusive stability: Essays in the history of international finance, 1919–1939 (Cambridge University Press, New York).

Frieden, Jeffry A., 1992, The dynamics of international monetary systems: International and domestic factors in the rise, reign, and demise of the classical gold standard, in: Jack Snyder and Robert Jervis, eds., *Coping with complexity in the international system* (Westview, Boulder, Colo.).

Graboyes, Robert F., 1990, The EMU: Forerunners and durability. *Federal Reserve Bank of Richmond Economic Review* 76, 8–17.

Griffiths, Mark, 1992, Monetary union in Europe: Lessons from the nineteenth century – an assessment of the Latin Monetary Union (unpublished).

Gros, Daniel, and Niels Thygesen, 1992, European monetary integration: From the European Monetary System to European Monetary Union (St. Martin's Press, New York).

Hodgman, Donald R., 1974, National monetary policies and international monetary cooperation (Little, Brown, Boston).

Jones-Hendrickson, S. B., 1989, Financial structures and economic development in the organisation of eastern Caribbean states. *Social and Economic Studies* 38, 71–93.

Kawai, Masahiro, 1987, Optimum currency areas, in: John Eatwell, Murray Milgate, and Peter Newman, eds., *The new Palgrave: A dictionary of economic theory and doctrine*, vol. 3 (Macmillan, New York).

Keohane, Robert O., and Stanley Hoffmann, 1991, Institutional change in Europe in the 1980s, in: Robert O. Keohane and Stanley Hoffmann, eds., *The new European Community: Decisionmaking and institutional change* (Westview, Boulder, Colo.).

Letiche, John M., 1974, Dependent monetary systems and economic development: The case of sterling East Africa, in: Willy Sellekaerts, ed., *Economic development and planning: Essays in honor of Jan Tinbergen* (International Arts and Sciences Press, White Plains N.Y.).

Martin, Lisa L., 1994, International and domestic institutions in the EMU process. This volume.

Martin, Guy, 1986, The Franc Zone, underdevelopment and dependency in Francophone Africa. *Third World Quarterly* 8, 205–235.

Masson, Paul R., and Mark P. Taylor, 1992, Issues in the operation of monetary unions and common currency areas, in: Morris Goldstein et al., *Policy issues in the evolving international monetary system* (International Monetary Fund, Washington, D.C.).

Mbogoro, D. A. K., 1985, Regional grouping and economic development: Some lessons from the East African integration scheme, in: W. A. Ndongko, ed., *Economic cooperation and integration in Africa* (CODESRIA, Dakar).

McClean, A., Wendell A., 1975, Money and banking in the East Caribbean Currency Area (Institute of Social and Economic Research, University of the West Indies, Kingston, Jamaica).

Meade, James E., 1956, The Belgium-Luxembourg Economic Union, 1921–1939: Lessons from an early experiment (International Finance Section, Princeton University, Princeton, N.J.).

Mintz, Norman N., 1970, Monetary union and economic integration (New York University Graduate School of Business Administration, New York).

Mugomba, Agrippah T., 1978, Regional organisations and African underdevelopment: The collapse of the East African Community. *Journal of Modern African Studies* 16, 261–272.

Mulhall, Michael G., 1899, The Dictionary of statistics, 4th ed. (Routledge and Sons, London).

Nielsen, Axel, 1933, Monetary unions, in: Encyclopedia of the social sciences, vol. 10 (Macmillan, London) 595–601.

North, Douglass C., 1990, Institutions and a transaction-cost theory of exchange, in: James E. Alt and Kenneth A. Shepsle, eds., *Perspectives on positive political economy* (Cambridge University Press, New York).

Ravenhill, John, 1979, Regional integration and development in Africa: Lessons from the East African Community. *Journal of Commonwealth and Comparative Politics* 17, 227–246.

Rothchild, Donald, 1974, From hegemony to bargaining in East African relations. *Journal of African Studies* 1, 390–416.

Tavlas, George S., 1992, The "new" theory of optimum currency areas (unpublished).

van de Walle, Nicolas, 1991, The decline of the Franc Zone: Monetary politics in Francophone Africa. *African Affairs* 90, 383–405.

von Hagen, Jürgen, and Michele Fratianni, 1994, The Transition to European Monetary Union and the European Monetary Institute. This volume.

Walter, Andrew, 1991, World power and world money (St. Martin's Press, New York).

Wendt, Frantz, 1981, Cooperation in the Nordic countries: Achievements and obstacles (Almqvist and Wiksell, Stockholm).

Yansane, Aguibou Y., 1978–1979, Some problems of monetary dependency in French-speaking West African states. *Journal of African Studies* 5, 444–470.

APPENDIX

| | Belgium-Luxembourg Economic Union (BLEU) | CFA Franc Zone (CFA) | East African Community (EAC) | East Caribbean Currency Area (ECCA) | Latin Monetary Union (LMU) | Scandinavian Monetary Union (SMU) |
|---|---|---|---|---|---|---|
| Date of origin | 1922 | 1959 | 1967 | 1965 | 1865 | 1873 |
| Membership | Belgium, Luxembourg | Benin, Burkina Faso, Cameroon, Central African Republic, Chad, Congo, Côte d'Ivoire, Equatorial Guinea (from 1985), Gabon, Mali (withdrew in 1962, rejoined in 1984), Niger, Senegal, Togo | Kenya, Tanzania, Uganda | Anguilla, Antigua and Barbuda, Dominica, Grenada (from 1967), St. Kitts-Nevis, St. Lucia, St. Vincent and the Grenadines | Belgium, France, Greece (from 1868), Italy, Switzerland | Denmark, Norway (from 1875), Sweden |
| Precursors | None | French franc zone (le franc des Colonies Francaises d'Afrique, 1945) | East African Currency Board (1919) | British Caribbean Currency Board (1950) | None | None |
| Currencies | Separate national currencies: Belgian franc, Luxembourg franc | Two regional currencies: franc de la Communauté financière Africaine and franc de la Cooperation financière en Afrique centrale (both called CFA francs) | Common currency (East African shilling) until 1965; then separate national currencies (shillings) | Common currency: East Caribbean dollar | Separate national currencies: Belgian franc, French franc, drachma, lira, Swiss franc | Separate national currencies: krone |
| Legal provisions | Belgian franc legal tender in both nations; Luxembourg franc legal tender in Luxembourg only | Each regional currency legal tender only in its own region | East African shilling legal tender in all members, until 1965; thereafter, national shillings exchanged at par | Legal tender in all members | Legal tender in all members | Legal tender in all members |
| Monetary institutions | Central bank (National Bank of Belgium) in Belgium; bank of issue (Luxembourg Monetary Institute) in Luxembourg | Two regional central banks: Central Bank of West African States (BCEAO) and Bank of Central African States (BEAC) | National central banks | Single central bank: East Caribbean Central Bank (established 1983; formerly the East Caribbean Currency Authority, established in 1965) | National central banks | National central banks |
| Related agreements | Benelux, European Community | West African Monetary Union (UMOA) and Customs and Economic Union of Central Africa (UDEAC) | None | East Caribbean Common Market (1968); Organization of East Caribbean States (1981) | None | None |
| Dissolution | Still in operation | Still in operation | 1977 | Still in operation | 1914–1927 | 1914–1931 |

# 9

## FISCAL POLICY AND EMU

### Barry Eichengreen

This chapter[1] takes stock of the literature on fiscal policy and European Monetary Unification and offers new evidence relevant to the debate. Following a critical review of the fiscal provisions of the Maastricht treaty, it considers the case for formal fiscal restraints and for fiscal federalism as a concomitant of monetary union. It concludes that the provisions of the treaty restraining fiscal behavior during Stage Two of the transition to monetary union are difficult to justify on any grounds. It argues that what the Maastricht treaty fails to say about fiscal policy is as significant as what it says. In particular, the treaty makes inadequate provision for fiscal federalism.

EUROPEAN MONETARY unification promises to transform the conduct of monetary policy in Europe. Under the envisioned Economic and Monetary Union (EMU) the separate monetary policies of the participating countries will be superseded by a single monetary policy upon the creation of the European Central Bank (ECB).[2] Less certain and more controversial are EMU's implications for fiscal policy. One view, advanced mainly by academics [e.g., Kenen (1969); Eichengreen (1993a)], emphasizes the need for fiscal flexibility to compensate for the loss of monetary autonomy. Proponents of this view point out that, because the national economies joined together in Europe's monetary union will continue to experience distinctive macroeconomic disturbances, once the option of an independent monetary response is foregone, the capacity to take stabilizing fiscal action will become all the more crucial. The opposing perspective, advanced mainly by government officials and incorporated into the Maastricht treaty on economic union [European Commission (1992)], emphasizes the importance of harmonizing and restraining fiscal policies to ensure the smooth operation of the monetary union. Allowing some EMU participants to run excessive budget deficits, in this view, threatens to distort intra-EMU real exchange rates, place upward pressure on interest rates, and subvert the ECB's commitment to price stability.

To reconcile these conflicting desires for budgetary autonomy and fiscal coordination, the Maastricht treaty instructs participating countries to coordinate their fiscal policies following guidelines established by the Council of

[1] An earlier version of this paper was published in Italian in *Stato e Mercato* (Winter, 1993). I thank Morris Goldstein and Geoffrey Woglom for data, Jeffry Frieden for comments, and Graham Schindler for research assistance.

[2] The word "participating" is critical, since not all signatories of the Maastricht treaty will necessarily join the monetary union. Who will participate is a complicated question that depends both on politics and on the appropriate interpretation of the treaty's "convergence criteria" governing entry.

Ministers. It specifies quantitative criteria (termed "reference values") against which the adequacy of fiscal performance may be judged. It vests existing and yet-to-be-created Community-level entities with responsibility for monitoring the fiscal conduct of member states, recommending adjustments, and sanctioning governments that fail to heed those recommendations. Whether these provisions are necessary and sufficient to ensure the pursuit of appropriate fiscal policies has emerged as a contentious issue in the debate over the Maastricht treaty.

Furthermore, the treaty makes no provision for fiscal federalism at the union level or for binding restraints on the debts and deficits of member states, both of which are identified by some commentators as essential concomitants of a smoothly functioning monetary union. Much discussion revolves around the question of whether these omissions are fatal flaws in the Maastricht blueprint.

This chapter takes stock of the literature on fiscal policy and EMU and offers new evidence relevant to the debate. The next three sections provide a critical review of the fiscal provisions of the Maastricht treaty; examine the case for formal fiscal restraints and present evidence on their effectiveness in an existing economic and monetary union, the United States; and present a parallel analysis of fiscal federalism. The concluding section returns to the implications of the findings for the EMU debate.

### FISCAL POLICY IN THE MAASTRICHT TREATY

The Maastricht treaty contains two classes of fiscal provisions: articles concerned with the conduct of fiscal policy during both the transition to monetary union (known in the language of the treaty as Stage Two) and monetary union itself (the so-called Stage Three), and articles that apply only to the latter phase.[3] In this section I argue that there is some justification for aspects of the "excessive deficits" procedures incorporated into the Maastricht treaty, although that justification may not be exactly the one the treaty's framers had in mind. Fiscal restrictions for Stage Three can be justified if one anticipates, under certain circumstances, a failure of monetary resolve on the part of the European Central Bank, but not if one has reason to be confident of the ECB's antiinflationary resolve. During Stage Two, in contrast, the excessive deficits procedures are difficult to justify on any grounds.

Stage Two commenced on January 1, 1994 (Stage One having begun on July 1, 1990). Member states are to abolish all restrictions on capital movements and to adopt multiyear programs designed to ensure the international convergence

---

[3] Useful introductions to these issues are Buiter, Corsetti, and Roubini (1993) and Goldstein and Woglom (1992).

of their public finances. They are to begin fortifying the independence of their central banks. In addition, members are to avoid "excessive deficits." Excessive deficits will be said to exist if the ratio of the planned or actual deficit of all levels of government exceeds 3 percent of GDP and in addition one of the following two criteria is not met: either the deficit ratio has not declined "substantially and continuously" to a level "close" to the 3 percent reference value, or that ratio cannot be regarded as "exceptional and temporary and . . . close to" the 3 percent threshold. A related precondition requires governments to avoid the accumulation of excessive debts. The ratio of total government debt to GDP will be said to be excessive if it exceeds 60 percent and is not "sufficiently diminishing and approaching the 60 percent level at a satisfactory pace." In the event of excessive deficits and/or debt accumulation under these definitions, the Commission, after taking into account the share of the deficit accounted for by capital expenditures and other relevant considerations, including the longer-term budgetary and economic position of the state, may declare that an excessive deficit exists, and so report to the Council of Ministers. The European Monetary Institute (EMI), a predecessor of the ECB set up at the beginning of Stage Two, is to collaborate with the Commission in reporting to the Council on the fiscal performance of the members.

The Council, after entertaining any observations that the member state wishes to offer, may then vote by qualified majority to confirm the Commission's determination that an excessive deficit exists. If it does, the Council will make confidential recommendations to the member state, with a view toward bringing that situation to an end within a specified period of time. If the Council subsequently determines that the member state has failed to take effective action in response to its recommendations within an appropriate period, the Council may make those recommendations public. The sanction implicit in such an announcement is that the member state will not qualify for admission to EMU at the outset of Stage Three.

In fact, the debt and deficit requirements comprise only one of four conditions that member states must satisfy to qualify for participation in EMU (the others concern the stability of exchange rates, the rate of inflation, and the level of interest rates). No later than December 31, 1996, the European Council must decide, by qualified majority vote, whether a majority of member states satisfy all four preconditions for participating in the monetary union; if they do, it may set a starting date for Stage Three. If the date for inaugurating Stage Three has not been set by the end of 1997, it will begin automatically on January 1, 1999 (so long as even a minority of member states satisfies the conditions).

The Council of Ministers is to coordinate the economic policies of the member states and to formulate "broad guidelines" for those policies. The treaty prohibits excessive deficits in Stage Three as well as in Stage Two, and the Council retains responsibility for assessing whether they exist. As in Stage Two, the council may submit recommendations to member states and, if the latter fail to take corrective action, make them public. Although member states not yet participating in EMU can be threatened with continued exclusion if they fail to take appropriate measures, other sanctions must be made available in the case of participants in the monetary union, since there is no provision for expelling them. In such cases, the Council may require the member state to submit a program of fiscal adjustment accompanied by an explicit timetable. If the country fails to do so, the Council may take steps to increase the difficulty for the member state in issuing bonds and securities, invite the European Investment Bank to reconsider its lending policy toward the country, require the member state to make noninterest-bearing deposits with the Community, and impose fines of "an appropriate size."

Is there a coherent rationale for this oversight of national fiscal policies? To put the point another way, why can't countries be relied upon to manage their fiscal affairs themselves?

Consider first the situation following the inauguration of monetary union. Economic and monetary integration creates a case for more closely "coordinating [national fiscal policies] within the Council" if such integration magnifies the international macroeconomic spillovers of national fiscal policies. This rationale has figured in some of the background papers to the Delors report and the Maastricht treaty [e.g. Emerson et al. (1990)]. But most theoretical and empirical studies of international fiscal transmission [e.g. Oudiz and Sachs (1984); Bryant et al. (1990)] conclude that the spillovers are both small and unlikely to be significantly magnified by further economic and monetary integration. An increase in public spending stimulates the absorption of foreign as well as domestic goods, which is a source of positive transmission; completion of the Single Market should strengthen this positive cross-border effect. At the same time, however, the higher domestic interest rates created by the increase in domestic public spending tend to raise interest rates abroad, which is a source of negative international transmission; since monetary union eliminates exchange risk and enhances the international integration of national financial markets, it should also strengthen this source of negative transmission. To the extent that the two effects are offsetting, further integration does not obviously strengthen the case for fiscal coordination.

This analysis ignores the implications for monetary policy of the change in fiscal incentives. But if economic and monetary integration magnifies the tendency for central bankers to monetize budget deficits, failure to restrain national fiscal policies may have inflationary consequences as well. Provisions for ascertaining the existence of excessive deficits and for sanctioning governments refusing to correct them could then be justified on these grounds.

Whether one believes that integration will create a bias toward excessive deficits, monetization, and inflation depends on the institutional setting and market structure one has in mind. Canzoneri and Diba (1991) model the problem in a particularly simple and appealing way. Starting from a benchmark world in which capital is immobile internationally and no exchange-rate stabilization agreement exists, they assume that deficit spending leads to the accumulation of debt that must be serviced through the imposition of distortionary taxes. Since capital is immobile in the benchmark model, all domestic debt will be held at home; only domestic interest rates will rise as a result of additional public spending, and only domestic residents incur the costs of additional distortionary taxes. In addition, so long as each country has its own money and no international arrangements for supporting national currencies exist, only domestic residents will incur the welfare costs of any inflation induced by domestic deficits. In deciding whether to use the inflation tax to help finance the government's deficit, an optimizing central bank would solve the Ramsey-Phelps optimal taxation problem, equalizing at the margin the costs of revenues raised with distortionary taxes and with seigniorage (where the cost of additional seigniorage is the deadweight loss associated with reductions in agents' money holdings due to inflation). Faced with a government engaged in high levels of spending and necessarily levying highly distortionary taxes, an optimizing central bank will rationally create additional inflation. Even so, a government concerned with the welfare of domestic residents should take into account the implications for future distortionary taxation and inflation of its current spending and set the level of government expenditure accordingly. It will balance, in other words, the benefits of its spending against the costs of the distortionary inflation and commodity taxes needed to finance it. In this benchmark world, there should therefore be no problem of excessive deficits, excessive monetization, and excessive inflation.[4]

But as capital becomes increasingly mobile internationally as a result of financial integration, interest rates will tend to move together at home and abroad. Deficit spending that drives up domestic interest rates will also drive up foreign interest rates as investors shift from assets with low yields to assets with higher ones. Some of the costs of additional spending by the domestic government will consequently be borne by foreign residents, since foreign governments will be forced to levy additional distortionary taxes to pay the increased interest charges on their outstanding debt. Individual governments have no

---

[4] This is the case only when the government's rate of time preference and taste for public goods is identical to the public's. As Canzoneri and Diba (1991) show, allowing government and private sector preferences to differ reintroduces the potential for inefficient levels of government spending, taxation and seigniorage. Note that while this setup presents no problems for the optimal conduct of monetary and fiscal policies, it may or may not be compatible with the maintenance of fixed exchange rates, one of the objectives of Stage Three of the Maastricht process (and, depending on one's interpretation of the treaty, Stage Two as well).

reason to take this international externality into account. In a noncooperative equilibrium, public spending will therefore be too high.[5]

When monetary union is added to the analysis, member states may have an even stronger incentive to spend and borrow excessively, insofar as they have reason to anticipate additional monetization of their deficits by the common monetary authority.[6] An additional ecu of public spending must still be financed by a fraction of an ecu of additional distortionary taxation and one minus that fraction of an ecu of additional seigniorage. But since the additional seigniorage revenues, raised through additional inflation, are now spread over a larger (unionwide) seigniorage tax base, their marginal costs are lower when viewed from the perspective of any one country. That country has an incentive to reduce taxes to the point where the welfare cost associated with the tax distortions thereby created fall to the reduced welfare cost of additional seigniorage. And an optimizing central bank, seeking to equate the costs of seigniorage and distortionary taxes at the margin, will raise its rate of debt monetization. In the new equilibrium, monetization and inflation will be increased as a result of the fact that national governments bear only a portion of the deadweight loss associated with central bank financing of their deficits. All participating governments can be expected to run larger deficits as a result.

This analysis, though based on a very particular set of assumptions, provides a coherent rationale for concern with the size of budget deficits in Stage Three.[7] The question is whether the excessive deficits procedures of the Maastricht

[5] Admittedly, this model is based on strong assumptions about international transmission. Canzoneri and Diba (1991), in the model from which this discussion is drawn, assume perfect substitutability of goods produced at home and abroad. In alternative models with imperfect substitutability, such as that of van der Ploeg (1989), fiscal policy in noncooperative equilibrium may be inadequately rather than excessively expansionary. If fiscal expansion leads to real appreciation (as it will upon relaxing the assumption of perfect substitutability), it will stimulate exports and increase employment in neighboring countries, swamping the negative effect of higher interest rates. Empirical studies suggest that fiscal spillovers are predominantly negative: that the interest rate effects emphasized in this discussion dominate [Roubini (1989); Masson and Melitz (1991)]. Even if the opposite is true, the case for fiscal coordination will remain (although not the justification for fearing "excessive deficits"). Note that it is financial integration, rather than monetary union per se, that would lead uncoordinated fiscal policies to be set at increasingly inefficient levels in the Europe of the future. It can be argued, of course, that monetary union is itself a consequence of financial integration. With the removal of capital controls, the argument goes, the European Monetary System of the 1980s, which reconciled divergent national policies with stable exchange rates through the maintenance of barriers to cross-border capital movements, was no longer viable. The only remaining options were floating exchange rates and monetary unification. Given Europe's aversion to floating, EMU followed.

[6] The intermediate case of high capital mobility and budgetary autonomy but no agreement on the centralization and coordination of national monetary policies is considered by Casella and Feinstein (1991).

[7] On the limitations of the assumptions, see note 5. In addition, Siebert (1992) shows that, when holdings of money depend on after-tax incomes, if an inefficiently high level of public spending, like that which obtains in the Canzoneri-Diba model with capital mobility, is financed partly out of taxation, it will reduce after-tax incomes and thereby increase the marginal cost of raising seigniorage revenues. This last fact may lead the central bank of the monetary union to reduce its rate of monetary creation, actually resulting in a deflationary bias.

treaty are an appropriate response to this concern. The incentive for governments to run excessive deficits derives from the central bank's willingness to finance some portion of their spending with seigniorage. If the central bank is unwilling to do this, the problem of excessive deficits dissolves, along with the need for the treaty's excessive deficits procedures. A solution would seem to be a firm declaration by the central bank of its refusal to finance budget deficits and of its commitment to price stability.

The problem with this approach is that even if the central bank is independent, such statements on its part will not be credible. A zero inflation rule will be time-inconsistent. The central bank may state its intention of maintaining price stability and of refusing to monetize additional budget deficits. But if such deficits accrue, the monetary authorities, upon solving the Ramsey-Phelps problem, will find it optimal to equate the deadweight loss of distortionary taxes and inflation at the margin, violating their preannounced rule. Knowing this, governments retain their incentive to run excessive deficits. Thus, central bank independence by itself is not sufficient to preclude monetization and excessive deficits.

Time-consistency and credibility consequently require that central bank independence be supplemented by an effective prohibition of debt monetization. If the central bank is prevented by statute from undertaking such policies, the excessive deficits problem evaporates.

In fact, the Maastricht treaty contains provisions that can be understood in precisely these terms. The ECB is prohibited from providing credit to the EC or to national, state, or local governments. A "no bailout" rule forbids it from buying up the debt of countries experiencing fiscal crises. Finally, the treaty specifies the maintenance of price stability as the primary objective of ECB policy.

The question is whether these measures suffice to counter the incentive the ECB would otherwise possess to renege on its commitment not to monetize budget deficits. The conviction that the excessive deficit procedures are still required may thus reflect a belief that the provisions in the Maastricht treaty prohibiting credit to governments and identifying price stability as the central bank's paramount goal will be less than completely effective in preventing debt monetization.

These possible justifications for the excessive deficits procedures are predicated on the incentive problems that may arise once the ECB begins operation. Until then, potential participants will retain their national currencies and national central banks, and nothing beyond existing European Monetary System (EMS) agreements will obligate other countries to monetize portions of any one government's budget deficit.[8] If a government runs deficits, only the domestic

---

[8] In fact, the EMS Act of Foundation requires other central banks to provide unlimited support for weak Exchange Rate Mechanism (ERM) currencies, which might be thought to entail an obligation to undertake deficit monetization in the event that such support weakens the exchange rate. But the implicit understandings surrounding the act effectively limit the requirement to extend foreign support. For details, see Eichengreen and Wyplosz (1993).

central bank will have any incentive to monetize a portion of its debt. Only domestic residents will suffer the inflationary consequences. Moreover, the argument that the case for fiscal policy coordination across countries is no stronger under monetary union than today applies equally to Stage Two. These arguments do not therefore provide an obvious rationale for excessive deficits procedures during the second, transitional stage.

The debt and deficit targets of Stage Two are more frequently justified on the grounds that they are useful for distinguishing disciplined from undisciplined governments and hence for identifying desirable participants in Europe's monetary union. Assume that it is wished to form a monetary union of only countries possessing fiscal discipline. Do the Maastricht treaty's reference values for debts and deficits adequately differentiate such countries from their undisciplined counterparts? There is a logic to considering stocks (debts) and flows (deficits) together: if the treaty set targets only in terms of debts, countries starting from unfavorable initial conditions (such as Belgium, with a debt/GDP ratio well in excess of 100 percent) would not be rewarded for having shifted their budgets into substantial surplus and thereby having moved onto a sustainable path; if the treaty considered only current deficits, countries would be encouraged to play games with current expenditures (for example, by converting outstanding obligations into zero coupon bonds, which require no debt service in the short run, thereby reducing the interest charges borne by the government and making the current budget balance look artificially strong).

There is no reason, however, why governments possessing fiscal discipline (in this context, those willing to finance their spending on a noninflationary basis) should be expected to keep their deficit ratio below any arbitrary fraction of national income. They will wish to run deficits in periods when the marginal utility of public and private expenditure is high, and to shift their budgets toward surplus in other periods to stem the growth of the public debt and mobilize the resources necessary to service it. When the marginal utility of private spending is high, the marginal cost of taxation is high as well, and governments wishing to maximize the welfare of domestic residents will run deficits, accumulating debt that is serviced and/or repaid in subsequent periods when the marginal utility of public and private spending is low [Frenkel and Razin (1987)]. From this perspective, a 3 per cent deficit limit is entirely arbitrary.[9] If the marginal utility of spending rises dramatically (for example, because incomes fall dramatically), it may be optimal for even a disciplined government to run larger deficits than this.

The same argument applies to the public debt limit of 60 percent of GDP.

[9] Buiter, Corsetti, and Roubini (1993) suggest that the negotiators at Maastricht may have settled on 3 percent as the reference value for deficits because Germany typically spends 3 percent of its GDP on public investment, and because they did not regard public investment as inflationary on the grounds that it should generate a stream of investment income that can be used in the future to service the corresponding public debt.

The appeal of this criterion, relative to the deficit threshold, is that it allows governments to run deficits in some periods and surpluses in others, as fiscally prudent governments facing unpredictable shocks to national income will be inclined to do. It attempts to distinguish disciplined and undisciplined governments according to the magnitude and persistence of those deficits, as reflected in their accumulation of public debt. Once again, however, the particular threshold selected at Maastricht – 60 percent of GDP – is entirely arbitrary.[10] There is no reason that a fiscally disciplined government of a country experiencing an extended sequence of negative shocks to national income would not choose to run deficits that cumulatively exceeded this threshold and remained above it for an extended period of time.

Such objections to the 3 and 60 percent reference values were not lost on the Maastricht treaty's negotiators, it would appear, since the fiscal conditions include loopholes, as described above, exempting countries whose excess over the reference values is "only exceptional and temporary," is declining toward the reference value "at a satisfactory pace," and so forth. While these qualifiers would appear to permit countries to pursue appropriate fiscal policies in response to their particular economic conditions, the looseness of the language implies that qualification for monetary union will be based on subjective political considerations rather than a precise assessment of fiscal performance.

Is there an alternative formulation that might combine the precision and objectivity of numerical reference values with the desirability of flexible application in light of the different economic circumstances in which countries find themselves? The obvious possibility is the solvency calculus pioneered by Buiter (1985) and Cohen (1991). This approach seeks to distinguish solvent countries (those whose ratio of debt to GDP stabilizes in the long run) from insolvent countries (those whose debt ratio rises without limit), essentially by taking the initial debt ratio and extrapolating its subsequent path on the basis of the primary deficit, the growth rate of real GDP, and the real interest rate. (If the real interest rate that must be paid on the debt exceeds the real GDP growth rate, then any initial debt ratio will rise explosively in the absence of a sufficiently large primary surplus.) One might object that a formula based on Commission and EMI forecasts of interest rates and GDP growth rates is less transparent than simple reference values for current debts and deficits, but as discussed above, the reference values in the Maastricht Treaty are qualified by provisions robbing them of their transparency.

To summarize, there is some justification for certain aspects of the excessive deficits procedures. There is a coherent rationale for the excessive deficits procedures during Stage Three (once EMU comes into operation) if it is believed

[10] Again, Buiter, Corsetti, and Roubini (1993) suggest that the Maastricht negotiators may have had Germany's public investment behavior in mind when selecting a 60 percent reference value for the public debt ratio. They show that 3 per cent deficits cumulate into a 60 percent debt ratio under conventional assumptions about the growth rate of nominal GDP.

that the provisions of the Maastricht treaty banning ECB financing of governments and debt bailouts will be incompletely effective and that they must therefore be buttressed by measures preventing governments from soliciting central
bank financing and bailouts in the first place. The case for provisions to promote coordination of national fiscal policies for stabilization purposes, though
unobjectionable, is not obviously strengthened by the advent of EMU.

During Stage Two, in contrast, the excessive deficits procedures are difficult
to justify on any grounds. If they are rationalized as a device for distinguishing
fiscally disciplined from fiscally undisciplined governments, then there exist
less subjective criteria better suited to the task.

### THE NEED FOR AND EFFECTIVENESS OF FISCAL RESTRAINTS

An alternative to guidelines and recommendations for deterring member states
from running excessive budget deficits is formal fiscal restraints.[11] If one
believes that fiscal policies must be restrained during Stage Three but that
the vague and subjective criteria of the treaty are not up to the task, European
policymakers may choose to opt for strict legislative restraints. They will then
want to look at the experience of other countries with the operation of such
restrictions.

It is not obvious that formal fiscal restrictions, whether statutory or constitutional, effectively limit the deficits and debts they are designed to control, or
that either type of restriction reduces the rate of return investors require to hold
public obligations. (The rate of return is relevant to the Maastricht debate insofar as that rate is a measure of the default risk investors attach to public obligations and hence of the perceived likelihood of the need for a bailout.) Most
analyses of fiscal restraints, using U.S. data, conclude that they have little if any
impact on fiscal outcomes. (As of 1987, forty-six U.S. states had balanced-
budget requirements of some sort, while some thirty states had limits on their
power to issue debt.) A recent study by von Hagen (1992), for example, compared levels of debt per capita and debt/income ratios in states with and without
formal fiscal restrictions, and found that the differences between the two groups
were statistically insignificant.

There are several reasons for reconsidering this question. For one, most work
on the issue, including that of von Hagen, utilizes bivariate tests, in which the
level of debt in states with and without fiscal restraints is compared without
controlling for other determinants. Moreover, von Hagen considered the impact
of balanced-budget restrictions on the level of debts, not on the budget deficits
to which they are most immediately directed. Finally, the data on state general
obligation yields recently obtained by Goldstein and Woglom (1992) allow
us to analyze the impact of fiscal restrictions on the cost as well as the quantity

---

[11] This section elaborates an analysis summarized in Eichengreen (1992b).

of borrowing, which provides an important check on the robustness of the results.

The econometric analysis reported here utilizes pooled time series/cross-section data for 1985 through 1989. I employed the specification estimated by the Advisory Commission on Intergovernmental Relations (ACIR) (1987) on state-level data for 1983.[12] The per capita general fund surplus (or deficit) is assumed to depend on agricultural output per capita (AgriPC), the per cent of state population aged 54 or older (Elders), federal aid to the state per capita (Grant), and a dummy variable (South) equaling one for states in the south. Grant should enter with a positive sign insofar as federal grants permit politicians to replace deficit spending with spending financed by federal aid. The dummy variable for southern states should enter negatively if the region, as sometimes asserted, is fiscally conservative. The agricultural output variable should similarly display a negative sign if farm states are fiscally conservative.

As shown in Table 1, the signs of the coefficients on all these variables are as predicted, although their statistical significance varies. A number of measures of the severity of balanced-budget restrictions are significantly associated with larger budget surpluses (smaller deficits). The first is a dummy variable equaling one for states prohibited from carrying over a deficit into the next fiscal year (Balance 1). The second (Balance 2) is an index designed to capture the relative stringency of state balanced-budget requirements (it ranges from one in the case of the least stringent requirements to ten for the most stringent).[13] The third, not considered by ACIR, is a dummy variable equaling one for states whose governors must sign a balanced budget by statutory or constitutional law (Balance 3).

The first two equations of Table 1 show that Balance 1 and Balance 3 are significantly associated with the magnitude of budget deficits. Their coefficients uniformly differ from zero at the 95 percent confidence level. The positive signs suggest that states whose governors must sign balanced budgets and states that cannot carry over deficits tend to run larger surpluses (smaller deficits). The coefficient on Balance 2, in the third equation, while also positive is not significantly different from zero. Since this index is an increasing function of Balance 1 and Balance 3 as well as of various weaker fiscal requirements, its insignificance suggests that it is mainly the more stringent restrictions that have noticeable effects on the size of deficits.

---

[12] One variable considered by the ACIR, mineral production per capita, is omitted because it did not prove possible to obtain data on a year-by-year basis.

[13] This index is constructed by assigning point values to the legislative status and relative stringency of balanced-budget restrictions, and then summing the totals for the two categories. One point is assigned if the requirement is a statutory provision and two points are assigned if it is constitutional. Values assigned to the specific features of the requirement are as follows: one point if the governor only has to submit a balanced budget, two points if the legislature only has to pass a balanced budget, four points if the state may carry over a deficit but it must be corrected in the next fiscal year, six points if the state cannot carry over a deficit into the next biennium, and eight points if the state cannot carry over a deficit into the next fiscal year.

TABLE I EFFECT OF FISCAL RESTRAINTS ON THE GENERAL FUND BUDGET BALANCE

| | (1) | (2) | (3) | (4) | (5) | (6) |
|---|---|---|---|---|---|---|
| C | 41.93 | 46.23 | 25.30 | −50.46 | 58.13 | 0.34 |
| | (1.10) | (1.02) | (0.52) | (−0.53) | (0.51) | (31.19) |
| BALNC1 | | 23.43 | | | 23.81 | |
| | | (2.06) | | | (1.97) | |
| BALNC2 | | | 3.16 | | | 3.44 |
| | | | (1.63) | | | (1.68) |
| BALNC3 | 19.65 | | | 20.45 | | |
| | (2.13) | | | (2.19) | | |
| ELDERS | −5.01 | −2.08 | −1.48 | −4.48 | −2.10 | −1.62 |
| | (−2.05) | (−0.74) | (−0.53) | (−1.82) | (−0.73) | (−0.56) |
| GRANT | 0.12 | 0.02 | 0.02 | 0.13 | 0.02 | 0.02 |
| | (3.15) | (0.37) | (0.46) | (3.30) | (0.41) | (0.49) |
| ITEM | | | | −4.53 | −2.10 | −6.14 |
| | | | | (−0.36) | (−0.14) | (−0.39) |
| SOUTH | −28.38 | −40.38 | −36.45 | −24.33 | −44.54 | −40.82 |
| | (−2.55) | (−2.91) | (−2.67) | (−1.86) | (−2.90) | (−2.66) |
| TEL | | | | −9.47 | −12.80 | −12.31 |
| | | | | (−0.96) | (−1.07) | (−1.02) |
| YEAR | | | | 0.04 | 0.01 | 0.01 |
| | | | | (0.97) | (0.15) | (0.18) |
| YPC | | | | 0.002 | −0.001 | −0.001 |
| | | | | (0.67) | (−0.37) | (−0.48) |
| AGRIPC | 0.01 | 0.01 | 0.01 | | | |
| | (1.56) | (1.31) | (1.18) | | | |
| 1986 | −12.94 | −10.92 | −11.12 | −13.27 | −10.43 | −10.34 |
| | (−0.92) | (−0.65) | (−0.66) | (−0.92) | (−0.61) | (−0.60) |
| 1987 | −9.21 | −2.92 | 0.17 | −11.53 | −1.86 | 2.28 |
| | (−0.64) | (−0.17) | (0.03) | (−0.79) | (−0.11) | (0.13) |
| 1988 | 2.37 | 18.53 | 19.60 | −1.40 | 21.06 | 22.77 |
| | (0.17) | (1.10) | (1.16) | (−0.09) | (1.16) | (1.26) |
| 1989 | 15.56 | 29.21 | 26.74 | 9.94 | 33.01 | 31.19 |
| | (1.10) | (1.71) | (1.56) | (0.61) | (1.70) | (1.58) |
| $N$ | 242 | 250 | 250 | 242 | 250 | 250 |
| $R^2$ | .14 | .09 | .08 | .17 | .09 | .08 |
| F-statistic | 5.34 | 2.58 | 2.39 | 3.91 | 1.88 | 1.78 |

Note: Values in parentheses are $t$-statistics.

The next three equations update the ACIR's alternative specification, which drops the insignificant measure of agricultural production and adds four additional regressors. The first is a dummy variable for states with tax and/or expenditure limitations (TEL), which typically limit appropriations to a share of personal state income. This variable should enter with a negative sign unless the limitations are set at such high levels as to be inoperative. The second regressor, the year in which statehood was granted (Year), should enter positively if special interest groups grow more entrenched over time and their lobbying leads to larger deficits. The third, a dummy variable for the presence of a line-item veto (Item), is hypothesized to have a negative effect on spending and hence on the size of the deficit, other things being equal. The final new term, state product per capita (YPC), is designed to pick up any tendency of richer states to run larger deficits.

The signs of the coefficients on these additional variables are as predicted, although none is significantly different from zero at standard confidence levels. More important for present purposes, none of the coefficients on the balanced-budget restrictions is much affected by the inclusion of these additional variables. Balance 1 and Balance 3 remain significant at the 95 percent level, while Balance 2 is now also significantly different from zero (at the 90 percent level). When agricultural output is added to this augmented specification, however, the coefficient on Balance 2 slips back below the 90 percent level.[14] I conclude therefore that balanced-budget restrictions are in fact conducive to budget balance only if they are relatively stringent.

Some advocates of restrictions on deficit spending argue that these laws are important for limiting the level of public expenditure as well as the size of the deficit.[15] I therefore estimated the determinants of own-source spending per capita, again employing a specification that follows ACIR (1987). The determinants of spending include, along with the variables previously described, the size of the state legislature (Size). If it is assumed that larger legislatures are subject to higher transaction costs, that transaction costs have a negative effect on legislative output, and that the lower the legislative output, the higher the budget deficit, then Size should be associated with larger deficits and higher expenditures.

These hypotheses are broadly supported by the point estimates in Table 2. Importantly, none of the balanced-budget restrictions has a significant effect on the level of per capita spending. Although the coefficients for states whose governors must sign a balanced budget and on the ACIR stringency index are negative as predicted, neither measure differs significantly from zero. Thus, even if sufficiently stringent balanced-budget restrictions are in fact conducive to budget balancing, they do not affect the level of public spending, implying that their impact on policy operates mainly on the tax side.

Table 3 turns from balanced-budget requirements to debt limits, again employing a variant of the ACIR specification. The dependent variable is the full-faith-and-credit debt of state governments. These multivariate tests indicate that

[14] Given this ambiguity about the significance of Balance 2, the ACIR index, I considered individually the effects of its other components, defining dummy variables equaling one for states that cannot carry over a deficit into the next biennium, for states that may carry over a deficit but must correct it in the next fiscal year, for states whose legislatures only have to pass a balanced budget, and for states whose governor must only submit a balanced budget. Adding these variables to the basic specification, either in addition and in lieu of Balance 1 and Balance 3, provided no indication that any of these measures had a discernible effect on deficit spending.

[15] See ACIR (1987, p. 52).

TABLE 2 EFFECT OF FISCAL RESTRAINTS ON OWN-SOURCE SPENDING

| | (1) | (2) | (3) | (4) | (5) | (6) |
|---|---|---|---|---|---|---|
| C | -253.67 | 281.72 | 366.47 | -390.63 | 196.42 | 307.48 |
| | (-1.23) | (0.98) | (1.18) | (-1.80) | (0.65) | (0.96) |
| BALNC1 | | 50.10 | | | 57.58 | |
| | | (0.72) | | | (0.83) | |
| BALNC2 | | | -2.46 | | | -4.19 |
| | | | (-0.21) | | | (-0.36) |
| BALNC3 | -12.40 | | | -11.49 | | |
| | (-0.28) | | | (-0.25) | | |
| ELDERS | -23.38 | -101.23 | -98.46 | -33.60 | -108.85 | -105.77 |
| | (-1.97) | (-6.70) | (-6.60) | (-2.89) | (-7.31) | (-7.15) |
| ITEM | | | | 66.41 | 77.13 | 76.54 |
| | | | | (1.06) | (0.88) | (0.87) |
| SIZE | -1.81 | -2.65 | -2.73 | -1.61 | -2.51 | -2.67 |
| | (-4.53) | (-4.60) | (-4.76) | (-3.83) | (-4.19) | (-4.42) |
| SOUTH | 95.29 | 155.43 | 165.28 | 132.00 | 171.46 | 185.31 |
| | (1.53) | (1.80) | (1.93) | (2.20) | (2.04) | (2.23) |
| TEL | | | | -42.08 | -61.64 | -63.36 |
| | | | | (-0.87) | (-0.91) | (-0.93) |
| YPC | 0.10 | 0.15 | 0.14 | 0.11 | 0.15 | 0.15 |
| | (7.33) | (7.90) | (7.75) | (8.83) | (8.80) | (9.54) |
| AGRIPC | -0.05 | -0.03 | -0.03 | | | |
| | (-2.02) | (-0.85) | (-0.91) | | | |
| 1986 | -20.82 | -66.01 | -64.01 | -23.04 | -66.96 | -64.48 |
| | (-0.30) | (-0.69) | (-0.67) | (-0.33) | (-0.70) | (-0.67) |
| 1987 | -21.45 | -82.77 | -81.69 | -30.04 | -86.50 | -86.64 |
| | (-0.31) | (-0.85) | (-0.84) | (-0.43) | (-0.89) | (-0.89) |
| 1988 | -59.22 | -185.61 | -179.67 | -80.03 | -195.28 | -189.21 |
| | (-0.80) | (-1.82) | (-1.76) | (-1.09) | (-1.93) | (-1.87) |
| 1989 | 898.09 | 724.98 | 736.64 | 868.05 | 708.88 | 722.85 |
| | (11.40) | (6.60) | (6.67) | (11.16) | (6.55) | (6.62) |
| N | 241 | 249 | 249 | 241 | 249 | 249 |
| $R^2$ | .70 | .61 | .61 | .70 | .61 | .61 |
| F-statistic | 53.09 | 36.72 | 36.60 | 47.41 | 33.44 | 33.31 |

Note: Values in parentheses are t-statistics.

constitutional debt limits (Dbtlim) exert a downward influence on full-faith-and-credit debt per capita. The coefficients on the debt-limit variable are significantly less than zero at the 99 percent confidence level; a point estimate of -250 suggests that a debt limit reduces state debt per capita by $250 dollars.

Von Hagen (1992) has suggested that the negative impact of debt limits on full-faith-and-credit debt may disguise a tendency for governments confronted with binding debt limits not to tighten fiscal policy but instead to substitute other debt instruments (bonds of utility districts, affiliated agencies, etc.). As a check on this possibility, Table 4 turns from quantities to prices, considering the impact of debt and deficit limits on the yields on state bonds (rather than on

TABLE 3   EFFECT OF FISCAL RESTRAINTS ON LEVELS OF DEBT

| | (1) | (2) | (3) |
|---|---|---|---|
| C | 964.39 | –1,153.36 | –1,084.98 |
| | (2.26) | (–1.45) | (–1.39) |
| DBTLIM | –293.95 | –255.19 | –224.90 |
| | (–3.11) | (–2.81) | (–2.53) |
| ELDERS | –107.23 | –53.51 | –34.47 |
| | (–5.39) | (2.54) | (–1.61) |
| GRANT | | 1.57 | 1.66 |
| | | (5.11) | (5.60) |
| ITEM | | –147.69 | –85.16 |
| | | (–1.26) | (–0.73) |
| SIZE | | –1.88 | –2.32 |
| | | (–2.45) | (–3.06) |
| SOUTH | –62.78 | 282.96 | 201.12 |
| | (–0.53) | (2.42) | (1.72) |
| TEL | | 81.64 | 24.17 |
| | (0.91) | (0.27) | |
| YEAR | | 0.18 | 0.22 |
| | | (0.53) | (0.67) |
| YPC | 0.10 | 0.15 | 0.13 |
| | (3.74) | (6.36) | (5.34) |
| AGRIPC | –0.09 | | –0.15 |
| | (–1.87) | | (–3.21) |
| 1986 | 63.62 | 4.28 | 5.28 |
| | (0.53) | (0.04) | (0.05) |
| 1987 | 135.02 | 66.23 | 77.34 |
| | (1.09) | (0.58) | (0.69) |
| 1988 | –147.80 | –301.42 | –255.90 |
| | (–1.23) | (–2.46) | (–2.12) |
| $N$ | 200 | 200 | 200 |
| $R^2$ | .34 | .44 | .47 |
| $F$-statistic | 12.06 | 12.29 | 12.69 |

*Note:* Values in parentheses are *t*-statistics.

stock or flow supplies).[16] A previous study by Goldstein and Woglom (1992) examined the effect of debt limits on yield spreads and found that debt limits reduced borrowing costs. The other principal variable included in their analysis was the outstanding debt. A problem with this approach, as these authors note, is simultaneity bias: the level of debt is likely to affect the cost of borrowing, but the cost of borrowing is also likely to affect the decision to borrow. Although Goldstein and Woglom (1992) and Bayoumi (1992) attempt to surmount this problem with instrumental variables, I take a different approach: rather than

[16] This alternative test will be informative if investors succeed in seeing through the veil that officials attempt to place in front of their eyes when substituting away from full-faith-and-credit debt.

TABLE 4   EFFECT OF FISCAL RESTRAINTS ON STATE BOND YIELDS

|        | (1)     | (2)     | (3)     | (4)     | (5)     | (6)     |
|--------|---------|---------|---------|---------|---------|---------|
| C      | −14.13  | −48.70  | −47.22  | −11.56  | −17.56  | −2.51   |
|        | (−1.23) | (−2.04) | (−1.97) | (−1.02) | (−1.70) | (−0.23) |
| BALNC1 |         |         |         |         | −12.52  |         |
|        |         |         |         |         | (−4.75) |         |
| BALNC2 |         |         |         |         |         | −1.53   |
|        |         |         |         |         |         | (−3.62) |
| BALNC3 |         |         |         | −0.14   |         |         |
|        |         |         |         | (−0.05) |         |         |
| DBTLIM | 0.16    | −2.68   | −2.96   |         |         |         |
|        | (0.06)  | (−1.00) | (−1.09) |         |         |         |
| ELDERS | 0.94    | 1.20    | 1.29    | 0.73    | 1.48    | 1.03    |
|        | (1.43)  | (1.89)  | (2.00)  | (1.05)  | (2.39)  | (1.66)  |
| GRANT  | 0.04    | 0.03    | 0.03    | 0.04    | 0.04    | 0.03    |
|        | (3.72)  | (3.20)  | (3.29)  | (2.73)  | (4.56)  | (3.53)  |
| ITEM   |         | 0.80    | 1.31    |         |         |         |
|        |         | (0.24)  | (0.38)  |         |         |         |
| SOUTH  | 3.89    | 1.32    | 0.78    | 4.19    | 9.53    | 5.87    |
|        | (1.24)  | (0.38)  | (0.22)  | (1.28)  | (2.99)  | (1.91)  |
| TEL    |         | 6.53    | 6.29    |         |         |         |
|        |         | (2.45)  | (2.35)  |         |         |         |
| YEAR   |         | 0.03    | 0.03    |         |         |         |
|        |         | (2.52)  | (2.57)  |         |         |         |
| YPC    |         | −0.001  | −0.002  |         |         |         |
|        |         | (−1.95) | (−2.15) |         |         |         |
| AGRIPC | 0.0002  |         | −0.002  | 0.0008  | −0.002  | 0.0007  |
|        | (0.12)  |         | (−0.89) | (0.33)  | (−0.74) | (0.35)  |
| 1986   | −1.04   | 0.90    | 0.96    | −0.99   | −1.35   | −0.94   |
|        | (−0.26) | (0.23)  | (0.25)  | (−0.24) | (−0.35) | (−0.25) |
| 1987   | −0.26   | 1.40    | 1.65    | −0.13   | −0.47   | −1.92   |
|        | (−0.06) | (0.35)  | (0.41)  | (−0.03) | (−0.12) | (−0.49) |
| 1988   | −3.26   | −0.28   | 0.33    | −3.41   | −3.41   | −4.22   |
|        | (−0.81) | (−0.07) | (0.08)  | (−0.82) | (−0.90) | (−1.08) |
| 1989   | −6.74   | −2.43   | −1.62   | −6.27   | −7.27   | −5.62   |
|        | (−1.64) | (−0.54) | (−0.36) | (−1.43) | (−1.89) | (−1.42) |
| $N$    | 200     | 200     | 200     | 192     | 200     | 200     |
| $R^2$  | .08     | .17     | .17     | .06     | .18     | .14     |
| F-statistic | 1.90 | 3.21   | 3.02    | 1.23    | 4.63    | 3.48    |

Note: Values in parentheses are t-statistics.

attempting to estimate a pair of structural equations representing the influence of the debt burden on the cost of borrowing and of that cost on the quantity of borrowing, I estimate the associated reduced forms. I solve the structural equations for the quantity of borrowing and the yield and relate these reduced forms to other (exogenous) variables utilized in the ACIR study. Given the questionable exogeneity of the available instruments, this approach may be more successful at producing an unbiased point estimate of the critical relationship, namely, the impact of fiscal restrictions on interest rates.[17]

The dependent variable in this analysis is the difference in basis points between the yield on twenty year general obligation bonds for a specific date and that on a twenty year New Jersey general obligation bond for the same date, again, for the years 1985 through 1989. The debt limit variable, in the first three columns of Table 4, has the anticipated negative sign in two of three cases but is not significantly different from zero. Thus, despite influencing the quantity of debt outstanding, debt limits do not appear to influence the required rate of return. Insofar as the rate of return is unaffected, this result is consistent with von Hagen's conclusion that debt limits lead mainly to a substitution of other instruments for full-faith-and-credit debt.

In contrast, the balanced-budget variables, in the remaining columns, generally do have a significant negative impact on yields. This is plausible if default risk increases with the rate of growth of the debt rather than with its average level.

The general conclusion to emerge from this analysis of the experience of U.S. states is that, contrary to frequently voiced skepticism, statutory and constitutional deficit restrictions, when sufficiently stringent, can restrain the fiscal behavior of governments. This is evident from the behavior of both deficits and yields. Evidence of the effectiveness of debt limits is less definitive. Thus, if it is concluded that monetary autonomy in Stage Three needs to be buttressed by fiscal restraints, the experience of other countries suggests that statutory or constitutional balanced budget restrictions would be up to the task.

## THE DEBATE OVER FISCAL FEDERALISM

If borrowing by states within a monetary union creates negative externalities and hence must be restrained, local jurisdictions may be left with very limited capacity to use fiscal policy to counteract macroeconomic shocks. Bayoumi and Eichengreen (1994) show that fiscal policy at the state level contributes significantly to macroeconomic stabilization in the United States, but that state governments subject to formal fiscal restraints are less able to undertake this

---

[17] This conclusion follows only if fiscal restrictions are exogenous with respect to the interest rate. This assumption seems innocuous. Note that there is no paradox in the fact that several of the exogenous variables enter with opposite signs in the equations explaining the level of debt and the yield. Consider, for example the coefficient on the share of the state population aged sixty five or older, which enters negatively in the equations explaining debt per capita but positively in those for yields, and visualize a (upward sloping) supply curve and (downward sloping) demand curve in stock-of-debt/yield space. If a high share of the elderly shifts the supply curve of debt to the left (on the grounds that the elderly demand fewer social services or support politicians who are fiscally conservative) but simultaneously shifts the demand-for-debt curve to the right (on the grounds that the elderly prefer government bonds to riskier assets), albeit by a relatively small amount, we would observe the variable Elders entering the debt and deficit equations negatively and the yield equations positively.

function. This suggests the need for an alternative mechanism for fiscal stabilization in monetary unions whose members retain only limited fiscal autonomy.

Herein lies the case for fiscal federalism. Sala-i-Martin and Sachs (1992) have revived the argument, originally set forth by Ingram (1959), that fiscal federalism is an important concomitant of monetary union in the United States, and that its absence in Europe may mean that regional problems will follow the transition to EMU. They estimate that the federal fiscal system in the United States, by reducing federal tax liabilities and increasing inward transfers, offsets roughly 35 percent of a state's income loss when it experiences a recession. Purchasing power is stabilized, diminishing regional problems that can no longer be redressed using the exchange rate.

Using data for U.S. census regions, Sala-i-Martin and Sachs estimate regressions relating tax and transfer payments to movements in pre-tax personal income (both measured relative to the national average), and then use the elasticities from these regressions to estimate the size of the stabilization effect on income.[18] They find that federal tax liabilities decline by roughly twenty-five cents for every dollar by which regional income falls short of national income, and that inward transfers rise by roughly ten cents. Thus, the stabilization effect occurs mainly on the tax side. It is substantial.

Sala-i-Martin and Sachs's case for fiscal federalism as a concomitant of monetary union is controversial [see, e.g., Frenkel and Goldstein (1991); Wyplosz (1991)]. Von Hagen (1992) emphasizes the need to distinguish transfers extended in response to temporary declines in state incomes from those extended in response to permanent declines. Most interstate transfers in the United States, he argues, are of a permanent nature designed to offset long-standing differences in state incomes ("equalization"), not temporary transfers extended in response to cyclical fluctuations ("stabilization"). Once permanent and temporary transfers are distinguished, he suggests, one finds that transfers extended in response to cyclical fluctuations in state incomes are relatively small.

Bayoumi and Masson (1991) have considered this refinement, using data for Canada and the U.S. They regress each region's per capita personal income net of taxes and transfers on its per capita personal income inclusive of taxes and transfers. Both regressors are normalized by the analogous national average. This equation measures the relationship between personal income before federal fiscal flows and personal income after federal fiscal flows, with the slope coefficient capturing the size of the offset. For the United States, the estimated coefficient of 0.80 indicates that, on average, federal fiscal flows reduce long-term income inequalities by twenty cents on the dollar. Thus, Bayoumi and Masson's estimate, while smaller than that of Sala-i-Martin and Sachs, still suggests a substantial stabilization effect.

---

[18] Real energy prices and a time trend are also included as determinants of state tax liabilities, and an effort is made to control for simultaneity due to the dependence of state income in taxes and transfers.

To get at the different responses to temporary and permanent income fluctuations, Bayoumi and Masson then estimate the same regression on detrended data (first differencing all variables to remove the trend). Regressions on differenced data yield a coefficient of .72, suggesting that the stabilization of short-term fluctuations, at twenty eight cents on the dollar, is even larger than the response to long-term differentials. This plausibly reflects the linkage between federal transfers and poverty, which is correlated with the cycle. The fact that the largest change in coefficients when detrended rather than trended data are used occurs when personal income is adjusted not for taxes but for social insurance, transfers and grants is consistent with the notion that the grant and transfer component of federal programs is particularly responsive to the cycle.

A similar analysis for Canada yields evidence of more equalization and less stabilization by that country's national budget. Bayoumi and Masson estimate that personal direct taxes provide five cents on the dollar of equalization, while transfers and grants provide fifteen cents each. The offset to long-term income differentials is therefore thirty-five percent, nearly twice the figure for the United States. This large transfer and grant effect plausibly reflects Canada's more extensive social service and regional equalization mechanisms.

In contrast to the results for the United States, then, the response in Canada to short-term personal income fluctuations is smaller – almost exactly half the response to long-term differentials. Thus, equalization payments reflecting the extent of responses to regional inequality in Canada play a larger role than in the United States. Offset of temporary income fluctuations, though still substantial, is less important than in the United States.

While documenting the need to distinguish equalization payments devised to moderate persistent income differentials from countercyclical transfers designed with stabilization and insurance in mind, this research ultimately confirms the importance in existing monetary unions of fiscal transfers extended in response to temporary income fluctuations. The question is whether the EC has the capacity to undertake them. In 1993 the Community budget was little more than 1 per cent of EC GNP; it is hard to see how it could quickly evolve into a fiscal mechanism with the redistributive capacity of the U.S. or Canadian federal budget. As far back as 1977, the MacDougall Report suggested, on essentially these grounds, that an EC budget of no less than 5 percent of Community GNP was needed for the viability of monetary union [European Commission (1977)]. In 1991 federal government spending as a share of consolidated government expenditure, another relevant comparison, was 69 percent in Belgium, 64 percent in the United States, 61 percent in Germany, 42 percent in Canada and 30 percent in Switzerland; by comparison, the EC budget was no more than 5 percent of the consolidated government spending of member countries.[19]

---

[19] Van Rompay, Abraham, and Heremans (1991, p. 115).

Again, the implication is that the EC budget, as of late 1993, possesses very limited redistributive capacity.

Williamson (1990) has advocated a Community-wide unemployment insurance system as a means of providing regional coinsurance. This proposal is not without problems, however. Consider the following example [from Eichengreen (1992a)]. National labor unions seeking to maximize the wage bill set the level of real wages, subject to which firms then choose the level of employment. Unions will trade additional unemployment for higher wages when their unemployed members receive more generous unemployment benefits. If the cost of those benefits is shifted from the national level to the Community, it is no longer a transfer exclusively from employed to unemployed residents of a given country. The union has an incentive to raise its wage demands, producing more unemployment. Not only does insurance thereby encourage the outcome, unemployment, whose effects it is designed to mitigate, but the magnitude of the distortion increases with the extent of fiscal federalism.

Institutional safeguards could conceivably mitigate these problems. In the United States, for example, the structure of unemployment insurance does exactly this. While each state administers its own insurance trust fund, states also pay a fraction of their payroll taxes into a federal unemployment trust fund, from which they are permitted to draw when their own trust funds move into deficit. Significantly, however, states must pay interest on the funds they borrow. This minimizes their capacity to shift the cost of unemployment benefits onto neighboring jurisdictions within the federal system.

Another potential conduit for fiscal transfers is the EC's Structural Funds. Targeted at depressed regions within the Community, these funds were recently doubled in size. Spain and other Mediterranean members of the EC have lobbied for expanding them further as a precondition for EMU. But the principal function of the Structural Funds is transferring resources to regions where incomes are persistently below the EC average; in other words, they are better suited to equalization than stabilization. Gordon (1991) estimates that a one dollar fall in a member state's per capita income increases its Structural Fund receipts by at most one cent. Since the size of the Structural Funds has recently been doubled, one might wish to double this effect. Still, unless their administration is fundamentally reformed, the Structural Funds are an unlikely source of regional coinsurance. To create a substitute for U.S.-style fiscal federalism, it would be necessary to increase not only the scale of the Structural Funds but also their elasticity with respect to current income fluctuations. This, however, would fundamentally alter their raison d'être, something that current recipients would resist.

One skeptical response to the case for fiscal federalism is that such monetary unions as the United States acquired a common currency long before they developed a federal budget with the capacity to transfer resources across regions in response to cyclical fluctuations. U.S. fiscal federalism is a twentieth-century innovation. Does history, thus, contradict the view that fiscal federalism is an essential concomitant of monetary union?

Advocates of fiscal federalism would respond that the economic conditions that make fiscal coinsurance an essential concomitant of monetary union were not so prevalent a century ago. Substantiating this assertion is not straightforward. The argument that nineteenth-century labor markets were less structured, rendering wages and prices more flexible and thereby reducing the unemployment response to cyclical fluctuations, finds only weak support in recent empirical studies. Though there is some evidence suggesting that the degree of wage and price flexibility has declined over time, recent research does not paint a picture of earlier historical periods as eras of perfect flexibility.[20] Nor is it plausible that region-specific disturbances were less prevalent before the twentieth century. The nineteenth century U.S. economy's regional specialization and dependence on interregional trade heightened the scope for shocks to affect different regions differently. Shocks to the price of primary commodities (such as cotton and tobacco) relative to that of manufactures surely had very different effects on New England and the South, for example.

Perhaps the main difference between the fiscal federalism era and earlier periods lies in the extent of labor mobility in response to cyclical disturbances. Blanchard and Katz (1992) document the importance of migration for regional adjustment in the postwar United States. In earlier periods, by comparison, high transport costs damped the migratory response. Regional problems could be severe, but until the Dust Bowl days of the 1930s, they did not provoke large-scale migrations. This minimized the social and political strains associated with regional disturbances, reducing the need for fiscal transfers to limit relocation.

For connoisseurs of the literature on optimum currency areas, this is an ironic conclusion. In his seminal article, Mundell (1961) argued that exchange rate changes (and by implication, fiscal federalism) were least necessary where a high degree of labor mobility provided an alternative adjustment mechanism. The conclusion here is that high labor mobility may make fiscal federalism more rather than less desirable when the decision is made to give up the exchange rate as an instrument of adjustment. In the absence of both exchange rate changes and fiscal transfers, adjustment *could* take place through labor mobility, but only at a political and social cost that most modern societies would regard as prohibitive – hence the argument for fiscal federalism to limit labor flows and their associated costs.

---

[20] For a discussion of this literature and a review of recent contributions, see Eichengreen (1993b). A recent study of this subject concludes: "Nominal prices in most industrial countries display symptoms of stickiness even in the gold standard period. Nominal price flexibility seems to have increased after World War II, but the evidence favoring this hypothesis is not overwhelming, and the extent of the increase may not be large" [Obstfeld (1993, p. 246)].

## IMPLICATIONS FOR EMU

The provisions of the Maastricht treaty concerning fiscal policy are among its most controversial. They make approval by the Council of Ministers of the fiscal policies of member states a precondition for participating in EMU. They empower the Council to recommend modifications of the fiscal policies of participating countries and to apply sanctions against governments that fail to take the recommended steps.

The provisions governing fiscal behavior following the inauguration of Stage Three (monetary union) are not without justification. (During Stage Two, in contrast, the excessive deficits procedures are difficult to justify on any grounds.) With the integration of European commodity and financial markets will come increasing international spillovers of national fiscal policies. Insofar as national fiscal policies are excessively expansionary because financial and monetary integration shifts some of the costs of deficit finance onto neighboring countries, central bank independence alone will not dispose of the problem. Statements by central bank governors, however independent, that they refuse to monetize government debts will not be taken at face value because such refusal is contrary to the central bank's self-interest. Other measures to restrain excessive spending, such as the treaty's provisions for coordinating national fiscal policies through the Council of Ministers, can be justified on these grounds. But the vague and subjective criteria of the treaty will prove difficult to enforce. If they are convinced of the need to buttress monetary union with fiscal restraint, European policymakers may want to opt for the type of formal restrictions prevalent in existing monetary unions.

What the Maastricht treaty fails to say about fiscal policy is as significant as what it says. It says nothing about fiscal federalism. Existing monetary unions, such as the United States and Canada, rely heavily on interregional fiscal transfers to compensate for the absence of internal exchange rates that can be adjusted in response to disturbances affecting different regions in different ways. Yet the Maastricht treaty makes no provision for fiscal federalism, and the small size of the EC budget leaves the Community a long way to go before it can engage in fiscal federalism on a North American scale. That the United States and Canada adjust to region-specific shocks through interregional labor flows, which are unlikely to be matched by labor mobility between EC countries, underscores the point.[21] This suggests that the restraints on national fiscal and monetary policies that will come with EMU may leave member states without adequate options for dealing with national macroeconomic problems.

---

[21] The importance of labor mobility to regional adjustment in the United States has been emphasized by Blanchard and Katz (1992).

## REFERENCES

Allen, Steven, 1992, Changes in the cyclical sensitivity of wages in the United States, 1891–1987. *American Economic Review* 82, 122–140.

Advisory Commission on Intergovernmental Relations, 1987, *Fiscal discipline in the federal system* (ACIR, Washington, D.C.).

Bayoumi, Tamim, 1992, State and local government finances in the current cycle (unpublished manuscript, International Monetary Fund).

Bayoumi, Tamim, and Barry Eichengreen, 1994, The political economy of fiscal restrictions: Implications for Europe from the United States. *European Economic Review* (forthcoming).

Bayoumi, Tamim, and Paul Masson, 1991, Fiscal flows in the United States and Canada: Lessons for monetary union in Europe (unpublished manuscript, International Monetary Fund).

Blanchard, Olivier, and Lawrence Katz, 1992, Regional evolutions. *Brookings Papers on Economic Activity* 1, 1–61.

Bryant, Ralph, Dale W. Henderson, Gerald Holtham, Peter Hooper, and Steven A. Symansky, eds., 1990, *Empirical macroeconomics for interdependent economies* (Brookings Institution, Washington, D.C.).

Buiter, Willem, 1985, A guide to public sector debt and deficits. *Economic Policy* 1, 4–69.

Buiter, Willem, Giancarlo Corsetti, and Nouriel Roubini, 1993, Excessive deficits: Sense and nonsense in the treaty of Maastricht. *Economic Policy* 16, 57–100.

Canzoneri, Matthew, 1985, Monetary policy games and the role of private information. *American Economic Review* 75, 1056–1070.

Canzoneri, Matthew, and B. Diba, 1991, Fiscal deficits, financial integration and a central bank for Europe. *Journal of the Japanese and International Economies* 5, 481–503.

Casella, Alessandra, and Jonathan Feinstein, 1989, Management of a common currency, in: Marcello De Cecco and Alberto Giovannini eds., *A European central bank?* (Cambridge University Press, Cambridge), 131–156.

Cohen, Daniel, 1991, *Private lending to sovereign states: A theoretical autopsy* (MIT Press, Cambridge, Mass.).

Eichengreen, Barry, 1990, One money for Europe? Lessons from the U.S. currency and customs union *Economic Policy* 10, 117–187.

———, 1992a, Is Europe an optimum currency area? in: Silvio Borner and Herbert Grubel, eds., *European economic integration: The view from outside* (Macmillan, London) 138–161.

———, 1992b, Should the Maastricht treaty be saved? *Princeton Studies in International Finance,* no. 74 (December).

———, 1993, European monetary unification, *Journal of Economic Literature* 31, no. 3, 1321–1357.

———, 1994, Prerequisites for international monetary stability, in: Proceedings of the Commission on the Future of the Bretton Woods Institutions (forthcoming).

Eichengreen, Barry, and Charles Wyplosz, 1993, The unstable EMS. *Brookings Papers on Economic Activity,* 1, 51–124.

Emerson, Michael, et al., 1990, One market, one money, *European Economy* 44 (special issue).

European Commission, 1977, *Report of the Study Group on the Role of Public Finance in European Integration* (European Commission, Brussels).

European Commission, 1992, *Treaty on European Union* (Office of Official Publications of the European Communities, Luxembourg).

Frenkel, Jacob and Morris Goldstein, 1991, Monetary policy in an emerging European economic and monetary union. *Staff Papers* 38, 356–373.

Frenkel, Jacob, and Assaf Razin, 1987, *Fiscal policies in the world economy* (MIT Press, Cambridge, Mass.).

Glick, R., and M. Hutchinson, 1992, Fiscal policy in monetary unions: Implications for Europe. *Open Economies Review* 4, 39–65.

Goldstein, Morris, and G. Woglom, 1992, Market-based fiscal discipline in monetary unions: Evidence from the U.S. municipal bond market, in: Matthew Canzoneri, Vittorio Grilli, and Paul Masson, eds., *Establishing a central bank: Issues in Europe and lessons from the U.S.* (Cambridge University Press, Cambridge), 228–270.

Gordon, James, 1991, Structural funds and the 1992 program in the European Community (unpublished manuscript, International Monetary Fund).

Ingram, James, 1959, State and regional payments mechanisms. *Quarterly Journal of Economics* 73, 619–632.

Kenen, Peter B., 1969, The optimum currency area: An eclectic view, in: Robert Mundell and Alexander Swoboda, eds., *Monetary problems of the international economy* (University of Chicago Press, Chicago), 41–60.

Masson, Paul, and Jacques Melitz, 1991, Fiscal policy independence in a European monetary union. *Open Economies Review* 2, 113–136.

Mundell, Robert, 1961, A theory of optimum currency areas. *American Economic Review* 51, 657–665.

Obstfeld, Maurice, 1993, The adjustment mechanism. in: Michael D. Bordo and Barry Eichengreen, eds., *A retrospective on the Bretton Woods system* (University of Chicago Press, Chicago), 201–268.

Oudiz, Gilles, and Jeffrey Sachs, 1983, Macroeconomic policy coordination among the industrial economies. *Brookings Papers on Economic Activity* 1, 1–64.

Roubini, Nouriel, 1989, Leadership and cooperation in the European Monetary union: A simulation approach. NBER Working Paper, no. 3044.

Sala-i-Martin, Xavier, and Jeffrey A. Sachs, 1992, Federal fiscal policy and optimum currency areas, in: Matthew Canzoneri, Vittorio Grilli and Paul Masson, eds., *Establishing a central bank: Issues in Europe and lessons from the U.S.* (Cambridge University Press, Cambridge), 195–220.

Siebert, Anne, 1992, Government finance in a common currency area. *Journal of International Money and Finance* 11, 567–578.

van der Ploeg, Frederick, 1989, Fiscal aspects of monetary integration in Europe. CEPR Discussion Paper, no. 340.

van Rompay, Paul, Filip Abraham, and Dirk Heremans, 1991, Economic federalism and the EMU. *The European Economy* special issue no. 1, 109–135.

von Hagen, Jürgen, 1992, Fiscal arrangements in a monetary union: Evidence from the U.S., in: Donald E. Fair and Christian de Boissieu, eds., *Fiscal policy, taxation and the financial system in an increasingly integrated Europe* (Kluwer, Dordrecht, Netherlands), 337–360.

Williamson, John, 1990, Britain's role in EMU (unpublished manuscript, Institute for International Economics).

Wyplosz, Charles, 1991, Monetary union and fiscal policy discipline. *The European Economy* special issue no 1, 165–184.

# About the Book

As the European Community moves fitfully toward economic integration, the problems underlying planned monetary unification have repeatedly come to the fore, as in the currency crisis of 1992–1993 and the continuing tribulations of the Maastricht Treaty. An inescapable lesson of these developments is that political problems have become as crucial as economic ones.

In this book, a distinguished group of economists and political scientists cover the central political and economic issues facing European monetary unification. Although the chapters are inspired by current developments and will prove essential to Europeanists, they also seek to derive general analytical and theoretical conclusions valuable to anyone concerned with international political economy.

# ABOUT THE EDITORS
## AND CONTRIBUTORS

**Alberto Alesina** is professor of economics and government at Harvard University. He has published articles in several major academic journals of economics and political science. He is the coauthor of a forthcoming volume on the American political economy.

**Benjamin J. Cohen** is Louis G. Lancaster Professor of International Political Economy at the University of California at Santa Barbara. His most recent books include *In Whose Interest?* (1986) and *Crossing Frontiers* (1991).

**Barry Eichengreen** is professor of economics and political science at the University of California at Berkeley, research associate of the National Bureau of Economic Research, and research fellow of the Centre for Economic Policy Research (London).

**Michele Fratianni** is AMOCO professor of business economics and public policy at the Graduate School of Business of Indiana University. He is the author of many books and articles on macroeconomics, monetary economics and international finance. He has been an economic adviser to the European Commission, senior staff economist with the U.S. President's Council of Economic Advisers, and is currently a director of the International Trade and Financial Association and managing editor of *Open Economies Review.*

**Jeffry Frieden** is professor of political science at the University of California at Los Angeles. His publications include *Banking on the World: The Politics of American International Finance* (1987), and *Debt, Development, and Democracy: Modern Political Economy in Latin America, 1965–1985* (1991).

**Geoffrey Garrett** is assistant professor of political science at Stanford University. His recent publications include *Partisan Politics in the Global Economy* (1994) and several articles on the political economy of European integration.

**Vittorio Grilli** is Woolwich Professor of Financial Economics at Birkbeck College, University of London. He is a research fellow of the Centre for Economic Policy Research (London), and research associate of the National Bureau of Economic Research (Cambridge, Massachusetts). He is currently senior adviser to the Italian Ministry of the Treasury.

**Jürgen von Hagen** is professor of economics at the University of Mannheim and a research fellow of the Centre for Economic Policy Research (London). He has served as research consultant at the International Monetary Fund, the Federal Reserve Bank of St. Louis, and the European Commission. With Michele Fratianni, he is the author of *The EMS and European Monetary Union* (1992).

**Lisa L. Martin** is John L. Loeb Associate Professor of the Social Sciences in the Government Department at Harvard University. She is the author of *Coercive Cooperation: Explaining Multilateral Economic Sanctions* (1992).

**John T. Woolley** is professor of political science at the University of California at Santa Barbara and Visiting Professor at the Georgetown University School of Business. His research involves the politics of monetary policy, including EMU, and the relationships of institutional structure and policy.

# INDEX